Easy Weekend Getaways in the
Hudson Valley & Catskills

EASY WEEKEND GETAWAYS IN THE

Hudson Valley & Catskills

Short Breaks from New York City

Carly Fisher

The Countryman Press
A division of W. W. Norton & Company
Independent Publishers Since 1923

For information about permission to reproduce selections from this book, write to
Permissions, The Countryman Press, 500 Fifth Avenue, New York, NY 10110

For information about special discounts for bulk purchases, please contact
W. W. Norton Special Sales at specialsales@wwnorton.com or 800-233-4830

Manufacturing by Versa Press
Series book design by Faceout Studio, Amanda Kreutzer
Production manager: Devon Zahn

Library of Congress Cataloging-in-Publication Data

Names: Fisher, Carly, author.
Title: Easy weekend getaways in the Hudson Valley & Catskills : short breaks
    from New York City / Carly Fisher.
Description: First edition. | New York : The Countryman Press, A division of
    W. W. Norton & Company Independent Publishers Since 1923, [2020] |
    Series: Weekend getaways | Includes index.
Identifiers: LCCN 2019055187 | ISBN 9781682683545 (paperback) |
    ISBN 9781682683552 (epub)
Subjects: LCSH: Hudson River Valley (N.Y. and N.J.)—Guidebooks.
Classification: LCC F127.H8 F56 2020 | DDC 917.47/304—dc23
LC record available at https://lccn.loc.gov/2019055187

The Countryman Press
www.countrymanpress.com

A division of W. W. Norton & Company, Inc.
500 Fifth Avenue, New York, NY 10110
www.wwnorton.com

10 9 8 7 6 5 4 3 2 1

For those who are ready to fall in love
where the sky meets the earth.

Contents

Welcome

Everything you've heard about the Hudson Valley and Catskills is true. Those rumors about its bucolic perfection and insane agriculture? Its centuries of fascinating history and mysterious ruins? Those *New York Times* Style section editorials waxing poetic about the relaxing holistic retreats, cool celebrity hideouts, hot restaurants, and up-and-coming galleries? Yep, it's all that, plus a splash of bizarre experimental art and unique local festivals to keep things weird. Add in year-round outdoor activities and a stunning seasonal landscape, and there's always a reason to head north.

Tackling it all, however, is another story. If you want to take advantage of something specific and get the best deal, you'll need to plan (and often book) way in advance—sometimes up to three or four months ahead. Much like other Tri-State Area regions, peak season travel

// Peak fall foliage season moves fast, so make sure to hit up places like the Upper Delaware Scenic Byway to peep leaves

is extremely competitive—not just among fellow city dwellers, but also among the multigenerational families who have vacationed upstate for decades and pretty much the entire Northeast (including a growing number of tipped-off Canadians and international travelers). All of this adds up to pricier weekend rates, more hiking trail foot traffic, and sold-out tours at popular museums and historic destinations.

On the other hand, there's a reason weekday travel is cheaper: it's sleepier. Many small-town businesses shutter Monday through Wednesday. Bars and restaurants close down way earlier than you'd expect. And if you've grown dependent on food delivery like many New Yorkers, just forget it. Last-minute trips and backup plans can be advantageous—even necessary—for weather-dependent outdoor activities like hiking, sports, and landscape art parks. Then there are those pesky details like transportation and gear rentals, because how many New Yorkers own a car, let alone camping gear? Exactly.

A lot to consider and a bit overwhelming, isn't it? Good thing you have this handy book! Along with the essentials, this guide is filled with helpful tips, lesser-known resources, and hidden gems off the well-worn path to give you a leg up on the masses (plus something to brag about to your friends).

Keep in mind that this book features only a slice of what's happening in this ever-growing region. Don't be afraid to ask locals for tips or lean hard into a wrong turn for a whole new adventure. Going off the map is usually one of the most memorable (and common) parts of travel. Plus, new businesses and attractions pop up seemingly every day—you might be among the first to discover the next coolest thing.

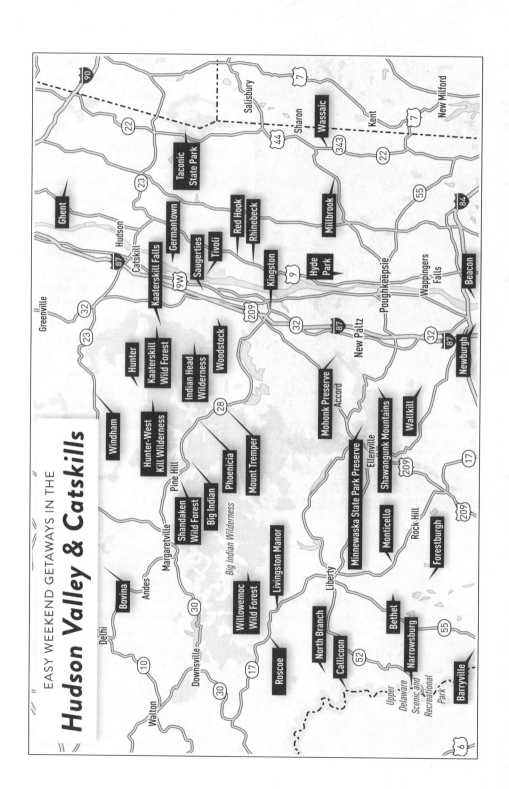

EASY WEEKEND GETAWAYS IN THE

Hudson Valley & Catskills

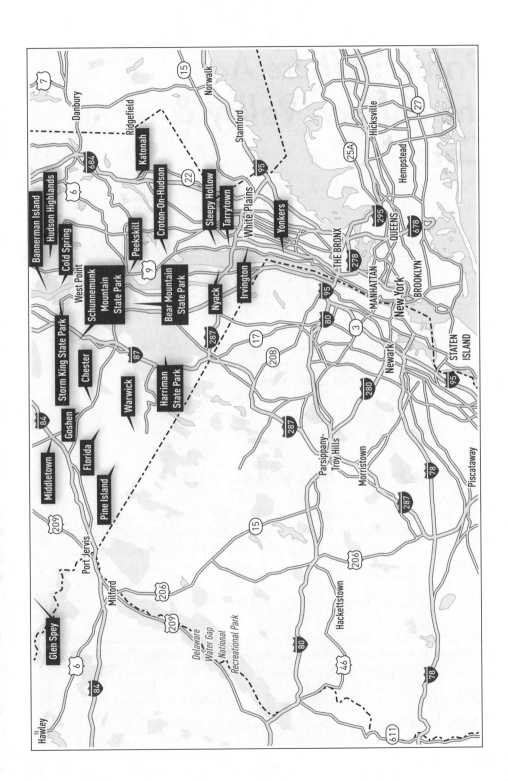

Primer: Where Are the Hudson Valley & Catskills?

Nearly everyone has heard of the Hudson Valley and Catskills, but ask any New Yorker where the areas' borders are and you'll receive the same shrug: "Upstate?" It makes sense to lump both regions into a nebulous "somewhere up there," considering these two massive territories overlap in a cross-section that includes hundreds of thousands of acres and more than a dozen counties.

Officially, the Hudson Valley region stretches across ten counties, from the border of the Bronx at Westchester and Rockland all the way north to Albany and Rensselaer. Meanwhile, the Catskill Mountain region spans 700,000 acres of the Catskill Park and five counties west of the Hudson Valley. Add in outliers, like the fact that Greene County is somehow located in both the Hudson Valley and Catskills, and it's hardly a shocker that most New Yorkers are just barely familiar with well-worn weekender destinations like Beacon and Hudson.

For the sake of ease, navigation, and time (clocking out on Friday afternoon and returning Sunday afternoon), all destinations are within 3 hours' travel time each way from New York City and separated into the following regions.

☰ Hudson Valley Regions

Stretching across 7,228 square miles from Westchester County to Albany, traveling from New York City can take anywhere from 30 minutes if you're going to Yonkers up to 2.5 hours if you're headed for Hudson and Ghent. Attractions within this book are organized into the following pockets: Lower Hudson Valley, Upper Hudson Valley, and Western Hudson Valley.

LOWER HUDSON VALLEY

WHERE IS IT?: Divided by the Hudson River, this region includes towns and attractions along the east bank from Yonkers to Poughkeepsie to the Connecticut border; and on the west bank from Orangeburg and Nyack, north to New Paltz, and west to Harriman State Park.

COUNTIES: Westchester, Rockland, Putnam, Orange, and lower Dutchess and Ulster

MAJOR STOPS: Yonkers, Peekskill, Cold Spring, Beacon, Newburgh

GOOD FOR: A quick 'n' easy getaway. Here, you'll find lots of commuter-friendly cities along the east side of the Hudson River that are serviced by the Metro-North Railroad, making for easy day trips to popular attractions like Dia:Beacon, Bannerman Castle, and Lyndhurst Mansion. If you're planning to head anywhere along the west riverbank, plan to rent a car or combine transit options (train or bus and car).

Getting There

BY TRAIN | 30 minutes–2 hours. Commuter-friendly towns with bustling main streets can be found on stops along the Metro-North Railroad and can easily be visited as a quick day trip ($15–32 each way, depending on peak/off-peak pricing). Unsurprisingly, that means these are among the most well-worn weekender destinations, meaning Saturday mornings are busier than you'd expect (you might find yourself standing on a packed train for an hour). Amtrak and VIA Rail both stop in Poughkeepsie, but don't bother with these—they both cost more and run less frequently than Metro-North.

BY CAR | 30 minutes to 1 hour 40 minutes. The Taconic State Parkway is the gateway to this section of the Hudson Valley, a straight shot from Manhattan via I-278 in the South Bronx. This is a good option if you want to go anywhere outside of a town's main strip or places not serviced by Metro-North, like Bear Mountain State Park or Harriman State Park. Keep in mind that most stations have Zipcar spots in the parking lot and decent Lyft and Uber service. So if you're going for a day trip or have minimal off-site excursions in mind, it's typically cheaper and less of a hassle to combine train and car service rather than going in on a weekend car rental.

BY BUS | 1 hour to 2 hours 30 minutes. The MTA offers bus service from NYC to Yonkers ($2.75–7.50), while some destinations farther north can be reached via the Coach USA Shortline Bus (coachusa.com/shortline). But that method will take more time and won't save you much money ($23–35) compared with the train.

TRANSIT TIP

You'll most likely want to get a car rental for destinations farther north and west of the Hudson River, but you can save money and time by taking Metro-North to towns like Beacon or Poughkeepsie. Not only are the rates on car rentals and gas a better value, but you'll skip paying that pesky $15 George Washington Bridge city toll. Off-peak travel times are always cheaper, but Metro-North's deals and Getaway packages offer additional discounts on inclusive train and ticket prices to popular destinations like Dia:Beacon, Wave Hill, and Bannerman Castle, as well as bike rentals in Peekskill. Check the Metro-North website (mta.info) to purchase ahead of time.

Getting Around

If you're traveling by Metro-North, many major attractions are within walking distance of the train stations. However, if you want to veer off-course, Lyft and Uber are both easily accessible and Zipcar locations are available at each Metro-North train stop.

UPPER HUDSON VALLEY

WHERE IS IT?: East of the Hudson River: from Hyde Park to Hudson and east to the Connecticut and Massachusetts borders. West of the Hudson River: from New Paltz to Catskill.

COUNTIES: Upper Dutchess and Ulster, lower Columbia, and Greene

MAJOR STOPS: Hyde Park, Rhinebeck, Kingston, and Hudson

GOOD FOR: A sampler platter of the Hudson Valley. This area includes a solid mix of cultural and natural attractions, from historical destinations like the FDR Library and Museum and Olana State Historic Site to art-centric venues like Basilica Hudson. Traveling by car, train, or bus are all easy options, so it's easy to size up budget-friendly transit based on activity and destination. Here, you can explore the rural back roads of the nearby Catskill Mountains, hike along the New York–Massachusetts border, visit off-the-beaten-path Hudson Valley enclaves like Tivoli or Art Omi, or tour destination breweries and distilleries like Suarez Family Brewing and Hillrock Estate Distillery.

Getting There

BY CAR | 1 hour 30 minutes–2 hours 30 minutes. If you plan to stick within towns like Rhinebeck and Hudson, just take Amtrak. To go anywhere beyond that, you'll need a car. Not only will this save you time by eliminating the perpetual wait for spotty Lyft and Uber service, it will also save you money, given that astronomical rates start at $40 for a one-way ride between some destinations. This area covers destinations along Route 9 from Poughkeepsie to Kinderhook (including Hyde Park, Rhinebeck, Tivoli, and Hudson), and rural highways to the east (Millbrook, Wassaic, Copake, Ghent).

BY TRAIN | 1 hour 40 minutes–2 hours. Rhinecliff and Hudson are both accessible via Amtrak's Empire Service (amtrak.com) for about $27–45 each way. This is a good option for a car-free weekender, sticking within these two destinations, or using it as a launch point after which you pick up a rental car to head for farther destinations within the Upper Hudson or Catskills.

BY BUS | 1 hour 30 minutes–3 hours 15 minutes. Cities like Kingston, Phoenicia, New Paltz, and Woodstock are all accessible via the NY Trailways regional bus service (trailwaysny.com)

for about $19–65. Luxury Charter Bus Line operates service between NYC and New Paltz, Kingston, Woodstock, Phoenicia, Hunter, and Windham for about $39 each way. Tour operators like Sourced Adventures (sourcedadventures.com) offer inclusive transit and tour pricing for outdoor trips like rafting and hiking ($99–250).

Getting Around

This depends on where you're going and what you're doing. It's probably best not to trouble yourself with limited public transit service (these are geared toward locals' needs, not tourists'). Services like Lyft and Uber are more robust in larger cities like Hudson, Kingston, and New Paltz (you won't need them for small, walkable villages like Phoenicia and Woodstock). But if you want to go off the grid or plan to split time among a few destinations, such as Rhinebeck, Kingston, and Woodstock, it's typically worth the investment to get a car rental.

WESTERN HUDSON VALLEY

WHERE IS IT: Heading west of the Hudson River at Harriman State Park, this agricultural region stretches north to New Paltz and west through the Shawangunk Ridge and Black Dirt Region.

COUNTIES: Orange, Sullivan, Ulster

MAJOR STOPS: Harriman State Park, Shawangunk Ridge, Black Dirt Region, New Paltz, Upper Delaware Scenic and Recreational Byway

GOOD FOR: Drinking and hiking. This is where you'll find most of the wineries, cider mills, distilleries, breweries, outdoor adventure, and general bounty of the Valley. It encompasses the rolling ranges through the peaks of Mohonk Preserve, Bear Mountain State Park, and Schunnemunk Mountain State Park, as well as the agricultural lowlands of the Wallkill River Valley. Because it's rural, this section is still considered more off the beaten path compared with the Lower Hudson Valley and the well-worn destinations nestled in the eastern Catskills, which means you'll definitely want a car to make the most of a weekend exploring the sprawling landscape and discovering hidden gems along the way.

Getting There

BY CAR | 1 hour 30 minutes–2 hours 20 minutes. It's possible to travel via train and bus, but a car is really your best bet. This region is far more rural than other commuter-friendly towns in the Lower Hudson Valley. Destinations are connected by back roads and rural highways west of I-87 and north of I-84.

BY TRAIN | 1 hour 30 minutes–3 hours. Areas in the Western Hudson Valley and Catskills, like Harriman State Park and towns such as Middleton and Warwick, connect to commuter bus and train lines through New Jersey Transit (njtransit.com), which cost about $18–23 each way. The upside is that this can cut down on time sitting in traffic; the downside is that you'll probably still need to arrange a car rental or taxi for when you get there.

BY BUS | 1 hour 30 minutes–2 hours 30 minutes. This is a good option for direct service to certain destinations like Goshen, Callicoon, and Hyde Park, as well as attractions like Bethel Woods Center for the Performing Arts for an easy round-trip day trip or weekender operated by Coach USA Shortline Bus (coachusa.com/shortline). But once you get to your destination, you'll still need to arrange a taxi or car rental, because this area is pretty rural and conducive to driving culture. Ultimately, it's still smarter to just get a rental car.

Getting Around

Can you get around the Catskills and Western Hudson Valley without a car? Sorta. Do you want to? Depends. Long roads weave through the forested back roads of this sprawling rural

SOMEWHERE IN BETWEEN . . .

Shawangunk Ridge

WHERE IS IT?: A mountain range starting at the Pennsylvania–New Jersey border in Port Jervis and stretching across Awosting Reserve, Minnewaska State Park, and Mohonk Preserve, all the way to New Paltz. Most destinations are nestled west of I-87 along Route 44 (Gardiner to Kerhonkson).

COUNTIES: Orange, Sullivan, Ulster

MAJOR STOPS: New Paltz, Minnewaska State Park, Mohonk Preserve

GOOD FOR: A weekend in the woods. The 47-mile ridge known as the Shawangunk Mountains, a.k.a. The Gunks, is where you'll find some of the more interesting natural attractions, like hiking through dwarf pitch pine forest inside Sam's Point Preserve to the Ellenville Fault Ice Caves and Verkeerderkill Falls.

Black Dirt Region

WHERE IS IT?: Beginning at the Delaware River Mountain region on the west New York–Pennsylvania state border and stretching to the eastern side of the Shawangunk Ridge. These destinations are clustered off I-87 via Route 6 (Chester, Goshen) with connecting back roads to Florida, Warwick, and Pine Island.

COUNTIES: Orange

MAJOR STOPS: Warwick, Goshen, Florida, Chester, Pine Island

region, so having a car is essential for these parts. Certain destinations like Harriman State Park, New Paltz, Goshen, and Warwick are accessible without a car. But it will cost you the time you kill between bus transfers and waiting for spotty Lyft or Uber service.

≡ *Catskills Regions*

The Catskill Mountain range spans 5,892 square miles across Sullivan, Delaware, Greene, and Ulster Counties. Trips here are roughly 2 to 3 hours from New York City, but it can take up to 1 hour 30 minutes to travel between Kaaterskill Wild Forest and Windham on the eastern border to the hamlet of Roscoe on the western border. Because of that, the regions have been separated into the following territories: Eastern Catskills, Western Catskills, and Upper Catskills.

GOOD FOR: The literal farm-to-table experience. This microregion is wedged between the Upper Delaware Scenic and Recreational River on the west and the Shawangunk Ridge to the east. It's defined by its rich, black soil formed by years of erosion from an ancient glacial lake and flooding from the Wallkill River. Because the ground is so fertile, it's incredibly distinctive from other nearby land formations and made for agriculture. This is where you'll find tons of farm stands, microbreweries, cider makers, apple orchards, and other artisanal producers.

Upper Delaware Scenic and Recreational River

WHERE IS IT?: From the Upper Delaware Scenic and Recreational River on the west New York–Pennsylvania state border along Route 97, starting at Port Jervis and going north to Callicoon.

COUNTIES: Orange, Sullivan

MAJOR STOPS: Barryville, Narrowsburg, Callicoon

GOOD FOR: Outdoor adventures. This portion of New York State technically isn't in the Catskills or Hudson Valley, but it's very close to both regions and is an incredible weekender attraction worth knowing about. Owned by the National Park Service, this scenic byway is the Big Sur of the Northeast: a winding 70-mile scenic stretch along the Upper Delaware River (hence the perfunctory name "scenic and recreational"—it's literally pretty and fun). You're here for the nature, whether it's a brisk hike during spring, camping and coasting along the river during the summer, or driving through during the fall foliage season.

EASTERN CATSKILLS

WHERE IS IT?: The forested regions of the eastern Catskill Mountains, including Kaaterskill Wild Forest, Indian Head Wilderness, Hunter-West Kill Wilderness, and the eastern side of Slide Mountain Wilderness bordered by the Esopus Creek.

COUNTIES: Sullivan, Ulster, Greene

MAJOR STOPS: Mount Tremper, Phoenicia, Woodstock, Hunter, Windham

GOOD FOR: Wilderness within reach of civilization. It's all here: mountains, hiking trails, and a creek for outdoor adventures, plus solid farm-fresh restaurants and boutique hotels. This means you can still get a decent craft cocktail after a day of hitting the trails.

Getting There

BY CAR | 2 hours 30 minutes. Most attractions are connected via I-87, cutting along Route 212 past the Ashokan Reservoir (Woodstock), heading north via Route 28 along the Esopus Creek (Mount Tremper and Phoenicia), northeast on Route 214 to Hunter Mountain, and on Route 23 to forested destinations within the Kaaterskill Wild Forest (Kaaterskills Falls Trail).

BY BUS | 2 hours 30 minutes. The only time you should bother messing with the bus is if you're taking an inclusive shuttle for skiing and resort events at Hunter or Windham Mountain or a weekend in Phoenicia on the Esopus Creek (see page 32 for more seasonal shuttle bus trips).

Getting Around

Rental car or bust. As a rule of thumb, it's best to get a car rental for any destination within the Catskills, unless you're taking advantage of popular spots like Hunter, Windham, and Phoenicia, which all have decent shuttle service during peak summer and winter times. The majority of this region is rural, mountainous, and geared toward car culture, with practically nonexistent public transit or Lyft and Uber service (in fact, mobile service is finicky here overall).

SIRI DOESN'T KNOW IT ALL

Once you hit the road, expect to go through at least one mobile dead zone (more realistically: many, many dead zones) and fair-weather GPS directions. Make sure to save a copy of the directions while you have reception or Wi-Fi, watch out for inefficient turns and routing, and most importantly, don't be afraid to ask locals for directions. Honestly, they usually have better information than your smartphone.

WESTERN CATSKILLS

WHERE IS IT?: The forested regions of the western Catskill Mountains, including Slide Mountain Wilderness, Big Indian Wilderness, Sundown Wild Forest, Balsam Lake Mountain Wild Forest, and Willowemec Wild Forest, west to the Neversink Reservoir, Willowemec Creek, and Beaverkill Creek.

COUNTIES: Sullivan, Delaware

MAJOR STOPS: Livingston Manor, Roscoe, North Branch

GOOD FOR: Crunchy outdoor weekenders and retreats. Much like the Eastern Catskills, this section has its fair share of mountainous landscapes and creeks ideal for hiking, camping, and fly-fishing (in fact, the town of Roscoe proudly wears the title of Trout Town, USA). Many boutique hotels have set up shop in Livingston Manor, North Branch, and Roscoe, bringing in tow farm-to-table restaurants, microbreweries, distilleries, and other cultural attractions backed by panoramic wilderness.

Getting There

BY CAR | 2–3 hours. Because there are so many wild forests scattered throughout this area, the majority of attractions are nestled in towns along Route 17. From New York City, take I-95 north to I-287 West to I-87 North to Route 17. From there, you can use small roads to head toward the Upper Delaware Scenic and Recreational River and explore towns like North Branch.

Getting Around

Absolutely rent a car. Unless you're signing up with an all-inclusive tour operator, everything in this area is geared toward going off the grid.

UPPER CATSKILLS

WHERE IS IT?: The forested regions of the northern Catskill Mountains, including Hunter-West Kill Wilderness, Shandaken Wild Forest, Big Indian Wilderness, and Delaware Wild Forest.

COUNTY: Delaware

MAJOR STOPS: Big Indian, Pine Hill, West Kill, Roxbury, Bovina Center, Andes

GOOD FOR: Exploring the hidden gems of the Catskills. These destinations are just a touch outside the 3-hour driving mark direct from New York City, but once you get to either the Eastern or Western Catskills, they're not a huge drive to tack on for a weekend. Find the best of all worlds here: picturesque mountains, rustic boutique hotels, great camping, lots of hiking, and peaceful retreats.

Getting There

BY CAR | 2 hours 30 minutes–3 hours. GPS will most likely direct you via I-87 or Route 17 to all destinations here, given that this area is perfectly centered above the Eastern and Western Catskills.

Getting Around

It's essentially impossible to get to this region without a car, as it is mostly composed of mountain back roads populated by tiny rural communities.

Top 10 Experiences

1 · Back-to-back art trips to Dia:Beacon and Storm King
(Chapter 2)

2 · Historical estate hopping through Hyde Park
(Chapter 5)

3 · Hiking through the dwarf pine forest, ice caves, and waterfall trails at Sam's Point Preserve
(Chapter 7)

4 · Summer outdoor adventures on the Upper Delaware River
(Chapter 7)

5 · The entire month of October in Lower Hudson Valley
(Chapter 9)

6 · Learning to fly-fish in the Catskills or ordering a plate of the region's prized, locally caught trout while you're in town
(Chapter 7)

7 · Enjoying the full cultural sampler platter of eating, drinking, gallery hopping, and shopping your way through Hudson
(Chapter 3)

8 · Biking and brewery hopping along the Heritage Trail
(Chapter 7)

9 · Drinking through the Black Dirt Region beverage trail— make sure someone else is driving!
(Chapter 4)

10 · Taking a tour during winter holiday season at Lyndhurst Mansion
(Chapter 9)

Planning Your Trip

What do I do? Where do I go? How do I get there? How much does it cost? Do I need a car? But what about hiking gear? Don't worry, it's all covered in this book. Between Hudson Valley and the Catskills, you're looking at roughly 13,000 square miles of variable landscape. Factor in a combination of cultural activities that continues to grow every year, thanks to the hordes of ex-city dwellers moving upstate, and it makes sense that planning is a necessity. Good news: this chapter breaks down all of these considerations.

There's a lot to tackle, so figure out your priorities. Start by narrowing down the following things.

☰ Choose Your Adventure

Do you want to visit a bunch of breweries or go hiking in the woods? Maybe a little of both? Perhaps you just want to know the best things to do in Hudson after months of envying your friends' Instagram pics? Either way, this book breaks down exploration by interest, be it visual and performing art, historical attractions, outdoor adventure, holistic retreats and spas, or just eating your heart out. At the beginning of each chapter, two or three cities conducive to an activity are listed, along with ideas of where to eat, drink, and stay to enhance the trip. So if you've always wanted to check out the modernist art museum Dia:Beacon but don't have a game plan beyond that, just flip to the chapter on art to find out where all the top galleries, hip restaurants, and art-centric hotels are located.

☰ When to Go?

Do you have a specific weekend in mind or do you just want to hit the road quickly? Depending on what you want to do, there are tips throughout this book to keep in mind when planning your trip. If you want to see fall foliage, for example, expect cider houses will have a wait during peak seasonal hours. But if you're just really into cider, it might be a better bet to wait a couple of weeks to avoid the masses or hit up the Hudson Valley Cider Festival in June with the locals. Read ahead to the next section for more details on peak/off-peak seasonal planning.

☰ How Long Do You Have?

It can take up to 3.5 hours to get end-to-end of both regions, which is why each chapter is divided between "day trips" and "weekenders." Day trips are typically stops along the Metro-North Railroad and lower Hudson Valley locations that take 1.5 hours or less by car. Any day trip can quickly turn into an overnighter, which is why choice overnight locations are at the end of each chapter. Of course, not every option can be listed in this book. Find additional accommodation resources on page 33.

☰ How to Travel and Get Around

Given that most New Yorkers can barely afford their overpriced shoebox apartments, it's safe to assume that many weekenders don't have a car. Read ahead to page 27 for a breakdown of the best destinations to see without a car, transit tips, hacks, and other resources for getting upstate.

☰ *Best Times to Go*

While there's no "bad time" to travel upstate, you can find plenty of unexpected perks and deals if you time your trip right.

HIGH SEASON: Late May–October

LOW SEASON: November–early May

SPRING

PROS: Excellent spring produce, blooming landscapes, less foot traffic from tourists, off-peak travel deals.

CONS: Unpredictable weather for outdoor activities, fewer community events and festivals.

After a long, heavy winter trudging through the city streets, there's nothing like seeing the Valley flourish with all its flowering glory. There are plenty of views to take in, whether you find them driving through the Upper Delaware Scenic Byway, taking a stroll through the manicured gardens at a historic estate, flying in a hot-air balloon, skydiving, or racing through a zipline course. That beautiful landscape doesn't just look good, it tastes good, too. It's where all that amazing agriculture at the Union Square Farmers' Market comes from, making this an ideal time for food-obsessed travelers to load up on the spring bounty and check out breweries, wineries, distilleries, and cider houses (particularly on a nice day, when you can drink outdoors). Off-peak travel nets a better deal on lodgings than summer and fall, when bouts of rain can make planned hikes and outdoor activities a muddy challenge. Of course, if you don't mind getting wet, spring is also the best time for fly-fishing, because this is when trout season picks up.

SUMMER

PROS: Perfect for outdoor activities like camping, hiking, and watersports; seasonal operations open extended hours; countless festivals to attend.

CONS: Heavily booked in advance; higher peak pricing; less of a "local" feel.

Memorial Day kicks off peak season, which means ideal conditions for massive outdoor festivals and nature activities like hiking, canoeing, swimming, kayaking, and biking—and the undeniable reality that you'll be competing with pretty much everyone in the Tri-State Area to take advantage of it all. Day trips usually require less planning, though tours and transit typically fill up quickly (seriously, you might find yourself standing on the Metro-North train from Grand Central until you hit Peekskill). Weekenders often book several weeks or months in advance, depending on the lodging, though this is also the best time to camp in the woods. Check ahead for conflicting events that book up faster than others, such as popular music festivals and graduation weekend at prominent schools like West Point, Bard, and Marist.

FALL

PROS: All the awesomeness of autumn: fall foliage, harvest and Halloween festivals, apple and pumpkin picking.

CONS: Insanely busy (especially with families); unpredictable and often muddy conditions for outdoor activities.

Don't be fooled by the peaceful, technicolor images you've seen plastered all over Instagram showcasing the beauty of fall foliage in Hudson Valley and the Catskills—it's absolute madness. There are nonstop lines of people buying fresh apple doughnuts and cider. Towns like Sleepy Hollow and Croton-on-Hudson transform into Halloween wonderlands. Notoriously haunted estates like the Burn Brae Mansion and Lyndhurst Mansion really justify the spooky rumors by hosting paranormal tours, hikes, and overnighters. In fact, fall is such a big deal that locals don't even bother with cider celebrations until June, when they can really enjoy Hudson Valley Cider Week in peace. That said, there's a reason these things are so popular: it's all pretty stunning. Peeping leaves doesn't take too long, so this is a good time to book a retreat or escape to a cabin outfitted with a solid hot tub.

WINTER

PROS: Prime time for winter mountain sports; better bargains with off-peak pricing; an ideal time for indoor activities like estate tours and museums.

CONS: Limited outdoor activities beyond mountain sports; reduced hours for businesses and seasonal operations.

Winter is the best time to get away from everyone. You'll find no shortage of winter sports, thanks to a naturally mountainous landscape that has made destinations like Hunter Mountain, Windham Mountain Resort, and Belleayre perennially popular, with frequent round-trip shuttle services for easy weekend day trips. If a weekend hibernating is more your speed, you can't beat cozying up in a firelit lodge or cabin with some local spirits, beers, or wines; touring historic estates (particularly around the holidays, when they're decorated for the festive season); or just finally going on that holistic retreat you've been eyeing. This is also a great time to find off-peak savings for weekend stays—everything slows down after the New Year.

BEST TOWNS TO VISIT WITHOUT A CAR

☰ *Lower Hudson*

YONKERS

Situated just outside of the Bronx, Yonkers is one of those commuter cities that's so close it almost doesn't feel like a getaway at all. That also makes it a super-easy, last-minute day-trip destination. In fact, you can even make it there and back for an impromptu gallery crawl. On the first Thursday of each month, cool galleries like Urban Studio Unbound and the Hudson River Museum open as a part of the Yonkers Gallery Hop. Head out early on Saturday or Sunday to get the most out of a weekend day trip, grabbing a drink at Yonkers Brewing or taking at bakery tour at Greyston Bakery. Bring your bike to explore paved trails at Tibbetts Brook Park. Before you head back, watch the sunset along the waterfront at X20 Xaviars on the Hudson or on the Yonkers Waterfront just across from the train station, featuring live music frequently through the summer.

Getting There

BY TRAIN | 37 minutes. Metro-North is the best option, a relative blip from Grand Central for $7.75–10.50 each way.

Getting Around

It's easy to get almost anywhere on foot, with many popular attractions within a square mile. Thanks to a convenient location near the Bronx, Lyft and Uber service here is decent if you need it.

Highlights

HUDSON RIVER MUSEUM • 511 Warburton Avenue, Yonkers • 914-963-4550 • hrm.org • Wednesday to Sunday, 12–5 p.m. • adults, $7; seniors, students, and veterans, $5; youth ages 3–18, $4; children under 3, free. Save by booking a Metro-North's Getaway package ahead of time, with inclusive train/ticket pricing. Get free admission on Friday and Saturday evenings (5–8 p.m.) July through August, which includes free planetarium shows at 7 p.m.

Celebrating its centennial anniversary, this unique museum features an expansive art gallery showcasing everything from 19th-century Hudson River landscapes up to contemporary art, a historic Gilded Age estate, a full planetarium, and an outdoor amphitheater.

continued

TIBBETTS BROOK PARK · 355 Midland Avenue, Yonkers

This sprawling 161-acre park is like the mini-version of Prospect Park, filled with woodland trails, playing fields, and lakes. Except Yonkers outdoes Brooklyn with its impressive waterpark (complete with a lazy river) and mini golf course.

URBAN STUDIO + UNBOUND · Main Street Lofts, 66 Main Street #B, Yonkers · urbanstudiounbound.org

A working studio and artist collective made up primarily of staff, faculty, and alumni from the Fine Arts Department at the Fashion Institute of Technology, Urban Studio + Unbound showcases innovative, contemporary works from artists based locally and throughout New York City. On the first Thursday of every month, US+U opens up its doors as part of a monthly downtown Yonkers Gallery Hop, which includes wine receptions at several local galleries.

Where to Eat and Drink

Okay, so Yonkers isn't a dining destination. But it's much more interesting than you'd give it credit for. Everything from house-made Italian pastas and no-frills Dominican food to upscale Pakistani, refined French, and farm-to-table fare are all within a half-mile radius from the train station. Here are a couple worth checking out:

For a Fancy Meal on the Riverfront

X20 XAVIARS ON THE HUDSON · 71 Water Grant Street, Yonkers · 914-965-1111 · xaviars.com · $$$

You really can't beat the views at this stalwart fine dining restaurant, which also happens to be on the only currently operational Victorian-era pier on the Hudson. Decked out with a massive "Yonkers" sign and an elaborate turn-of-the-century design, it's a hard one to miss as you exit the Yonkers train station. Expect to pay on par with upscale steakhouse prices in Midtown for its menu of European-inspired classics. If the phrase "white tablecloth" gives you wallet anxiety, head to The Dylan Bar and Lounge at X2O for a craft cocktail and a round of oysters.

For the Beer You Can't Find in Your Borough

YONKERS BREWING COMPANY · 92 Main Street, Yonkers · 914-226-8327 · yonkersbrewing.com · $

New York State is filled with so many craft breweries that it's sort of a rite of passage to drink your way through them all. This brewery, founded by two proud Yonkers locals, features a mix of solid staples and a handful of cool experimental styles, like a hoppy tangerine German pilsner and a mai tai–inspired kettle sour with orgeat, fresh lime, and orange zest.

For Feel-Good Baked Goods

GREYSTON BAKERY • 104 Alexander Street, Yonkers • 914-375-1510 • greystonbakery.com • $

Not only does this bakery make solid brownies and blondies good enough to sit on the shelves at Whole Foods, but it's a company with a sweet story. Originally started by a Brooklyn-born Zen Buddhism teacher as a café operation to help support students, the bakery has grown and evolved over the past 37 years, becoming the state's first registered Benefit Corporation and setting the tone for social justice employment practices for the homeless and unemployed via the Open Hiring Model.

TARRYTOWN AND NYACK

Plan it right, and you can try to fit a little of these two destinations into one weekend without a car. Situated conveniently off the Metro-North Hudson line, Tarrytown is only an hour's ride from New York City, making it an easy day-trip destination.

Soak up history at legendary Victorian and Gilded Age properties like Lyndhurst Mansion and Kykuit, colonial heritage site Philipsburg Manor, and Washington Irving's fascinating Sunnyside estate (see Chapter 6 for Lower Hudson historical destinations). Get in touch with the outdoors by taking a stroll along the water at RiverWalk Park or renting a bike to ride along the along the Old Croton Aqueduct Trail. You can even take a peek at original stained-glass works by French masters Marc Chagall and Henri Matisse at the Union Church of Pocantico Hills.

Take a quick bus ride across the Tappen Zee Bridge to Nyack, where you can snap some scenic pictures of the waterfront before heading to the Edward Hopper House Museum to learn about the roots of American art. Bounce around the restaurants and shops along Broadway Street before heading back to Tarrytown, then pat yourself on the back for effectively managing a whole weekend in the Hudson Valley without a car.

Getting There

About 1 hour via Metro-North from Grand Central Train Station to Tarrytown for $9–19 each way.

Getting Around

From the Tarrytown train station, it's a 15-minute bus ride on the Hudson Link to Nyack ($3) or an 8-minute Lyft or Uber ride. Pick up an electric bike rental at Sleek eBikes (sleekrides. com), which is a good option for those who haven't been on a bike in a while, for $25/hour or $65/day rental.

continued

Highlights

EDWARD HOPPER HOUSE · 82 North Broadway, Nyack · 845-358-0774 · edwardhopperhouse.org · Wednesday to Sunday 12–5 p.m. · free the first Friday of each month;. adults, $7; seniors, $5; students, $2; free for ages 16 and under

Best known as the Grandfather of American Realism, Edward Hopper painted the iconic *Nighthawks*, a moody portrait of a downtown New York diner in 1942. His childhood Queen Anne–style home in Nyack now serves as a museum, gallery, exhibition space, and performing space.

OLD CROTON AQUEDUCT TRAIL · Tarrytown

Converted from a historic waterway, this 26.2-mile bike path trails the east side of the Hudson River from Yonkers to Croton-on-Hudson, passing several cool Tarrytown stops along the way, including Washington Irving's Sunnyside, the Lyndhurst Mansion, the Kykuit Rockefeller Estate, and the Tappan Zee Bridge. At the tail end is Croton Gorge Park, where you can stop off to see the 200-foot Croton Dam along the reservoir.

RIVERWALK PARK · 250 West Main Street, Tarrytown

You can't—and shouldn't—miss this half-mile scenic promenade nestled along the Hudson River, a short 6-minute walk from the Tarrytown train station at Pierson Park. Along with those picturesque waterfront views, the park features a flora- and fauna-filled "eco-corridor" made entirely of native plants.

UNION CHURCH OF POCANTICO HILLS · 555 Bedford Road, Tarrytown · tours run seasonally April 3 through December 3, open Wednesday through Monday · $7

This Gothic Revival church was built by John D. Rockefeller after he built his Kykuit estate. Aside from its historic architectural importance, the church is most famously known for its stained glass, including Henri Matisse's final piece, the Rose Window, and nine windows by Marc Chagall. Because of its small size, this is an easy one to tackle on your own, but guided tours also run roughly every 30 minutes.

Where to Eat and Drink

Most of the action is between the strips on Broadway and Main, about a 10-minute walk from the train station.

For a Solid Cup of Coffee

COFFEE LABS ROASTERS · 7 Main Street, Tarrytown · 914-332-1479 · coffeelabs.com · $

It's a quick half-mile walk from the Tarrytown train station to this indie coffee roastery and café, best known for its sustainable brews from around the world that earned it second place in the 2013 America's Best Espresso competition.

MUDDY WATER COFFEE AND CAFÉ · 52 Main Street, Tarrytown · 914-909-2826 · muddywatercoffeehouse.com · $

Crowned by locals as *Westchester Magazine*'s Best New Coffee Shop in 2017, this contemporary café features organic brews and baked goods just 6 minutes from the train station.

For Fancy Farm-to-Table on the Hudson

EQUUS RESTAURANT · 400 Benedict Avenue, Tarrytown · 914-631-3646 · castlehotelandspa.com/attraction/equus-restaurant · $$$

Not like anyone needs much of an excuse to eat in a castle, but incredible views of the Hudson River over an elegant farm-to-table dinner doesn't hurt, either. Housed within the historic turn-of-the-century Carrollcliffe Castle (better known now as the Castle Hotel & Spa), you can turn your fancy dinner into an overnight stay.

Where to Stay

Major hotel chains and Airbnbs tend to dominate the area, but for a special weekend, check out:

For One Night in a Castle

CASTLE HOTEL & SPA · 400 Benedict Avenue, Tarrytown · 914-631-1980 · castlehotelandspa.com

Originally built at the turn of the century under the moniker Carrollcliffe Castle, this historic estate is now a top-rated luxury hotel, spa, and restaurant. It's not cheap, and rooms book up fast, but summer is among the best times to go, for its seasonal outdoor swimming pool, whirlpool, and mile-long landscaped jogging trail.

For a Taste of the Past

TARRYTOWN HOUSE · 49 East Sunnyside Lane, Tarrytown · 914-591-8200 · tarrytownhouseestate.com

This historic estate dating back to the mid-1800s has all the charm of Hudson Valley's past, but with the benefit of modern amenities better than your New York City apartment, like temperature-controlled heating/cooling and an indoor/outdoor pool.

For a Modern Boutique Vibe

THE TIME NYACK · 400 High Avenue, Nyack · 845-675-8700 · thetimehotels.com/nyack

Yes, The Time is a chain hotel, but it has a modern, boutique design with some personality, a brand-new pool, a central location within walking distance of all the downtown Nyack landmarks, and typically cheaper rates than other Lower Hudson Valley destinations like Beacon.

☰ *Other Resources*

TRANSIT

Before you settle on a destination, it's important to figure out how you're going to get there. City dwellers without driver's licenses will have a harder time reaching rural areas that require a car rental, but you can skirt the issue by hopping on a shuttle service to popular destinations like Hunter Mountain or taking an organized tour.

Researching transit options can also make or break your budget and schedule. Combining transit can sometimes save money and/or time, such as picking up a Zipcar rental at a local train station, having a rental car company pick you up for a weekend reservation, or using Lyft/Uber for destinations within a short distance. Not sure of the best route? Sites like **Rome2Rio** and **Wanderu** search through train schedules, bus routes, ferries, and flights to find the best transit options and pricing.

Pick the situation that works for you by checking out all the available transit options below.

TAXI/RIDE SHARE: Okay, the ubiquitous ride-hailing services of Lyft (lyft.com) and Uber (uber.com) are a no-brainer. But they're a welcome addition for many Hudson Valley and Catskills tourists traveling without a car. Keep in mind that coverage is much spottier than in New York City, so save the numbers of local taxi services handy as backup, just in case.

CAR RENTAL: Popular car-sharing service Zipcar (zipcar.com) has locations scattered throughout select Metro-North train stops if you want the flexibility of having a car for a few hours without the commitment and price of renting one in the city. Peer-to-peer app Turo (turo.com) has competitive rates for grabbing a cool car (convertible BMW, anyone?) or economic standard for the day/weekend. But if you want a car for the whole weekend, after fees, tax, and insurance, it's often still a better deal to stick with a major car rental company like Enterprise or Avis (especially when picking up a car outside the city).

SHUTTLE: Ride to Hudson Valley and the Catskills in style with **Line** (ridewithline.com), a luxury charter shuttle running service Thursday through Monday between Manhattan and destinations like New Paltz, Kingston, and Woodstock, as well as stops at boutique hotels Scribner's Lodge and The Graham & Co. Along with perks like cushy leather seats and Wi-Fi, each bus has a personal attendant serving refreshments and swag for purchase. Bonus: the price is a steal—tickets start at $39 round-trip.

TOUR OPERATORS: Sidestep traffic and reduce costs by looking into destination-based shuttle service operators like Urban Sherpa (urbansherpatravel.com), Sourced Adventures (sourcedadventures.com), and NYC Snow Bus (nycsnowbus.com). Along with easy day-trip service between the city and popular destinations these operators typically offer inclusive outdoor adventure packages like skiing, rafting, and hiking for $49–250.

LODGING

At the end of each chapter there is a curated list of standout lodgings, but check out these sites to discover additional housing options that fit your style and budget.

INSTAGRAM-WORTHY BOUTIQUE HOTELS: Snag last-minute deals on boutique hotels on smartphone apps like HotelTonight or One.Night.

HOME AWAY FROM HOME: Find unique apartments, vacation rentals, and even airstream trailers on booking websites like Airbnb, Red Cottage Inc., and VRBO.

SLEEP OUTDOORS WITHOUT SCHLEPPING THE EQUIPMENT: When you want to camp but don't want to invest in pricey camping equipment (that you have no room to store anyway), check out websites like Tentrr, Hipcamp, or Glamping Hub. Each site specializes in permanent outdoor rentals like platform tents, glamping sites, yurts, tepees, trailers, and cabins equipped with everything you might need for a weekend. Rent backpacking and car camper tents, sleeping pads, and the rest of your camping gear from outfitters like Duffle Out, Outdoors Geek, LowerGear, and Gear To Go (learn more on page 171).

NATURE INTEL

Before you venture into the woods, download the AllTrails (alltrails.com) and Offline Survival Manual smartphone apps. AllTrails features extensive user-submitted hiking trail information, photos, and maps to plan your perfect hike. Offline Survival Manual (Android only) has more information than you'd ever need to know about going off the grid, such as preparing fires, useful power sources, and how to identify plants.

STEAL THIS DEAL

Cut the drive and cost for getting to the Catskills by hitching a ride with one of the regular daily charter bus services heading to Monticello casino **Resort World Catskills**. Because it's so new (and a casino), it's an overlooked and less-trafficked shortcut compared to the regular fleet of tour operators. Besides, the casino has some genuinely decent entertainment and dining options once you get there before you start bouncing around Sullivan County. Check out rwcatskills.com for the most up-to-date schedule and pricing, which often includes free game-play and other incentives once you arrive.

LOCAL PUBLICATIONS

Want to know what's on this weekend? Snag a copy of *Dveight*, *Edible Hudson Valley*, *Chronogram*, *The Valley Table*, and *Hudson Valley Magazine*, which can usually be found lying around at area hotels, coffee shops, and restaurants and are always dialed into the latest local happenings and new openings.

TOURS

Want to drink your way through the wineries and breweries of the Shawangunks, but don't have anyone who wants to play designated driver? Thinking about going on a nature walk, but not sure where to start? Tour operators take the work out of planning and driving, and they typically have good local connections for those who want to pack everything into a short time frame.

THE LITTLE WINE BUS/THE LITTLE BEER BUS

thelittlewinebus.com/thelittlebeerbus.com

Pick your poison—wine, beer, spirits, or combining the best of all three worlds—then let this guided bus tour do the rest. Jump on a scheduled public tour or book a custom private trip with a group of friends, which picks up and drops off in Midtown and includes a visit, a tour, and a tasting at three Hudson Valley wineries, breweries, or distilleries; an organized lunch; and a swag bag. They even have a karaoke bus available, which is always fun after a drink or three.

HUDSON VALLEY BUCKET LIST

hvbucketlist.com

How does drinking wine in Hudson Valley during fall foliage season sound? A food and drink crawl around Beacon? Roaming through a field of sunflowers before a wine and cheese tasting? This tour operator focuses on bespoke experiences that capture the best of the Valley's artisanal producers in day and weekend getaways, picking up at the Beacon Metro-North train station and whisking travelers away to prime destinations.

HUDSON VALLEY CRAFT BEER BUS

hudsonvalleycraftbeertours.com

Craft beer fans, this is your tour. Grab your friends and book a tour that picks up from the Poughkeepsie or Beacon Metro-North train station and shuttles to private tastings at coveted breweries like Sloop Brewing Company, Keegan Ales, and Newburgh Brewing Company.

TOUR WITH DONOVAN

tourwithdonovan.com

Whether it's bouncing around wineries, distilleries, cider mills and breweries; a hiking tour in Shawangunks; a bachelorette weekend; or a personalized trip around Hudson Valley's biggest events, Donovan is your man with the van. This local tour operator knows the Valley like the back of his hand and can make a custom trip tailored to your ultimate checklist.

EVENT ATLAS

eventatlasco.com

Taste your way through mid-Hudson Valley with this indie tour operator that has established relationships with up-and-coming wineries, distilleries, and breweries like Tuthilltown Distillery, Tousey Winery, and Suarez Family Brewery.

THE OUTSIDE INSTITUTE

theoutsideinstitute.org

Nature is everywhere in Hudson Valley and the Catskills, but knowing how to navigate it can get complicated. Take an expert-guided walk through the woodlands or go on a foraging adventure with naturalist Laura Silverman, who hosts off-road excursions rooted in the beauty of the great outdoors.

FREESTONE EXPEDITIONS

freestonexp.com

From hiking and fly-fishing day trips to foraging with a professional wood-fire chef and campfire overnighters, this outdoor-centric tour operator specializes in personalized small-group outings for those who want to learn more about plant life and nature.

2

Art Worth Name-Dropping

Weekend Escapes for Art Lovers

Long before the *New York Times* began writing trend pieces on hipsters heading up north to launch open studios, Hudson Valley and the Catskills were a hub for the arts. Artists, craftsmen, writers, filmmakers, musicians, performers, and other experimental visionaries have set up camp here, from the earliest Dutch pioneers to contemporary tastemakers. Sure, antique shops, craft fairs, and family-friendly farm activities will always be part of any rural town, but it's really the weirdos that make this region special.

For a start, it's the birthplace of America's first arts and crafts community, Byrdcliffe Arts Colony, which opened in 1902 and still operates in Woodstock today, with artist residences and exhibitions. That spawned the country's original fine arts movement in the mid-19th century, the Hudson River School, which groomed landscape painters to depict dreamy scenes from the Hudson Valley, Catskills, and beyond. Among them, the estates of renowned painters Thomas Cole and Frederic Edwin Church continue to anchor both sides of the Hudson River, connected today by the Rip Van Winkle Bridge, just outside the city of Hudson. Nyack native Edward Hopper, who became the face of American Realism in the early 20th century, is immortalized in his hometown at the Edward Hopper House Art Center.

Legendary psychedelic 1960s music festival Woodstock might have grabbed its name from the Hudson Valley town, but if you want to plan a pilgrimage, you'll have to head to the landmark farmland where it actually happened, in the Catskills town of Bethel. Along with its fascinating immersive rock 'n' roll museum, the Bethel Woods Center for the Arts includes a performing arts venue that hosts everyone from Elvis Costello and the Imposters to the Zac Brown Band. It's no surprise, then, that musicians like Jimi Hendrix, Van Morrison, and Bob Dylan all took up residencies here in the 1960s and 1970s at places like the Big Pink House in Saugerties, where Dylan recorded *The Basement Tapes* with The Band in 1975 (it's now an Airbnb destination for fans).

If you're more likely to hit up MoMA, Chelsea gallery openings, and avant-garde noise concerts than pay patronage to fossilized hippie buses, don't worry—you can find all of that here, too. Contemporary art museums Storm King Art Center, Art Omi, and Dia:Beacon house some of the world's most acclaimed art from Louise Bourgeois, Richard Serra, Bruce Nauman, Alexander Calder, and Roy Lichtenstein. Hudson newcomer Basilica Hudson, a performing arts venue located within a railroad factory, hosts biannual experimental music and art events that bring out folks like Patti Smith, Eileen Myles, Angel Olsen, and Swans. Scratch beneath the surface and you'll find lesser-known enclaves, too, like Opus 40, a 40-year sprawling sculptural project independently built by sculptor and quarryman Harvey Fite, tucked away on his private residence in Saugerties.

Emerging art is still thriving throughout the region, thanks to writers' and artists' residencies, forward-thinking creative schools, and performing arts centers. Beacon, Kingston, and Hudson are among the best destinations for an art-filled weekender, crammed with plenty of emerging galleries, indie shows, vintage film screenings, and events like live band karaoke. This means no matter how you spin it, it's easy to fill up a weekend searching out the next big thing in art with the cool crowd without getting hit with a case of urban FOMO.

☰ *Best Destination for Art Nerds*

BEACON/COLD SPRING

Renowned contemporary art museum Dia:Beacon and massive outdoor sculpture park Storm King are probably both on your radar, but if you want to soak up a whole weekend of art, that's just the beginning. Stroll down Main Street in Beacon to pop into independent galleries like Matteawan Gallery, Marion Royael, The Clutter Gallery, Maria Lago Studio 502, and artisan glassmaking Hudson Beach Glass.

If you plan to make a whole weekend in Beacon, spend a day one stop away in Cold Spring, where you'll find the lesser-known Magazzino, which features an impressive collection of Italian art, and Manitoga, the 75-acre woodland garden, house, and studio of mid-century designer Russel Wright.

Getting There

1 hour 40 minutes via Metro-North to Beacon or Cold Spring. Save on admission to popular art attractions by purchasing an inclusive Metro-North Getaway package at Grand Central Terminal.

Getting Around

Once you get off the train, it's a short walk to the attractions along Main Street in Beacon or to Dia:Beacon. Lyft and Uber both operate here, though service is spottier than what you'd find around New York City. Local taxi services usually have cars by the train station, so bring cash in the event you need to pick up a ride.

Artsy Highlights

DIA:BEACON

3 Beekman Street, Beacon • 845-440-0100 • diaart.org • check the website for its latest monthly schedule • adults, $15; students and seniors, $12; free for members and children under 12

Neon lights? Check. Massive interactive steel sculptures? Check. A serene garden interrupted by a woman screaming bird calls? Yup, that too. Bring your external battery, because you're going to run your smartphone into the ground taking photos at this avant-garde art museum. Explore immersive experimental and conceptual works from groundbreaking artists like Louise Bourgeois, Richard Serra, Bruce Nauman, and Walter De Maria. Don't miss Bruce Nauman's famed work, *Body Pressure*, sitting on permanent display in the basement, featuring a stack of free pink prints to take home.

HUDSON BEACH GLASS

162 Main Street, Beacon • 845-440-0068 • hudsonbeachglass.com • Monday to Saturday 10 a.m.–6 p.m., Sunday 11 a.m.–6 p.m.

Watch live glassblowing at this working artist's studio and shop, that has been going strong in Beacon for over 20 years. Browse through functional and sculptural hand-cast pieces from local artisans, and pick up a bespoke ornament, decorative bowl, or entire stemware set to take home.

MAGAZZINO ITALIAN ART

2700 Route 9, Cold Spring • 845-666-7202 • magazzino.art • Thursday to Monday 11 a.m.–5 p.m. • free

Most people know of Dia:Beacon, but not everyone knows that a couple towns over is this warehouse gallery space boasting a massive collection of Postwar and Contemporary Italian art. With contents handpicked from the Olnick Spanu Collection, this free 20,000-square-foot museum provides a unique opportunity to see formal, conceptual, and immersive pieces from solely Italian contemporary artists outside of Italy. Magazzino provides a free shuttle from the Cold Spring Metro-North train station to the museum. Book in advance via their website.

MANITOGA

584 Route 9D, Garrison • 845-424-3812 • visitmanitoga.org • public tours run seasonally May through November, Friday to Monday 11 a.m. and 1:30 p.m.; select Saturdays at 3:30 p.m. • suggested donation of $5

Design nerds and crunchy hikers converge at the studio and home of modernist industrial designer Russel Wright. Dubbed "Dragon Rock," the stunning, experimental, glass-walled estate was built into the site of an abandoned quarry overlooking a 30-foot waterfall, pool, and 75 acres of natural woodland landscape. Take a tour of Wright's architectural home or hit the hiking trails that wind throughout the property and connect to extensions of the Osborn Loop Trail and Appalachian Trail. Tours are 90 minutes and are considered moderate, traversing uneven ground, rustic bridges, and stepping stones. Make sure to wear comfortable hiking or athletic shoes and prepare to be in the outdoors without protective covering. Summer through early fall, the property hosts a monthly late afternoon sunset tour of the house, studio, and Woodland Garden. Find up-to-date tour and ticket information via their website.

GETTING THERE: 1 hour 30 minutes via Metro-North to Cold Spring. Save $5 by purchasing a Metro-North Getaway package via the Manitoga website. On Saturday and Sunday, trolley service operates between the Cold Spring train station and Manitoga for $4 round-trip.

// *Three Legged Buddha* by Zhang Huan is among the permanent collection at Storm King Arts Center

STORM KING ART CENTER

1 Museum Road, New Windsor • 845-534-3115 • stormking.org • check the website for the latest monthly schedule • adults, $18; seniors 65+, $15; college students with valid ID and K–12, $8; free for members and children 5 and under

Listen: no one really conquers this massive 500-acre outdoor sculpture park in one day, so don't worry about leaving unfulfilled. It just means you have reason to come back, and it's so easy that you'll be a pro at getting there your second time around. Developed by the late landscape architect William A. Rutherford, this art park is best known for using brilliant landscape design to serve as a natural gallery space for massive sculptural installations for more than 75 contemporary artists. Sprawling through meadows, woodlands, water, and 100 acres of native grass, Storm King provides the unique experience of interacting with art outside the confines of gallery walls, so you can actually have a grassy picnic next to an Alexander Calder or Richard Serra sculpture.

GETTING THERE: Coach USA operates round-trip buses to Storm King from Port Authority Terminal seasonally (April–November) on Wednesday through Sunday. Alternatively, you can purchase a Metro-North Getaway package that includes admission to Storm King by taking the Hudson Line train to Beacon and getting a ride to Storm King from there.

>> **Know Before You Go:** The park is entirely outdoors, so wear comfortable shoes and plan for a day of extensive walking while exposed to the elements. If a long stroll isn't in the cards, rent a bike on-site or take the free tram that operates every hour.

Where to Stay
For a Design-Centric Hotel
ROUNDHOUSE BEACON

2 East Main Street, Beacon • 845-765-8369 • roundhousebeacon.com

This renovated property inside a former textile manufacturing warehouse captures the modern, design-centric vibe of nearby Dia:Beacon and Studio Row in Beacon. Rustic and industrial touches like exposed ceilings and factory windows blend seamlessly with elegant, minimalist furnishings tapped from local contemporary artists. It's not filled with the kind of frills that make you want to plan a staycation here, but it's comfortable enough if you end up doing just that. Bonus: the complimentary buffet breakfast inside the hotel's restaurant is exceptionally good, featuring house-baked pastries, egg dishes, freshly squeezed juices, and waterfall views from its floor-to-ceiling windows.

For When You Don't Want to Leave Storm King
STORM KING LODGE BED & BREAKFAST

100 Pleasant Hill Road, Mountainville • 845-534-9421 • stormkinglodge.com

If you're tacking on a day to visit Storm King Art Center, why not make it an overnighter? Stay at this immaculately maintained lodge located just around the corner, which features sweeping views of the pastoral landscape, a seasonal fireplace and pool, and a made-to-order breakfast.

// Storm King Lodge Bed & Breakfast is only a 2-minute drive from the famous sculptural art park that shares the same name

☰ *Under the Radar*

Go off the well-worn path to these super-cool but lesser-known art destinations.

MUSEUMS AND ART INSTALLATIONS

Upper Hudson Valley

FRANCES LEHMAN LOEB ART CENTER AT VASSAR COLLEGE

124 Raymond Avenue, Poughkeepsie • 845- 437-5237 • fllac.vassar.edu • Tuesday to Wednesday and Friday to Saturday 10 a.m.–5 p.m.; Thursday 10 a.m.–9 p.m.; Sunday 1 p.m.–5 p.m. • free

If you plan to hit up the Samuel Dorsky Museum in New Paltz (see page 44), make it a double art weekend by fitting in this Vassar College art museum across the river. Most notable is its impressive collection of original works from the Hudson River School, but if American realism and landscapes are of less interest than wandering through a gallery of modern masters like Georgia O'Keeffe and Willem de Kooning, the museum features more than 21,000 pieces of art spanning all genres and countries, from Japanese antiquities to 21st-century tastemakers.

HESSEL MUSEUM OF ART AT BARD COLLEGE

33 Garden Road, Annandale-on-Hudson • 845-758-7598 • ccs.bard.edu • Thursday to Sunday 12 a.m.–6 p.m. • free

Perpetually rotating exhibitions make every visit feel brand new at this 9,500-square-foot art museum within private liberal arts institution Bard College. Fans of New York City's New Museum and MoMA PS1 should take a second look; the Hessel Museum frequently showcases subversive contemporary art exhibitions within immersive large-scale playrooms. Works from notables like Cindy Sherman and Gillian Wearing often make cameos alongside selections from international art festivals like Venice Biennale.

OPUS 40

50 Fite Road, Saugerties • 845-246-3400 • opus40.org • open seasonally May through October, Thursday to Sunday 10:30 a.m.–5:30 p.m. and holiday Mondays • adults, $10; seniors, $7; children ages 6–12, $3; children under 6 free with an adult

Nestled behind a labyrinth of back roads on private property, sculptor Harvey Fite spent the last 37 years of his life quietly transforming a 6.5-acre former quarry into his life's work: a permanent art installation. Staring at the thousands of individually stacked slabs of blue stone, it's hard to believe he did it entirely himself without modern machinery, relying solely on ancient dry-key stone masonry techniques right until he died three years short of completion. His work might have faded into memory were it not for his wife, who opened it up to the public after Fite passed. Along with its stunning array of ramps, terraces, passageways, and pools, he also created the Quarryman's Museum dedicated to the working men that populated Saugerties in the 19th century. The property frequently hosts theater, dance, and other performing arts events throughout the year.

>> **Know Before You Go:** Along with being entirely outdoors and subject to the elements, the slab grounds aren't secured by mortar, making this slightly unstable ground to walk on and particularly rough for people with mobility issues. Walk carefully and make sure to wear secure athletic shoes.

>> **Secret Stay Alert:** Fite's stunning private residence at Opus 40, dubbed The House on the Quarry, is actually available to book as an Airbnb (starting at only $145). Because it's not listed on the website, this is an overlooked treat, providing a unique opportunity to experience a portion of the property that most visitors never see.

SAMUEL DORSKY MUSEUM OF ART

1 Hawk Drive, New Paltz • 845-257-3844 • newpaltz.edu/museum • Wednesday to Sunday 11 a.m.– 5 p.m. • $5 suggested donation

This college campus art museum might not be the first spot on your gallery-hopping checklist, but don't overlook this underrated gem hiding in plain sight. Its collection spans across all mediums and centuries, from rare antiquities and works by European masters to subversive contemporary installations.

ARTSY DAY TRIPS FROM NYC

Dip into these Lower Hudson Valley artistic institutions for a quick day trip.

EDWARD HOPPER HOUSE • 82 North Broadway, Nyack • 845-358-0774 • edwardhopperhouse.org • Wednesday to Sunday 12–5 p.m. • free the first Friday of each month; adults, $7; seniors, $5; students, $2; free for ages 16 and under

Visit the childhood home of Edward Hopper, the Grandfather of American Realism, best known for *Nighthawks*, his iconic, moody portrait of a downtown New York diner in 1942. Along with a historic glimpse into his life and work, the museum also features rotating exhibitions, installations, art talks, and lectures. Learn more on page 30.

KATONAH MUSEUM OF ART • 134 Jay Street, Katonah • 914-232-9555 • katonahmuseum.org • Tuesday to Saturday 10 a.m.–5 p.m.; Sunday 12–5 p.m.; closed Mondays and select holidays • adults, $10; seniors and students, $5; free for members and ages 12 and under

Veer off the well-worn paths in Beacon and Hudson to the hamlet of Katonah, where you can find amazing experimental works from artists like Nick Cave, Arman, and Mark di Suvero at this contemporary art museum.

THE WASSAIC PROJECT

Maxon Mills, 37 Furnace Bank Road, Wassaic • 855-927-7242 • wassaicproject.org • May through September, Friday 3–5 p.m., Saturday 12–7 p.m., Sunday 12–5 p.m.; October–April Saturday 12–5 p.m. • free to visit exhibitions; most lectures are free; event pricing varies

You never know what you'll find at this artist-run nonprofit organization housed within restored rustic buildings at Maxon Mills and Luther Barn. Weirdos are warmly welcomed here for its forward-thinking year-round artist residencies, drop-in art activities, music festivals, immersive performances, installations, lectures, educational activities, and more. In October, Maxon Mills transforms into a creepy-cool haunted house that has somewhat of an immersive art installation vibe. Learn more on page 199.

>> **Transit Pro-Tip:** Purchase a Metro-North Getaway package to save up to $20 on admission, with $5 of the ticket price donated to The Wassaic Project.

LITERATURE

Lower Hudson Valley

BINNACLE BOOKS

321 Main Street, Beacon • 845-838-6191 • binnaclebooks.com

Browse new and used titles at this progressive bookshop, including popular and niche works spanning everything from award-winning literature to graphic novels, poetry, art, and philosophy. Events here are worth attending, with discussions ranging from Afrofuturism and queer comics to movie screenings in the garden.

BRUISED APPLE BOOKS

923 Central Avenue, Peekskill • 914-734-7000 • bruisedapplebooks.com

Love the well-worn feel of an old-school bookstore stocked with an eclectic mix of new, used, and rare titles? You'll feel right at home at this Peekskill gem that has been going strong since 1993, filled with thousands of curated books plus a selection of vinyl, CDs, and movies to browse through.

Upper Hudson Valley

INQUIRING MINDS COFFEE HOUSE AND BOOKSTORE

68 Partition Street, Saugerties • 845-246-5775 • inquiringbooks.com

Tucked away along the Esopus Creek in Saugerties is one of the Hudson Valley's largest independent bookstores, housed within a historic building built in 1895. Between the endless array of books, the cozy enclaves, and the full-service café, this is an excellent spot to shack up for a long afternoon of reading, playing chess, or sticking around for one of their many community events.

OBLONG BOOKS & MUSIC

6422 Montgomery Street, Rhinebeck • 845-876-0500 • oblongbooks.com

A Rhinebeck institution since 1975, this beloved bookstore is best known for its curated selection of incredible new titles from top-name and emerging authors who often pop in for a reading, including famous folks like H. Jon Benjamin, Craig Ferguson, and Neil Gaiman.

RODGERS BOOK BARN

467 Rodman Road, Hillsdale • 518-325-3610 • rodgersbookbarn.com

True to its name, it's a bookstore within an actual barn. Book lovers might consider it more of a treasure trove or an opportunity for antique hunting for bibliophiles, carrying about 50,000 used and rare titles split between two floors, making it worth going out of the way for a visit.

ROUGH DRAFT BAR & BOOKS

82 John Street, Kingston • 845-802-0027 • roughdraftny.com

Come for the books, stay for the bar—it's the writerly way. Housed in historic Kingston, this bookstore-bar is a hot spot for browsing through the latest releases over a local craft beer, cider, or wine, plus artisanal snacks. Regular workshops with Kingston Writers' Studio and readings from visiting talent bring in the lit crowd, but casual events like trivia, bagel brunch, and streaming soccer games keep things lively.

SPOTTY DOG BOOKS & ALE

440 Warren Street, Hudson • 518-671-6006 • thespottydog.com

Shopping for books is great, but cozying up with a paperback and a beer is even better. More than a bookstore, this hybrid lit-and-lager spot lets you do both, showcasing emerging titles from lesser-known authors and frequently hosting events like live music, readings, coveted craft beer release parties, and trivia nights.

Catskills

HOBART BOOK VILLAGE

Main Street, Hobart • hobartbookvillage.com

There are more books than people in this Upper Catskills village of less than 500. It might have been a blip on the radar were it not for the collection of five bookstores that make up its Main Street, offering everything from antique bindings to feminism and African American studies.

MAGPIE BOOKSHOP

392 Main Street, Catskill • 518-303-6035 • magpiebookshop.com

Browse through gently used books at this bright and cozy two-floor shop, where you're as likely to stumble across a first edition of Nancy Drew as you are to find best-selling titles, all at super-affordable prices (including a stack of free books, typically out in front).

ONE GRAND BOOKS

60 Main Street, Narrowsburg • 845-252-3541 • onegrandbooks.com

Why does this tiny bookshop in the middle of Narrowsburg have international acclaim? Perhaps it's because its entire collection is curated by some of the world's most famous people, from Eileen Myles and Tilda Swinton to Bill Gates and Ta-Nehisi Coates. If you happen to find this book on the shelf, consider this author a made woman!

PERFORMING ARTS

Lower Hudson Valley

PARAMOUNT HUDSON VALLEY THEATER

1008 Brown Street, Peekskill • 914-739-0039 • paramounthudsonvalley.com

Originally opened as a cinema subsidiary of Paramount Pictures, this landmark theater continues to host music headliners like Ani DiFranco, Arlo Guthrie, and Chris Isaak; comedians Paul Reiser, Lewis Black, and Kathleen Madigan; and everything in between.

Upper Hudson Valley

BARDAVON 1869 OPERA HOUSE

35 Market Street, Poughkeepsie • 845-473-2072 • bardavon.org

As the oldest continuously operating theater in New York State (as well as one of the oldest in the US), this historic venue has seen its share of operatic greats, acclaimed musicians, politicians, and public speakers. That list hasn't shortened over time, now bringing in contemporaries like Neko Case, John Cale, and Joan Baez. In addition to an incredible bill, the theater also houses one of the last remaining—and still playable—Wurlitzer pipe organs in the country.

CRANDELL THEATRE

48 Main Street, Chatham • 518-392-3331 • crandelltheatre.org

One of the Valley's oldest theaters, this 534-seat cinema opened in 1926 and has been chugging along ever since. Only one film screens daily for a week at a time, showcasing a curated selection of independent and award-winning titles.

RICHARD B. FISHER CENTER FOR THE PERFORMING ARTS

60 Manor Avenue, Annadale-On-Hudson • 845-758-7900 • fishercenter.bard.edu

Even if you don't come for a show, it's worth driving by to see this behemoth 107,000-square-foot steel venue inside Bard College designed by legendary architect Frank Gehry. The center comprises four theaters and studios under one roof: the Sosnoff Theater, LUMA Theater, The Felicitas S. Thorne Dance Studio, and the Stewart and Lynda Resnick Theater Studio. Beyond its impressive exteriors, this is a fantastic venue for catching everything from opera, dance, and jazz to experimental theater, educational talks by Bard College students, and performances by international artists.

SPIEGELTENT AT THE FISHER CENTER 60 Manor Avenue, Annandale-On-Hudson • fishercenter.bard.edu/spiegeltent • 2-hour drive by car; during select Summerscape and Bard Music Festival series events, the theater offers round-trip chartered coach service from Lincoln Center in Manhattan for $40 • tickets and additional information are available via their website

While you're at the Fisher Center, check out Bard College's annual pop-up venue The Spiegeltent: an authentic 1900s traveling circus tent from Belgium. Catch outstanding cabaret, DJ, music, and other evening performances hosted by Mx. Justin Vivian Bond, a Tony Award–nominated musician and artist.

Western Hudson Valley

PARAMOUNT THEATRE

17 South Street, Middletown • 845-346-4195 • middletownparamount.com

Not to be confused with the Peekskill theater sharing its name, this massive 1,500-seat theater opened in 1930 was first intended for talkies (its original Wurlitzer pipe organ is still intact). The air conditioning and screen quality have improved since then, making this ideal for catching first-run movies, limited releases, local plays, and theater performances.

Western Catskills

BETHEL WOODS CENTER FOR THE ARTS

200 Hurd Road, Bethel • 866-781-2922 • bethelwoodscenter.org

Long before there was Coachella, Lollapalooza, or the seemingly never-ending list of new summer music festivals, there was Woodstock: the first rock festival that manifested as a phenomenon during the Summer of Love in 1969 on a small farm in Bethel, New York. The site is commemorated now in the form of Bethel Woods, a performing arts center, Woodstock rock history museum, and national landmark. Throughout the summer, catch touring performances from notables like Steve Martin and Martin Short, Judas Priest, and Lucinda Williams.

// Middletown's historic Paramount Theatre is home to an original Wurlitzer organ

THE FORESTBURGH PLAYHOUSE

39 Forestburgh Road, Forestburgh • 845-794-1194 • fbplayhouse.org

Love Broadway musicals but hate the idea of fighting Times Square tourists to get there? Sidestep the lines at this Catskills performing arts house, which has been hosting summer Broadway performances since 1947—and for a fraction of Manhattan prices. Tuesdays through Thursdays preshow or Friday and Saturday postshow, catch a buffet dinner cabaret performance to make an evening of it (the food isn't much to write home about, but it's a pretty good deal).

NACL THEATRE

110 Highland Lake Road, Highland Lake • 845-557-0694 • nacl.org

Short for North American Cultural Laboratory, this nonprofit theater hosts a rotating event calendar featuring thought-provoking stage work from actors, playwrights, musicians, and other performers. Catch everything from experimental theater tackling controversial topics to dinner-dance parties and burlesque.

FILM

Drive-In Movies

Catch the last vestiges of this dying American institution by paying a visit to one of these drive-in movie theaters for a double feature.

Western Hudson Valley

WARWICK DRIVE-IN

5 Warwick Turnpike, Warwick • 845-986-4440 • warwickdrivein.com

Dating back to the 1950s, this three-screen drive-in theater shows daily double features from box office toppers to throwback flicks.

FAIR OAKS DRIVE-IN

365 Bloomingburg Road, Middletown • 845-361-5686 • fairoaksdriveintheatre.com

This Middletown seasonal drive-in theater, which dates back to the 1970s, shows the latest releases and classic films on its two digital screens.

Upper Hudson Valley

HYDE PARK DRIVE-IN

4114 Albany Post Road, Hyde Park • 845-229-4738 • hydeparkdrivein.com

If you're heading to historic estates like Franklin D. Roosevelt's, Eleanor Roosevelt's, or Vanderbilt, make an evening pit stop at this 12-acre, seasonal drive-in theater.

Indie Cinemas

Check out up-and-coming foreign, indie, and art films at these theaters.

Lower Hudson Valley

DOWNING FILM CENTER

19 Front Street, Newburgh • 845-561-3686 • downingfilmcenter.com

Once considered a sleepy industrial town, Newburgh is gaining recognition for its growing arts scene, which includes this beloved small art house cinema, known for screening riveting selections of emerging, foreign, and classic films.

Upper Hudson Valley

UPSTATE FILMS

6415 Montgomery Street, Rhinebeck • 845-876-2515 • upstatefilms.org

This nonprofit local cinema operating since the early 1970s expanded from one screen to this newer location with three in the late '90s. It frequently showcases popular indie flicks, classic cinema, and special events. Try to show up early: the last showing is usually around 8 p.m.

CRANDELL THEATRE

48 Main Street, Chatham • 518-392-3331 • crandelltheatre.org

One of the Valley's oldest theaters, this 534-seat cinema opened in 1926 and has been chugging along ever since. Screening only one daily film per week, Crandell focuses on independent films over box office hits.

Eastern Catskills

UPSTATE FILMS

132 Tinker Street, Woodstock • 845-679-6608 • upstatefilms.org

The second addition to its flagship in Rhinebeck, Upstate Films' Woodstock location is housed within a former church, screening films only once or twice per day on a single screen.

ART WALKS

Lower Hudson Valley

MANITOGA

584 Route 90, Garrison • 845-424-3812 • visitmanitoga.org • public tours run seasonally May through November, Friday to Monday at 11 a.m. and 1:30 p.m.; select Saturdays at 3:30 p.m.

Design nerds and crunchy hikers converge on the 75-acre Woodland Garden, the studio and home of modernist industrial designer Russel Wright. Dubbed "Dragon Rock," the stunning, experimental, glass-walled estate was built into the site of an abandoned quarry overlooking a 30-foot waterfall, pool, and wooded natural landscape, subsequently marked as an official National Historic Landmark. The property is surrounded by beautiful hiking trails, with extensions connecting to the Osborn Loop Trail and Appalachian Trail. Tours are 90 minutes and considered moderate walks, traversing uneven ground, rustic bridges, and stepping stones. Make sure to wear comfortable hiking or athletic shoes and prepare to be in the outdoors.

GETTING THERE: 1 hour 15 minutes via Metro-North to Cold Spring. Get $5 off by purchasing tickets via the Manitoga website, then purchase train tickets through Metro-

North. For Saturday and Sunday 11 a.m. tours, you can catch a $4 round-trip trolley from the Cold Spring train station to Manitoga.

>>   **Manitoga at Sunset:** Once a month from summer through early fall, the property hosts late afternoon sunset tours of the house, studio, and Woodland Garden. Check their website for dates and tickets.

STORM KING

1 Museum Road, New Windsor • 845-534-3115 • stormking.org • check the website for the latest monthly schedule • adults, $18; seniors 65+, $15; college students with valid ID and K–12, $8; free for members and children 5 and under

Trying to conquer this massive 500-acre outdoor sculpture park in one day is setting yourself up for a challenge. But don't worry, that just leaves more areas to explore on your next visit. Late landscape architect William A. Rutherford had the vision behind this stunning outdoor park that uses a carefully arranged natural backdrop of forests, rolling hills, ponds, and meadows as the installation space for more than 75 artists, including Louise Bourgeois, Alexander Calder, Zhang Huan, and Roy Lichtenstein.

GETTING THERE BY BUS: 1 hour 30 minutes via Coach USA seasonal bus service from Port Authority Terminal ($48). The bus is the most direct option for an easy day trip.

GETTING THERE BY TRAIN: 1 hour 20 minutes via Metro-North to Beacon, then a shuttle to Storm King. Buy a Metro-North Getaway package ($40.50) for discounted train fare to Beacon and admission to Storm King, then take a taxi from the train station or book a weekend-operating shuttle ride via stormking.org/shuttle.

>>   **Know Before You Go:** Storm King is entirely outdoors, so wear comfortable shoes for extensive walking and clothing to protect against the elements. If you don't want to go by foot, rent a bike through the visitor center or take the free tram that operates every hour.

Upper Hudson Valley
ART OMI

1405 County Route 22, Ghent • 581-392-4747 • artomi.org • sunrise to sunset • free

Storm King usually gets all the fanfare, making this massive 300-acre outdoor sculpture park located 20 minutes northwest of Hudson a perpetually well-kept secret (not to mention free of charge). Explore a rotating exhibition of large-scale sculptural installations from emerging and established contemporary artists nestled within a sprawling landscape of pastoral fields, shady forests, and secluded natural trails.

>>   **Know Before You Go:** Ditch the heels, check the weather, and be prepared to walk extensively outdoors on unpaved, natural landscape. While there's a small café at the welcome center, food options are mostly limited, so it's best to pack a lunch.

≡ *Artsy Accommodations*

If you're not staying at boutique hotels worth bragging about on social media, are you even doing it right? Shack up somewhere nicer than your own cramped pad at these enviable interior-designed boutique hotels.

Upper Hudson Valley

VANDERBILT LAKESIDE

161 Main Street, Philmont • 518-672-7070 • vanderbiltlakeside.com

Often overlooked by weekenders due to its location about 20 minutes east of the main Hudson strip, this is one of those perfect gems that most weekenders wish they knew about. It's got it all: the right blend of modern-meets-rustic style, a peaceful and breathtaking lakeside view, nearby access to prime hiking trails, and a restaurant serving creative and healthy dishes loaded with local ingredients. On top of all that, the prices for all of this are shockingly much more affordable than you'd expect.

WING'S CASTLE

717 Bangall Road, Millbrook • 845-677-9085 • wingscastle.com

An architectural anomaly, Wing's Castle is one of Hudson Valley's most bizarre and fascinating bed-and-breakfasts. Constructed mostly out of scavenged and recycled materials, this hodge-podge estate that looks like a Jim Henson or J. R. R. Tolkien fantasy is the 47-year living artwork and dream home project of artists Peter and Toni Ann Wing. In 1970, the Wings sought to build a grand castle on a hill. After being turned down by contractors who found the project too complicated, they decided to take matters into their own hands and have made the project a continuous lifelong pursuit. What results is an incredible Gothic-inspired fairy-tale castle and Hobbit-like country cottage that includes a myriad of intricate details like hand-tiled mosaic art, a cauldron bathtub in the Dungeon basement suite, a "Stonehenge" sunset terrace, and a pool "moat."

WM. FARMER & SONS

20 South Front Street, Hudson • 518-828-1635 • wmfarmerandsons.com

It's like a home away from home—but probably better than the one you already have. Part restaurant, part boarding house, this historic property has become a hot ticket for city dwellers escaping to Hudson. Situated steps from the town's train station, the inn is split among three buildings, each with apartment-sized rooms and suites uniquely decorated with antiques and vintage-inspired knickknacks. Considering how stylish and in-demand the property is, the pricing is extremely reasonable (particularly for groups willing to split the two-bedroom).

Bonus: the ground floor restaurant is ridiculously good, with a seasonal menu boasting the best of Hudson Valley and an impressive bar menu developed by the late Sasha Petraske of renowned NYC craft cocktail bar Milk & Honey.

THE WOODHOUSE LODGE

3807 County Route 26, Greenville • 518-893-1511 • thewoodhouselodge.com

So stylishly mid-century modern, yet so deliciously rustic Catskills—exactly the kind of thing that makes designers swoon. This 10-room cabin lodge is all about the details, like handmade custom felt-and-leather headboards, Brooklinen bedding, down alternative pillows, and luxe natural bathroom amenities. Tucked away in the northern Catskills, about 30 minutes north-west of Hudson, it's just country enough to disconnect for a weekend in nature, but with all the modern conveniences, so you don't come home with a funky hiking smell.

Eastern Catskills

FOXFIRE MOUNTAIN HOUSE

72 Andrew Lane, Mount Tremper • 845-688-2500 • foxfiremountainhouse.com

Ever wish you could steal a hotel's interior designer? You might start fantasizing about redoing your whole home after staying at this adorably Bohemian boutique property in the Catskills. Between the beautiful furnishings and its incredible, seasonally driven menu at the hotel's restaurant, the idea of starting a new life up in the mountains doesn't sound so crazy. In the meantime, you'll have to settle for purchasing one of their signature handcrafted candles or soaps before a nice weekend dinner. And if you're into baths, make sure to ask for the room on the third floor, which has a deep soaking tub with excellent woodland views.

HOUSE ON THE QUARRY

50 Fite Road, Saugerties • 845-681-9657 • airbnb.com

Not everyone has heard of Harvey Fite's independent 40-year art installation quarry project, Opus 40. But even fewer people know that you can stay overnight at his former residence, The House on the Quarry, which overlooks the grounds. Two bedrooms are available to book through Airbnb (starting at the insanely reasonable price of $145). Because it's not listed on the website, this is an overlooked gem, providing a unique opportunity to experience a portion of the property most visitors never see.

KATE'S LAZY MEADOW

5191 Route 28, Mount Tremper • 845-688-7200 • lazymeadow.com

There's no shortage of swanky new spots dripping with modest mid-century design, but this campy Catskills destination is all about groovy vibes. That's because its owner is none other than Kate Pierson of the B-52s and her partner, Monica Coleman, who have built a veritable "love shack" appropriately situated just outside Woodstock. Each cabin is outfitted with its own bespoke retro interior, bursting with wild colors reminiscent of *Pee-wee's Playhouse* and plenty of space to spread out for group weekends. And for fine art geeks, look into snagging one of the two suites designed by artist Phillip Maberry.

THE ROXBURY MOTEL

2258 County Road 41, Roxbury • 607-326-7200 • theroxburymotel.com

Maybe the thought of sleeping in a room decorated like a coconut cream pie never occurred to you, but if the idea sounds appealing, you can actually do that at The Roxbury Motel. Despite an unassuming exterior, each of the rooms at this Catskills lodge is notoriously kitschy and thematic, from the Fred Flintstone-inspired caveman room to an over-the-top baroque suite that would have made Liberace proud. On-site is the property's co-ed Shimmer Spa, where you can use the hot tub and sweat lodge for only $20 per day.

SCRIBNER'S CATSKILL LODGE

13 Scribner Hollow Road, Hunter • 518-628-5130 • scribnerslodge.com

A resort relic that survived from the Catskills' Borscht Belt days of the 1960s, the property freshened up with modern renovation in 2016 reflective of its surrounding area's current design-focused digs. There's rarely a bad view, because most of its 38 rooms have private balconies and large windows overlooking its 20-acre mountainous landscape and expansive pool. Even if you aren't shacking up here, it's worth stopping by for dinner at the lodge's acclaimed restaurant, Prospect, which offers upscale takes on seasonal, local ingredients.

>> **Transit Pro-Tip:** A luxury charter shuttle, **Line**, offers drop-off service to Scribner's from Manhattan Thursday through Monday (646-798–8116; ridewithline.com).

Western Catskills

THE ARNOLD HOUSE

839 Shandelee Road, Livingston Manor • 845-439-5070 • thearnoldhouse.com

Harkening back to the heyday of the Catskills' 1950s and 1960s resort era, this 13-room vintage revival boutique hotel meshes mid-century modern chic with rustic cabin coziness. For vintage design and antique geeks, this stylish property will give you all the feels. This is kind of the MO of their hospitality group, Foster Supply, which owns a handful of other Catskills properties like North Branch Inn, Nine River Road, and The DeBruce. Overlooking seven acres of scenic landscape, nature is right at your fingertips for a secluded weekend hiking through the woods, sitting on the river, exploring local sights, or hibernating indoors next to the wood stove fireplace in the sun room.

EASTWIND HOTEL & BAR

5088 Route 23, Windham • 518-734-0553 • eastwindny.com

Channeling the trendy rustic-meets-minimalist-chic aesthetic of Scandinavia, this hip Catskills lodge just outside Windham Mountain is outfitted with mid-century modern furnishings and boasts a unique addition: three Lushna-style cabins (an intimate 220-square-foot enclosed triangular hut; essentially a form of glamping you'd most likely hear about from your coolest friend) with sauna access. If you prefer to keep things indoors, opt for a suite or the writer's room, both of which have sweeping mountainside views. There's no in-house restaurant, but the property has a weekend High Spirits craft cocktail bar that pops up Friday through Sunday.

NORTH BRANCH INN

869 North Branch Road, North Branch • 845-482-2339 • northbranchinn.com

Not far from The Arnold House is its quieter, off-the-beaten-path sister concept, North Branch Inn. Divided among three properties (including a former post office) along the small

// Take a spin on the North Branch Inn's authentic antique bowling alley

rural strip in the hamlet of North Branch, each of its 14 renovated rooms has a cozy, bespoke, vintage feel that's better than your run-of-the-mill bed-and-breakfast. Despite its secluded location, the property is blessed with an incredible restaurant where chefs often pull vegetables and herbs straight from North Branch's garden for farm-to-table dinners. Bonus: the main house is home to an authentic turn-of-the-century wooden bowling alley where you can still bowl.

THE RED ROSE MOTEL + TAVERN

21677 Old Route 17, Roscoe • 607-290-4333 • theredrosemotel.com

Built in 1938, this storied motel and tavern has seen many transformations throughout the years. Its most recent iteration finally opened its doors in 2018, a stunning renovation channeling the timeless rustic aesthetic of the Catskills and vintage Americana. Think: wood-paneled walls, sportsman motifs, cozy wool blankets, antiques peppered throughout, and endless views of the great outdoors. Downstairs in the tavern, you'll find a full selection of local wines, beers, spirits, and tasty bar bites made with farm-fresh ingredients.

SILENT G FARMS

169 Stewart Road, North Branch • silentgfarms.com

When you want to stay in a farmhouse, but prefer something a little more Restoration Hardware rustic chic instead of Laura Ashley country cottage, this is your rural getaway. Suites range from a massive three-bedroom converted barn house outfitted with a gentleman's bar to a refinished guesthouse furnished with a generously sized soaking tub with a sunroof shower. Upscale details are scattered throughout, like an authentic black leather Eames chair and wood stove fireplace. On-site amenities are nothing less than fabulous. Along with hiking trail access and a game room, Silent G has its own freestanding, wood-burning cedar sauna, eight-person hot tub, a private music studio you can reserve for recording sessions, and the ability to book a private chef dinner.

SPRUCETON INN

2080 Spruceton Road, West Kill • 518-989-6404 • sprucetoninn.com

Bed-and-breakfasts are so yesterday. This is the vision of the future: a bed and bar. You'll be happy to have it, because this destination property is way off the grid, located five miles down a seven-mile dead-end road surrounded by the wilderness of Catskills Park. You guessed it: no Wi-Fi. It's the kind of undistracted retreat that makes it a major draw for its regular artist residency program where writers like Stephanie Danler and Carmen Maria Machado have been among the alum to bang out their award-winning books at the property. Stay here when you want to enjoy the great outdoors without diving headfirst into a tent; where you can make s'mores over a fire, go hiking, take a fly-fishing class, or just nap in a hammock.

// Sleep in style at Catskills hideaway the Stickett Inn

STICKETT INN

3380 Route 97, Barryville • 845-557-0913 • stickettinn.com

Yes, the name is intentional, and it's exactly the kind of tongue-in-cheek welcome you should expect from its incredibly charming husband-owners, Roswell Hamrick and Johnny Pizzolato. An intimate property with only five suites, each stylish space is dressed with locally made Shibori bedding and themed by interest: "Eat" is outfitted with a kitchen and geared toward the traveler who wants to cook local farm fresh produce; "Steam" is equipped with a private steam shower and a cold plunge basin. In the courtyard, there's a four-seat jacuzzi with disco lights for hot-tubbing under the stars. Pick up a cup of coffee in the morning or end the evening with a nightcap of their proprietary cider (aptly named Stickett Inn Cider Dry and Hard) at the small bar/welcome center, where there's great swag for purchase that's worth toting home.

⩵ Food as Art

A streak of sauce here, a dash of spice there—for some chefs, a blank plate is a place for edible art. Put these destination fine dining spots on your list for food that looks as good as it tastes.

Lower Hudson Valley

BLUE HILL AT STONE BARNS

630 Bedford Road, Pocantico Hills • 914-366-9600 • bluehillfarm.com • $$$$

Farm-to-table pioneer Dan Barber put Hudson Valley on the map with this fine dining spot that has picked up virtually every culinary award under the sun. Situated within the innovative Stone Barns Center for Food and Agriculture, this establishment offers unique access to some of the freshest and most experimental ingredients around, all on-site. Book well in advance and make sure to dress appropriately—this is among the few places in the area with a jacket requirement.

>> **Deal Alert:** Score a better deal at **Blue Hill's Café and Grain Bar** for affordable, casual farm-to-table food during a visit to the Stone Barns agricultural center.

INN AT POUND RIDGE BY JEAN-GEORGES

258 Westchester Avenue, Pound Ridge • 914-764-1400 • theinnatpoundridge.com • $$$$

If it's a restaurant from internationally renowned chef Jean-Georges Vongerichten, then it's a given that it's going to be fine, fancy, and worth the trip. True to form, you can expect JGV's signature New French-meets-Pan-Asian cuisine infused with Hudson Valley's top-notch produce nestled within an intimate, historic inn, dating back to 1833.

Upper Hudson Valley

THE AMSTERDAM

6380 Mill Street, Rhinebeck • 845-516-5033 • lovetheamsterdam.com • $$$

Bringing a NorCal approach to Hudson Valley ingredients, this popular Rhinebeck restaurant is helmed by Chef Alex Burger, a vet of Daniel Boulud, and is best known for making magic with the local bounty for its seasonally changing menu that might include anything from pork belly with summer beans, crispy bacon, and smoked tomato to house-made charcuterie.

WILDE BEEST

310 Wall Street, Kingston • 845-481-4181 • wilde-beest.com • $$$

Wilde Beest is the kind of tweezer-food restaurant where there's bound to be some kind of esoteric foam or gel splashed across the plate, but they'll also probably have an album from someone like Patti Smith or Kurt Vile or Boy George on the record player, so it's kind of fancy . . . but also not. This is exactly the type of place that chefs love and Brooklynites fawn over, making this an essential stop for any food-obsessive traveling near Kingston.

Western Hudson Valley
BUTTERFIELD

3805 Main Street, Stone Ridge • 845-687-0887 • butterfieldstoneridge.com • $$$

Just off the beaten path in the small hamlet of Stone Ridge is this rustic farm-to-table restaurant with an elegant approach to seasonal ingredients. Think peach and burrata with guanciale, basil, and sherry vinaigrette, or black trumpet–crusted venison with parsnips, hazelnuts, and black currant jus.

Western Catskills
THE DeBRUCE

982 Debruce Road, Livingston Manor • 845-439-3900 • thedebruce.com • $$$

Every dish on this restaurant's nine-course tasting menu features locally hand-foraged ingredients painstakingly prepared from scratch each day and delicately plated in a way that rivals any top-level Manhattan fine dining spot.

Northern Catskills
BRUSHLAND EATING HOUSE

1927 County Highway 6, Bovina Center • 607-832-4861 • brushlandeatinghouse.com • $$

Brushland isn't as buttoned up or pricey as other fine farm-to-table spots, but there's an undeniable craft approach to its super-fresh and locally sourced ingredients, inventive flavors, and creative plating that anyone with an appreciation for food will love. Bonus: the property doubles as an inn, so you can make a whole weekend of it.

3

Will Travel for Food

Weekend Escapes for Foodies

Eating seasonal and local has become the norm, and you can't get much fresher than the produce, craft beverages, and artisanal snacks you'll find upstate (hey, that rolling agricultural landscape has more uses than just enhancing your Instagram). Unlike the sprawling cookie-cutter strip malls you might expect, New York State is unique in that its rural communities have become saturated with countless restaurants, cafés, tasting rooms, and specialty shops worth talking about.

City dwellers have become downright spoiled with producers toting goods directly to the five boroughs, setting up booths at Union Square Farmers' Market, stocking the nearest boutique grocer, and even Hudson Valley-inspired restaurants. In fact, the upstate food scene has acquired such notoriety that it's luring prominent talent away from Manhattan and Brooklyn. Chefs that trained at the Culinary Institute of America in Hyde Park are now viewing the area as a final destination rather than a career stopover.

Culinary innovators are already at work determining the future of renewable farming at Lower Hudson Valley destinations like Stone Barns Center for Food and Agriculture in Pocantico Hills, where award-winning chef-owner Dan Barber puts sustainable produce and

// Wake up with a French press at Nine River Road

meats to good use at the top-rated restaurant Blue Hill at Stone Barns. World-renowned chef Jean-Georges Vongerichten, whose Michelin-rated restaurants have outposts from Soho to Singapore, has set up shop in Westchester County at the Inn at Pound Ridge. And thanks to the growing art gallery scene in Beacon, discerning foodies can find an impressive number of artisanal makers hawking everything from freshly roasted coffee beans and rare game jerky to house-made marshmallows, locally made gin, and incredible pastries all within a 15-minute walk. Plus, Beacon is an easy day trip if you don't want to commit to a whole weekend.

Of course, Hudson is among the top dining destinations in the Upper Hudson Valley, with block after block filled with incredible eats. After making a name for himself in Manhattan (and picking up a prestigious James Beard Award to boot), chef-owner Zakary Pelaccio ditched the expensive downtown rents for the quieter life in Hudson. His restaurant, Fish & Game, and cocktail bar, BackBar, have both garnered attention, locally and beyond. Lil' Deb's Oasis, a quirky, hipster-centric Latinx restaurant and bar, proves that local ingredients don't have to be used for humble New American cuisine. The James Beard Foundation agrees, and that's why the restaurant is among the number of Hudson Valley establishments gaining national nominations for culinary excellence.

Even smaller towns in the Eastern Catskills are creating their own culinary microcosms, where you can shop for local cheeses at Main Street Farm and try award-winning beers at Catskill Brewery in Livingston Manor, or have an elegant nine-course tasting menu made entirely from foraged ingredients at The Debruce in Livingston Manor.

Craft beverages have exploded across the state, thanks to the Farm Brewery law that encourages wineries and breweries to use locally grown farm products. Nearly every town has its own craft brewery, warranting its own biking trail through Orange County. Beer collectors from beyond New York are willing to make regular trips across state lines for the latest releases at Equilibrium Brewery, Suarez Family Brewery, and Sloop Brewing Co. Orchards that were once a family-friendly seasonal draw for cider doughnuts and apple picking are now churning out European-style farmhouse hard ciders, brandy, and pommeau. And while Hudson Valley viniculture isn't quite outshining the countless wineries of the Finger Lakes, the quality has improved significantly beyond its former bad reputation for sweet wine. Best of all, the craft beverage trail has given rise to a number of tour operators so that no one has to play designated driver for the weekend.

Best Towns for Foodies

WOODSTOCK

Summed up best as "aging hippie with upscale tastes," this precious small town in Ulster County features a mix of touristy bohemian shops branded with logos from the eponymous 1969 music festival (which was actually held in the town of Bethel), sunny cafés, crunchy farmers' markets, and adorable bed-and-breakfasts. It also happens to have an incredibly impressive food scene despite its small size, which can give you a true taste of modern Hudson Valley dining.

In the morning, get Montreal-style wood-fired bagels from **The Mud Club** or fresh artisanal baked goods from **Bread Alone** (the seasonal Danish is legit). For a more substantial brunch, check out eclectic breakfast/lunch spots **Shindig**, **Joshua's Café**, and **Oriole 9**. Prefer a solid lunch over breakfast? You'll have your pick of options like pan-Asian spot **Yum Yum Noodle Bar**, meatball shop **Sharkie's Meatballs**, rustic comfort spot **Provisions Restaurant & Pub**, or pies from **Catskill Mountain Pizza**.

Walk it off with a hike at nearby **Overlook Mountain**, or if you're able to keep the momentum going, try a miniature artisanal ice cream crawl at **Nancy's of Woodstock** and **Sweet Dreams Organic Ice Cream**. Take a stroll through the organic **Sunflower Market**, where you can load up on fresh kombucha and find locally made snacks, then look for area wines and spirits at **Woodstock Wine & Liquors** (they host free wine tastings on Saturdays, 2–5 p.m.). For dinner, keep it casual at places like **Tinker Taco Lab**, **A&P Bar**, or **The Lodge at Woodstock**. If you'd rather treat yourself to something a little nicer, check out elevated farm-to-table restaurant **Silvia**. End with a nightcap at a local craft beer spot like **R&R Taproom** or **Station Bar & Curio**. It's really hard to fit all of this into one day, but you're making a weekend of it, so feel free to relax.

Getting There

Two hours via car is your best bet. If you just plan to do Woodstock, it's possible to go without a car, but it will require a 2.5-hour bus ride on Trailways NY (with a bus transfer in Kingston or a $30 Lyft/Uber) and limit your travel options. Opt for the car, if you can.

Getting Around

Most of the major attractions in Woodstock are within walking distance, though if you'll want to go hiking or reach certain lodging options, you might need to drive or hail a Lyft/Uber.

Where to Eat and Drink

For a Day-Starter

BREAD ALONE BAKERY

22 Mill Hill Road, Woodstock • 845-679-2108 • breadalone.com • $

Woodstock isn't the first Bread Alone location (that's in Kingston), and it's definitely not the last (check out sister spots in Boiceville and Rhinebeck), but it's required that you stop by any one of their cafés when spotted in the wild. If the name Bread Alone sounds familiar, it's probably because you've seen their loaves floating around New York City at fine grocers and neighborhood farmers' markets. But this coveted bakery has so much more waiting at this Woodstock café, where you can find their whole bread catalog, plus incredible pastries and brunchy things packed with local ingredients.

SHINDIG

1 Tinker Street, Woodstock • 845-684-7091 • woodstockshindig.com • $$

This sunny little all-day spot features solid brunch items made with local produce and from-scratch ingredients like a fried egg, ham, and cheddar cheese breakfast sandwich on a buttermilk biscuit; a healthy breakfast wrap with egg whites, quinoa, sautéed kale, and sriracha aioli; and seasonal pies, because there's never a bad time for a slice.

For Weird That Works

A&P BAR

83 Mill Hill Road, Woodstock • 845-684-5395 • aandpbar.com • $$

German Flammkuchen, elotes, spaghetti, and steak frites aren't dishes you'd expect to find on the same menu. But they're all quintessential comfort foods and easy crowd-pleasers, so there's no use in knocking a good thing. In the evening, stick around for a craft cocktail and regular events like screenings of throwback movies or sports games.

For Solid Farm-to-Table

SILVIA

42 Mill Hill Road, Woodstock • 845-679-4242 • silviawoodstockny.com • $$

The menu changes frequently at this chef-driven restaurant, but you can count on it being something fresh and farm-focused. Using mostly sustainable, local ingredients, Silvia puts woodfire to work for New American with a splash of Asian influence, including a solid amount of plant-based dishes, cool craft cocktails, and trendy natural wines, so there's something for everyone.

For a Nightcap

EARLY TERRIBLE

45 Mill Hill Road, Woodstock • 845-684-7226 • earlyterrible.com

New to the Woodstock food scene is this sexy-cool European wine and tapas bar that has a modern-meets-rustic Bohemian vibe for an intimate date night or a quieter spot to sink into an evening nightcap over a few Hudson Valley–fueled bar bites.

R&R TAPROOM

104 Mill Hill Road, Woodstock • 845-684-5928 • rrtaproom.com

Craft beers, cool snacks, and the occasional drag bingo, karaoke, or unplugged Celtic night—what more could you ask for? This popular Woodstock bar features 10 rotating taps from top-notch brewers near and far, plus farm-fresh bar bites like baked broccoli rabe with tomato sauce and mozzarella, white bean spread with pita and carrots, and guilty pleasures like Frito pie and cupcakes.

Where to Stay

There are plenty of classic bed-and-breakfasts, Airbnb properties, and Red Cottage lodgings, but if you want to roll in with some Woodstock vibes, there are indie hotels for that, too.

For Something in the Country, but Rock 'n' Roll

WOODSTOCK WAY HOTEL

10 Waterfall Way, Woodstock • 845-684-5911 • woodstockway.com

Like many of the new crop of Hudson Valley and Catskills boutique properties, this renovated spot, nestled along Woodstock's Tannery Brook, has a luxe Bohemian vibe with design features unique to each room, like hanging handmade textiles, exposed wooden beams, Brooklinen bedding, and a curated LP collection and record player.

HOTEL DYLAN

320 Maverick Road, Woodstock • 845-684-5422 • thehoteldylan.com

Is there anything more fitting than a Bob Dylan-inspired hotel in the middle of Woodstock? Hotel Dylan is much nicer than the scrappy setups of the Summer of Love, but it has a sunny vintage revival design with touches like in-room record players and a seasonal pool that make it a comfortable spot where you can drop in and tune out.

KINGSTON AND RHINEBECK

Between these two neighboring cities along the Hudson River, there are plenty of great restaurants to hop around. Despite its small footprint, Rhinebeck manages to pack plenty in. **The Tavern at Beekman Arms** is among the oldest, dating back to the Colonial era and hosting Presidents George Washington, Franklin D. Roosevelt, and Bill Clinton since then. Stick with the historic theme and hit up their neighbors **Foster's Coach House Tavern** and **Liberty Public House** just across the street, or you can get a taste of modern Rhinebeck at places like **The Amsterdam**, **Terrapin**, or **Spice Room**. Snacks are always a good idea, so make sure to factor in pit stops at **Bread Alone**, **Grand Cru Beer & Cheese Market**, and **Le Petit Bistro**.

That said, Rhinebeck is definitely pretty small (not to mention tending to draw an older crowd), so make sure to set aside time to check out the younger dining scene in **Kingston**. The up-and-coming city has major Brooklyn vibes with places like the café-and-antique shop concept **Outdated**, locavore grocer **Duo Pantry**, and bookstore-bar **Rough Draft Bar & Books**. Keep it casual at places like **Yum Yum Noodle Bar**, **Le Canard Enchaine**, or **Duo Bistro**. If there's nice weather, hit the back patio for sweeping views of the Catskills and projector movies at local favorite **Boitson's** (the fried chicken here is fab). For something a little fancier: check out farm-to-table newcomer **Wilde Beest**. And end with a nightcap at **Stockade Tavern**, **öl Beer and Bites**, or the **Brunette** wine bar.

Getting There

Two hours via car. Renting a car will be your best bet for exploring the area, but New York Trailways offers direct service from the Port Authority Bus Terminal. Amtrak offers direct service from Grand Central Terminal to Rhinebeck.

Getting Around

Kingston is an expansive city, with hotspots divided between the historic district (where New York Trailways drops off) and by the waterfront. Lyft and Uber both operate here, though service is spottier than what you'd find around New York City. Downtown Rhinebeck is located within walking distance of the main Amtrak train station, but if you want to venture beyond that, you'll need a car.

Where to Eat and Drink
Rhinebeck
THE AMSTERDAM

6380 Mill Street, Rhinebeck • 845-516-5033 • lovetheamsterdam.com • $$$

It's a classic story: New York City weekenders fall in love with Hudson Valley and decide to open up shop in a 1798 Dutch townhouse (hence the name). But their secret weapon? Luring a chef and general manager trained under the best at Michelin-rated restaurants to develop a menu of turned-up Hudson Valley farm-to-table dining. Think top-notch local ingredients, house-made charcuterie, inventive cocktails, and a cutesy back patio where you'll want to enjoy it all.

TERRAPIN

6426 Montgomery Street, Rhinebeck • 845-876-3330 • terrapinrestaurant.com • $$$

When a restaurant manages to stay open two decades, it's safe to assume they're probably doing something right. Housed within a renovated former church, Terrapin's recognizably cool façade anchors the town (and has a great New American menu to match). During the summer, catch a seat on the al fresco patio for a glass of wine, or cozy up inside when the weather cools off. Bonus: this is one of the few restaurants with a late-night menu, staying open until midnight, which you can bet you'll appreciate when the city shuts down early.

Kingston
BOITSON'S

47 North Front Street, Kingston • 845-339-2333 • boitsons.com • $$

You'd never know from the exterior, but this lively little joint has a downright incredible view of the Catskills on its back patio. That is definitely where you should eat if the weather holds up (especially during fall foliage, obviously), and when there's a scheduled live band or movie screening. Expect approachable bar bites like cauliflower "hot wings" and fried oysters with substantial portions (don't miss the honey-soaked fried chicken), along with solid drinks.

DUO BISTRO

299 Wall Street, Kingston • 845-383-1198 • duobistro.com • $$

Centrally located along the main strip in Kingston's trendy Stockade District is a sunny bistro staple worth putting on your weekend bucket list. Approachable and seasonally driven New American dishes are gently studded with inventive touches like tempura fried squash with berbere spice and mushroom risotto with roasted seitan. Don't have time for a full sit-down dinner? Pop into Duo Pantry, the sister grocer conveniently set up next door, which offers fresh pastries, bread, and curated items from across the Hudson Valley and Catskills.

OUTDATED CAFÉ

314 Wall Street, Kingston • 845-331-0030 • outdatedcafe.com • $

Don't be surprised if you walk in with the intention of only buying a cup of coffee and walk out with a handful of antiques. It's the blessing and curse of a curated café and antique shop, where everything is beautiful and most of it is for sale. Spare some time to dine in, so you can try creative sweet and savory vegetarian breakfast items like polenta with eggs or tofu, heirloom tomatoes, greens and tomato jam, or a sample from their rotating selection of baked goodies like peach lemon doughnuts or matcha cupcakes with orange buttercream. While you wait, rifle through the antiques decorating the café, which include things like vintage art supplies, signs and trinkets, and other curios.

WILDE BEEST

310 Wall Street, Kingston • 845-481-4181 • wilde-beest.com • $$$

A relative newcomer to the Kingston dining scene, Wilde Beest is among the latest hot spots driving farm-to-table into the next generation. Think: inventive combinations brimming with unique ingredients like smoked trout with goat cheese mousse and fresno piri piri; black bass with cucumber-dill syrup, sour cream, and lemon skordalia; and cardamom panna cotta with

WHILE YOU'RE IN KINGSTON, DON'T MISS:

KINGSTON WINE CO. • 65 Broadway, Kingston • 845-340-9463 • kingstonwine.com

If there's something special you've been eyeing to take home from Hudson Valley, chances are this curatorial wine shop has it, along with unique ciders and spirits from near and far.

ROUGH DRAFT BAR & BOOKS • 82 John Street, Kingston • 845-802-0027 • roughdraftny.com

Hanging out in a bookstore would be so much better if you could cozy up with a beer or glass of wine—which is why this place was invented. Thumb through the latest curated titles while unwinding with a little booze at this historic Stockade District shop.

BSP KINGSTON • 323 Wall Street, Kingston • 845-481-5158 • bspkingston.com

Indie bands like The Black Lips and Thurston Moore routinely grace this rock club, along with events like zodiac-themed dance parties, live band karaoke, and screenings of cult classics like *The Dark Crystal*.

spiced beer cake and apple pudding. The dishes might be preciously plated à la fine dining, but the atmosphere has a breathable Brooklyn vibe, typically backed by a rotating soundtrack of handpicked records ranging from David Bowie to Erykah Badu.

Where to Stay

You're better off scoring a deal by booking at a chain hotel or Airbnb in both cities, but for something a little more personal (albeit pricier) check out intimate properties like the historic spots below.

THE BEEKMAN ARMS

6387 Mill Street, Rhinebeck • 845-876-7077 • beekmandelamaterinn.com

Want to stay in a place with character? Book a room at the oldest inn in America. Standing tall since 1766, The Beekman Arms has hosted countless famous guests, dating back to the American Revolution, including former presidents George Washington, Franklin D. Roosevelt, and Bill Clinton. The property may be old, but the accommodations have fortunately received a modern upgrade with plush bedding and air conditioning. Bonus: as a nice gesture, the property stocks each room with a complimentary decanter of sherry.

THE RHINECLIFF

4 Grinnell Street, Rhinecliff • 845-876-0590 • therhinecliff.com

If it's a view you're after, you can't get much better than this small National Register historic railway hotel that directly overlooks the Hudson River. Each of its nine rooms has a water-facing private balcony and deep-set whirlpool tubs large enough for two, perfect for catching the sunset over a bottle of wine.

THE FORSYTH B&B

85 Abeel Street, Kingston • 845-481-9148 • theforsythkingston.com

This *Vogue*-approved property combines the comfort of a historic home with style and modernity worth humblebragging about on Instagram. Luxe touches like a California king bed, deep-soaking tub, and fresh-made breakfast from a trained chef make it so comfortable that if you end up staying in all weekend, you won't even be mad about it.

(ALMOST) BETTER THAN A BODEGA

Nothing could ever beat the awesomeness of a New York City bodega, but these curated general stores and markets are great places to stock up on all the best local goods.

Lower Hudson Valley

COLD SPRING GENERAL STORE · 66 Main Street, Cold Spring · 845-809-5522 · coldspringgeneralstore.com

Be careful when shopping here—you might blow your whole wallet. A curated selection of all-American-made local wines and artisanal snacks, handcrafted beauty products, and an entire floor of boutique fashion make this better than any general store you've been to.

Upper Hudson Valley

DUO PANTRY · 297 Wall Street, Kingston · 845-340-1237 · duobistro.com

It's the pantry you always dreamed of: fully stocked with New York State goodness. Freshly baked pastries and breads made right on-site, market-fresh items from local producers, unique condiments, and kitchenware.

OTTO'S MARKET · 215 Main Street, Germantown · 581-537-7200 · ottosmarket.com

Midway between Rhinebeck and Hudson, Germantown is one of those less bustling, more residential towns often overlooked by New York City weekenders taking the train. But if you're exploring with a car, this is a fantastic longstanding market taken over and revitalized a few years ago, now focusing on local, artisanal producers.

OLDE HUDSON · 449 Warren Street, Hudson · 518-828-6923 · oldehudson.com

Would you really expect anything less than awesome for a Hudson market? Didn't think so. If it's a high-quality, gourmet pantry item, chances are this place has it. Olde Hudson is perfect for stocking up on snacks, gifts, and ingredients to tote home.

Western Catskills

FORESTBURGH GENERAL STORE · 2841 Route 42, Forestburgh · 845-707-4862 · forestburghgeneral.com

Long stretches of rural highway make this general store easy to bypass. But then you'd miss out on all the items you really want to stock up on: local cheeses and maple syrup, craft beers and ciders, and potential impulse buys like jewelry, clothing, and bath bombs.

☰ *Destination Restaurants*

Lower Hudson Valley

BLUE HILL AT STONE BARNS

630 Bedford Road, Pocantico Hills • 914-366-9600 • bluehillfarm.com • $$$$

If there's an award, chances are this restaurant already has it: Michelin, World's 50 Best Restaurants, James Beard Foundation. The country outpost of Dan Barber's iconic fine dining New York City restaurant, Blue Hill was among the pioneers of upscale farm-to-table cuisine—bucking the Hudson Valley trend about a decade before everyone else. Conveniently positioned at the innovative Stone Barns Center for Food and Agriculture, the restaurant has unique access to some of the freshest and most experimental ingredients available for its opulent tasting menu.

This is definitely a driving-only destination, so consider making a day of it, with a combined insider's tour of the farm before your dinner. Be sure to book in advance; all of those accolades mean reservations go quickly. Jackets required; no shorts or flash photography allowed.

>> **Deal Alert:** Love food but can't afford the hefty price of a tasting menu? Check out **Blue Hill's Café and Grain Bar**, where you can pick up pastries and salads during a visit to the agricultural center.

EQUUS RESTAURANT

400 Benedict Avenue, Tarrytown • 914-631-3646 • castlehotelandspa.com/attraction/equus-restaurant • $$$

Not like anyone needs much of an excuse to eat in a castle with incredible sweeping views of the Hudson River, but having a beautiful fine dining menu presenting the bounty of local farmers really sweetens the deal. This restaurant is housed within the historic turn-of-the-century Carrollcliffe Castle, now a top-rated luxury hotel and spa. Here, you'll find elegant prix-fixe menus brimming with local, seasonal ingredients. Score a better deal at brunch, when the three-course menu is only $35.95, including most of the dishes from the prime time offerings.

HARVEST ON HUDSON

1 River Street, Hastings-On-Hudson • 914-478-2800 • harvesthudson.com • $$

When the weather is just right, you'll want to make sure that you hit the patio at this upscale Italian-Mediterranean restaurant. Particularly during fall foliage season, the sunset hitting the brilliantly colored leaves along the Palisades is jaw-dropping. But it's not just all perfect backdrops here—the menu is stellar, too, earning a nod from *Wine Spectator* for its curated bottle list—and with ingredients pulled right from the restaurant's on-site vegetable and herb garden.

INN AT POUND RIDGE BY JEAN-GEORGES

258 Westchester Avenue, Pound Ridge • 914-764-1400 • theinnatpoundridge.com • $$$$

With more than two dozen international restaurants and countless awards and books, Jean-Georges Vongerichten is one chef who hardly needs an introduction. That is why it goes without saying that his Westchester County restaurant is one worth traveling to. Expect JGV's signature New French cooking style infused with Pan-Asian influences, but nestled within a former historic inn dating back to 1833 (the key word here is *former*: unfortunately you can't sleep off your dinner here afterward).

PURDY'S FARMER & THE FISH

100 Titicus Road, North Salem • 914-617-8380 • farmerandthefish.com • $$

Farms and fish: that pretty much sums up the terroir of the Hudson Valley and explains what makes this market-fresh restaurant so special. Slurp on East Coast oysters and dig into locally driven, seasonal produce, then peek into the sustainable 4-acre farm located next door, which includes a hydroponic greenhouse, six beehives, and plenty of space for growing items that are for sale in the on-site farm shop.

SUSHI NANASE

522 Mamaroneck Avenue, White Plains • 914-285-5351 • $$$

With no website and a reservations-only policy that has meant it has been booked constantly for over a decade, there's something of an alluring secrecy to this omakase Japanese restaurant. But if you can score a seat, it's worth the trek to experience the incredible knife skills of owner Yoshimichi Takeda, a vet of legendary Manhattan restaurants Nobu and Masa. Only 18 seats are available, and you'll have to place your trust in Chef's hands because there's no menu, but the adventurous eaters are rewarded with ridiculously fresh fish, premium sake, and one of the best hidden gems for sushi outside of Japan.

SALTAIRE OYSTER BAR

55 Abendroth Avenue, Port Chester • 914-939-2425 • saltaireoysterbar.com • $$

Fresh shucked oysters, towers stacked with seafood, giant steamed Maine lobster tails, and free-flowing wine and craft beers—doesn't sound too shabby, does it? Then hit up this swanky raw bar nestled within a historic grain warehouse and outfitted with a Grand Central-meets-Montauk modern maritime vibe that received a major thumbs up from the *New York Times*. Conveniently two blocks from the Port Chester train station, it's a great spot to dip in for premium seafood after walking along the Byram River, or if you're driving, it's only 20 minutes east of estates like Lyndhurst Mansion and Kykuit, along the Hudson River.

>>   **Deal Alert:** Net a deal during their daily Wine and Brine Happy Hour when oysters, clams, and drinks are all on special.

// The Grange is among Hudson Valley's culinary pioneers of the local farm-to-table scene

Western Hudson Valley

THE GRANGE

1 Ryerson Road, Warwick • 845-986-1170 • thegrangewarwick.com • $$

Mention the town of Warwick to area locals, and you'll hear a round of dreamy praise. The cutesy rural town tucked near the Pennsylvania–New York border might look like a quick hit, but it's filled with hidden pockets of excellent dining like this incredible farm-to-table restaurant. Encompassing the first floor of a turn-of-the-century building, it's easy to bypass this intimate restaurant as someone's home. Then again, with only 19 seats and usually one cook working in the back, it really does have that home kitchen vibe. The majority of ingredients on its seasonally changing menu are locally sourced, and plenty of those same vegetables and artisanal products are available in the restaurant's market store.

IRON FORGE INN

38 Iron Forge Road, Warwick • 845-986-3411 • ironforgeinn.com • $$

While you're making the trek to Warwick, don't miss this elegant farmhouse restaurant and taproom housed within a historic Colonial-era inn. Its surroundings might be old (dating back to 1760), but the menu couldn't be fresher. This is the epitome of Hudson Valley farm-to-table, overseen by Culinary Institute of America graduate and chef-owner Erik Johansen, who puts local ingredients to good use with impressive Modern American fine dining applications.

>> **Know Before You Go:** Keep that GPS handy; the cell phone reception around Warwick isn't the strongest, and it is surrounded by long country stretches that make it easy to get lost.

EAT AND LEARN

Farms and culinary educational centers for a deeper dive into the local agriculture scene.

Lower Hudson Valley

STONE BARNS CENTER FOR FOOD AND AGRICULTURE · 630 Bedford Road, Pocantico Hills · 914-366 6200 · stonebarnscenter.org

Think of it as Willy Wonka's wonderland, but with vegetables. A working farm and agricultural institute, this is where you'll find the forefront of food innovation. Walk the fields with a self-guided tour or take an insider's tour with a local expert. Of course, if you're not a total ag nerd, it's still worth scheduling a visit to Dan Barber's coveted on-site restaurant, Blue Hill, or dropping in at the more casual farm-to-table café.

Upper Hudson Valley

CULINARY INSTITUTE OF AMERICA · 1946 Campus Drive, Hyde Park · 845-452 -9600 · enthusiasts.ciachef.edu

Brush up your knife skills by taking an immersive weekend or weeklong boot camp at one of the best culinary schools in the world. Courses range from seafood and grilling to skill development and working with specialized flavors of the Hudson Valley. If you only have time to pop in, the school has five restaurants open to the public and an excellent gift shop for finding cool kitchenware.

DRESSEL FARMS · 271 Route 208, New Paltz · 845-255-0693 · dresselfarms.com

On your next trip to New Paltz, swing by this fifth-generation pick-your-own farm stand that doubles as the home for Kettleborough Cider House. After stocking up on apples (and cider doughnuts, if you really want to go all out), hit the tasting room to try their handful of dry, European-style, farmhouse ciders and then grab a scoop of their house-made ice cream.

FISHKILL FARMS · 9 Fishkill Farm Road, Hopewell Junction · 845-897-4377 · fishkill farms.com

There's no shortage of pick-your-own farms around Hudson Valley, but this one is special in that they let you pick vegetables instead of your run-of-the-mill apples and also have an on-site garden for sipping hard cider among the orchards. The events here are pretty special, too, like fresh air yoga on the farm and an ongoing seasonal fall harvest festival featuring live music and food trucks. And if you just want to stop in for the good stuff and then bounce, you can pick up cider doughnuts and artisanal products at the farm store.

HAWTHORNE VALLEY FARM STORE · 327 County Route 21C, Ghent · 518-672-7500 · store.hawthornevalley.org

If you've been to a New York City Whole Foods or the Union Square Farmers' Market within the past few years, you've probably come across this upstate farm with brand-name appeal. Situated near the city of Hudson in Ghent, this biodynamic and organic farm includes a creamery, bakery, and fermentation area that churns out good-for-you products (yogurt and sauerkraut are good for your gut!). Learn more about the biodynamic agricultural process by scheduling a tour, or pop into the café to stock up on locally made foodstuffs.

Western Hudson Valley

BLOOMING HILL FARM · 1251 Route 208, Monroe · 845-782-7310 · bloominghill.farm

Want the legit Hudson Valley farm-to-table experience? This organic farm and restaurant should definitely be on your bucket list. Chefs from top-rated restaurants like Momofuku Ssäm, Lupa, and Cookshop are among the outspoken fans who stock up on Blooming Hill's produce to showcase at the center of the plate. Get vegetables at their freshest by dining right at the source Friday through Sunday, with a weekly changing menu that puts the harvest to good use in wood-fired pizzas, market fish and meat dishes, and vegetarian-friendly items worthy of standing on their own.

WEED ORCHARDS · 43 Mount Zion Road, Marlboro · 845-236-7848 · weedorchards.com

Short on time? Squeeze a winery visit and a pick-your-own farm visit into one stop at this century-old orchard. Vegetables, fruits, and flowers are all up for grabs, with a regularly maintained growing schedule available on their website so you know what's in season. Taking advantage of all that fresh fruit, the farm has its own winery and cider house (the cider is decidedly better than the wine) with a rotating list of infused cider blends like blood orange, blackberry, and peach.

Upper Hudson Valley

BARTLETT HOUSE

2258 Route 66, Ghent • 518-392-7787 • bartletthouse.com • $$

Ghent isn't a top travel destination in the Valley, but it should be, considering how incredible this restaurant is. Those in the know, however, are certainly willing to make the trek, considering the owners are none other than the co-founders of the luxury skincare line Fresh, who opened this up as a culinary dream project in 2016. Part bakery, part restaurant, the menu is fresh, seasonal, and inventive as hell. Think basil and orange polenta cake, pistachio croissants, and their signature pear rosewater muffin (just plan to order all three). Before you leave, browse through the café's pantry shop, featuring their unique jams and other items to tote home.

THE BOCUSE RESTAURANT AT CULINARY INSTITUTE OF AMERICA

1946 Campus Drive (Route 9), Hyde Park • 845-451-1010 • bocuserestaurant.com • $$

Get a taste from the star chefs of tomorrow at a fraction of the price by dining at this white tablecloth restaurant inside the prestigious Culinary Institute of America. Named after renowned French chef Paul Bocuse, this is the school's fine dining restaurant, where students bust out the skills they'll use at top-rated restaurants after graduation. Dishes are fresh, French, and decidedly fancy. You'll find black truffle soup, poached halibut, pot-au-feu, and Instagram-worthy desserts. Tuesday through Thursday offers the best deal, with a three-course prix-fixe menu for $35 at lunch and $45 during dinner.

Eastern Catskills

PEEKAMOOSE RESTAURANT AND TAPROOM

8373 Route 28, Big Indian • 845-254-6500 • peekamooserestaurant.com • $$

If you're heading to Belleayre Mountain for a ski weekend or Shandaken Wild Forest to go hiking, make a detour to the small town of Big Indian for a rustic Catskills meal that's more refined than your campfire cookout. Think: fisherman's stew with pan-seared scallops, golden snapper, and charred tomato broth; wild mushroom risotto laced with pecorino and white truffle oil; and local rainbow trout with spaghetti squash.

PHOENICIA DINER

5681 Route 28, Phoenicia • 845-688-9957 • phoeniciadiner.com • $$

Mention the word *Catskills* and undoubtedly someone will wax poetic about Phoenicia Diner. Rightfully so, as it's absolutely perfect. Nestled along the long rural stretch of Route 28, it makes every first-timer feel like they've found a secret spot (despite the fact that this is definitely a destination restaurant every weekender should know). Not much has changed from its

// That farm fresh flavor at Henning's
Local comes straight from the garden

original 1962 façade, except the menu, which puts elevated riffs on classic Catskills diner food, and a selection of craft cocktails. Attached to the restaurant is a head-turning vintage airstream trailer that serves as the kitchen for their seasonal outdoor pop-up bar, The Lot, which serves food and hosts a weekly lineup of live music. Don't bypass the cool gift shop swag, including retro-inspired shirts, totes, key rings, and other souvenirs.

Western Catskills

HENNING'S LOCAL

6 Old County Road, Cochecton • 845-252-3008 • henningslocal.com • $$

Given that it is wedged between Narrowsburg and Bethel, getting to this culinary anomaly requires some intention (then again, most things in the Catskills do). But make the schlep and you'll be rewarded with a menu full of local ingredients infused into Old World classics like seared Beaverkill rainbow trout, Chateaubriand, and Hungarian goulash. Want to dig deeper? Check ahead of time to see if one of their monthly cooking classes is available, where you can learn how to bake breads, make fresh pasta, ferment beverages, and more.

// Be forewarned: you'll probably want to every dish on the menu at The Heron

THE HERON

40 Main Street, Narrowsburg • 845-252-3333 • theheronrestaurant.com • $$

The love child of two New York City culinary vets, this charming New American restaurant is among the hot spots putting the tiny hamlet of Narrowsburg on the map as a premier Catskills culinary destination. Dig into comforting, feel-good New American dishes with local ingredients and inventive tweaks like baked Malpeque oysters, caramelized onion mac and cheese, and Tonjes blue cheese ice cream (don't be freaked out—it's great!). After dinner, take advantage of the restaurant's prime location along the Upper Delaware River, which twinkles with outdoor lights at night.

THE LAUNDRETTE

20 5th Street, Narrowsburg • 845-588-2004 • thelaundrette.xyz • $$

Another trendy restaurant adding to Narrowsburg's growing dining scene, this wood-fired pizza joint serves up more than your run-of-the-mill margherita. Local ingredients are put to work with inventive global riffs as in the Korean bulgogi pizza with corn, olives, mozzarella, mushrooms, and kimchi or the Indian saag paneer pizza. Even if you don't have an appetite, it's worth swinging by to grab a drink and take advantage of their incredible patio overlooking the Upper Delaware River.

UPSTATE SHOPPING LIST

Who needs a kitschy keychain or shot glass as a souvenir when you can stock up on delicious snacks from local artisans? Start with this shopping list as you taste your way through the Valley.

CROWN MAPLE SYRUP · crownmaple.com

Better than your average sugar shack variety, these premium maple syrups are lovingly infused with ingredients like Madagascar vanilla and cinnamon, then barrel-aged in apple wood and bourbon casks.

DRINK MORE GOOD · drinkmoregood.com

Spike your seltzer or house-made cocktail with these super-cool syrups in unique flavors like jalapeño black tea, cassia cream, and cucumber mint Earl Grey, all made in Beacon.

HUDSON VALLEY FOIE GRAS · hudsonvalleyfoiegras.com

Along with top-notch foie gras, this Hudson Valley producer sells a variety of duck products, ranging from duck fat and torchon to charcuterie and prime cuts. HVFG is also proud to be the only USDA certified cage-free producer of foie gras.

HUDSON VALLEY MARSHMALLOW COMPANY · hudsonvalleymarshmallow.com

Step up your s'mores game with these gourmet marshmallows and graham crackers made in Beacon.

MCGRATH CHEESE COMPANY · mcgrathcheese.com

Vermont might get all the glory, but Hudson Valley is just a little more modest when it comes to its exceptional cheeses. This premier cheesemaker taps local dairy farms to create beautiful fresh and aged cheeses prime for pairing.

NOBLE PIES · noblepies.com

What began as a roadside operation to save a family farm has turned into a full-on bakery with a cult following. Apple, pecan, chicken pot pie, quiche, and everything in between—the pies here are loaded with local ingredients, ridiculously good, and totally worth the trek.

continued

// Ridiculously good food is always worth traveling for, especially if it's from Noble Pies in Warwick

NORTHERN FARMHOUSE PASTA • northernfarmhousepasta.com

The formerly sleepy town of Roscoe is on the up-and-up thanks to a slew of breweries, distilleries, and inns starting to open, including this artisanal pasta shop that sells seasonally driven noodles packed with ingredients like wild ramps, zucchini blossoms, and roasted summer corn.

PAWLING BREAD COMPANY • pawlingbreadco.com

These specialty sourdough loaves are so pretty, you'll have a tough time sacrificing them to the knife. Inside, the bread is often studded with ingredients like roasted garlic, rosemary, and black pepper that beg for a slab of good butter and a pinch of salt before shoving into your mouth.

TONJES FARM DAIRY

You'll become acquainted with this small multigenerational dairy producer simply by seeing it all over the menus at restaurants throughout the Catskills. It's not just lip service—the grass-fed and pasture-raised cheeses ranging from fromage blanc to kefir and Greek yogurt are fabulous and worth toting home.

4

Boozy Stopovers

Weekend Escapes for Tipplers

Where there is food, there's always drink to follow. Given that both the Hudson Valley and Catskills are lush agricultural regions, it shouldn't come as too much of a shocker that the region is flush with winemakers, spirits producers, breweries, and cider houses. It's ingrained in its history, after all. In fact, Brotherhood Winery lays claim to being America's oldest continuously operating winery, weathering Prohibition by producing sacramental wine.

As the region has evolved, so has generational taste, which is why younger makers are moving toward drier, more experimental styles of production. Think bone-dry heritage-style ciders, infused and barrel-aged spirits, complex sour beers, and lighter-bodied wines skewing away from the classic sweet kind that once dominated these regional wineries.

Anyone can try to become a beverage producer, but not everyone is worthy of being showcased in top-rated New York City restaurants. However, take a look at any bar or beverage menu, and you'll find an increasing number of sections devoted entirely to New York State. And that's only if they were lucky enough to get their hands on some of these coveted bottles (places with a cult following like Equilibrium Brewery often sell out during weekend can sales before anything even leaves the warehouse).

// Brotherhood Winery holds the crown for being America's oldest winery

No matter which region you visit, there's bound to be something in reach. Almost every town has its own brewery, and there's even an increasing number of microfarm-breweries popping up in the rural outskirts, like Long Lot Farm Brewery in Chester or Plan Bee Farm Brewery in Poughkeepsie, that specialize in using fresh ingredients straight from the land surrounding them. Small craft breweries are starting to outgrow their spaces due to demand, which is why places like Sloop Brewing Co. and Clemson Brewing Co. have opened outposts.

Most of the wine production happens in the Shawangunk Region in Western Hudson Valley, a fertile section of lowlands backed by a mountain range, where you'll find more than a dozen wineries like Whitecliff Vineyard and Winery in Gardiner and Robibero Winery in New Paltz. It's a popular area, for sure, which is why booking a tour guide as a designated driver is usually a good idea, so you can actually enjoy yourself (see page 34 for a list of booze tours).

One of the most popular areas for all production is in the Black Dirt Region, another Western Hudson Valley microregion known for its distinctive nutrient-dense black soil that grows everything from the incredible produce you'll find at the farmers' market to corn, wheat, and apples. Naturally, this is where all the cider houses and distilleries tend to be concentrated, making it easy to hit several in a weekend (see page 215 for an itinerary of biking and boozing through the Heritage Trail).

Whether you're just picking up a growler or indulging in a full crawl, play it safe, and most importantly: don't drink and drive!

≡ *Boozy Highlights*

BREWERIES

Lower Hudson Valley

CAPTAIN LAWRENCE BREWING COMPANY

444 Saw Mill River Road, Elmsford • 914-741-2337 • captainlawrencebrewing.com

Even if you're not a beer nerd, Captain Lawrence is such a tap fixture at New York City bars that it's likely you at least know of it. So if you want to see where the magic is made (or are traveling with someone who would), make the pilgrimage to their award-winning brewery in the lower Hudson Valley. Whether you're a newbie who wants to learn more about the brewing process or a seasoned snob willing to travel for a one-of-a-kind pour, this brewery and beer hall works for everyone. A massive location makes it a safe bet for group outings, with enough frequently changing beer styles that even picky drinkers can find something safe. Bar bites aren't half bad either, featuring trend-forward snacks spiked with southeast Asian flavors like vegan buns with oak-smoked eggplant and sweet soy sauce, or a crispy chicken sandwich with ginger-garlic glaze, crispy shallots, jalapeño, and sambal mayo.

GETTING THERE: 30 minutes via Metro-North to Tarrytown (Hudson Line) or Valhalla stop (Harlem Line). From the station, catch a taxi or Lyft/Uber to the brewery.

>> **Know Before You Go:** Public brewery tours are held Saturday and Sunday at 1 p.m. and 2 p.m. for $7 per person. Tours are about 30 minutes long and include beer sampling at the end (an extra $2 is required for a take-home sample glass).

2 WAY BREWING COMPANY

18 West Main Street, Beacon • 845-202-7334 • 2waybrewingcompany.com

Barely a 10-minute walk from the Beacon train station, this is an easy brewery to check off the list (and not a bad place to kill some time if you miss a train). Tap handles change frequently at this microbrewery, with anything from saisons and sour ales to IPAs, brown ales, and seasonal pours likely to end up on draft. The food menu isn't mind-blowing, but it is approachable, with vegetarian and gluten-free options that should please picky eaters. If the weather's nice, grab a seat on the outdoor patio.

HUDSON VALLEY BREWERY

7 Main Street, Beacon • 845-218-9156 • hudsonvalleybrewery.com

Not to be confused with the similarly named Hudson Brewing Company in Hudson, this Beacon microbrewery has some of the most insane experimental brews you'll find. Big on sour and fermented styles, HVB has created wild flavors like apple cider doughnut sour IPA, farmhouse ales fermented with sourdough yeast and aged in oak, and a sour black double IPA. Unfortunately, you'll have to act fast because they never stick around long (can release days are highly coveted). Beer isn't the only thing that rotates around here; the kitchen is frequently handed off to different pop-ups from local restaurants like Allan's Falafel, Momo Valley, and Samosa Shack.

NEWBURGH BREWING COMPANY

88 South Colden Street, Newburgh • 845-569-2337 • newburghbrewing.com

Beacon usually gets all the glory, but its sister city across the river is starting to break out on its own, thanks to pioneers like this popular brewery and taproom housed within a massive, historic warehouse. Massive isn't an exaggeration, either—the tap house can easily fit 270, making this a great place to bring a group without having to knock elbows. But you're here for the beer, and there are a lot of them. Along with its six core brews, there's a shifting selection of seasonal and limited edition beers like a sour brewed with Ethiopian coffee, a Russian imperial stout brewed with cinnamon and pomegranate juice, and a farmhouse ale with blueberries and mint. If you plan to stick around for a while, the brewery serves bar bites, has a restored shuffleboard for gaming, and frequently hosts live music and events.

GETTING THERE: There is a weekday ferry that runs between Beacon and Newburgh, but if you arrive on the weekend, you'll need to take a taxi or ride-hailing service like Lyft or Uber between both cities. If you have a Zipcar membership, you can also reserve a car at the Beacon train station.

Upper Hudson Valley
CROSSROADS BREWING COMPANY

201 Water Street, Catskill • 518-444-8277 • crossroadsbrewingco.com

Take a detour from the weekend masses descending on Hudson by hopping across the river to the lesser-trafficked town of Catskill, where you'll find beers so good that it warranted opening this offshoot tasting room from its flagship brewpub in Athens (21 Second Street, Athens). Housed in the former printing facility of the local paper, *Daily Mail*, just along Catskill Creek, the taproom is connected to Crossroads' expansive 20-barrel brewhouse that produces beers worthy of multiple awards from state competitions like TAP NY and is on the national radar at the Great American Beer Festival. The tasting room is definitely geared toward those who are in it for the beers, given there's no food on-site (food trucks, however, are often lingering just outside). So, if you want a full menu, head to the Athens brewpub.

KEEGAN ALES

20 St. James Street, Kingston • 845-331-2739 • keeganales.com

Keegan Ales isn't the newest kid on the block, but they've been going hard since 2003, so they must be doing something right. It's hard to imagine now, but back then you couldn't give the space away. Owner Tommy Keegan happened upon an empty building with a defunct brewery, shined it up, and turned it into one of Hudson Valley's favorite craft breweries. Stop by for a weekend tour, or just pop into the brewpub to taste the taps (their Mother's Milk stout is coveted) and chow down on a menu of bar favorites.

HUDSON BREWING COMPANY

99 South 3rd Street, Hudson • 518-697-5400 • hudsonbrew.com

Don't be fooled by its small size; this farm brewery is big on flavor. Situated a few blocks from the Hudson Amtrak station in a revitalized warehouse, the tasting room has 11 brews on tap—an impressive selection, considering the compact size of its microbrewing facility. Brews like Widow's Walk IPA, Wayward Woman kolsch, and Shady Sadie New England IPA allude to Hudson's storied past as a rough shipping city (ask the bartender for a quick and fascinating history lesson). Though the brewery is known for its beers, one of its most interesting brews is actually its State St. Swill, a pineapple cider made in a similar fermentation style to the Mexican street drink tepache, using whole fruit. It's absolutely delicious, and you should definitely stock up on cans of it, because you probably won't find it outside the brewery walls.

MILL HOUSE BREWING COMPANY

289 Mill Street, Poughkeepsie • 845-485-2739 • millhousebrewing.com

Heading to a show at the historic Bardavon theater? Pregame at this cool brewery and brewpub known for its solid classics and eclectic originals like cucumber cream ale (don't knock it till you try it; it's picked up several awards). Cheffed-up bar bites like green chorizo arepas; poutine; and pizzas dressed with fig, mozzarella, and house-made duck bacon walk the line between approachable and funky well enough that there's always something that works for everyone.

PLAN BEE FARM BREWERY

115 Underhill Road, Poughkeepsie • 765-307-8589 • planbeefarmbrewery.com

"Farm" is the key word at this brewery, committed to sourcing 100% of its ingredients from New York State (including some grown on-site) to make super-fresh, agriculture-focused beers. Its tasting room, a rustic little space tucked away on a bucolic farm, provides the perfect rural backdrop for a sip of the Valley. Drinking local has its perks, specifically the opportunity to try creative seasonal beers infused with incredible heirloom flavors like wild ale made with organic rainbow carrots and ginger or a farmhouse ale made with fresh lemon verbena, lemon thyme, and lime basil. If beer isn't your jam, the tasting room also features wines from the brewery's friends at nearby Fjord Vineyards.

SLOOP BREWING @ THE BARN

1065 County Route 19, Elizaville • sloopbrewing.com

Sloop has two tasting rooms that are completely different experiences, so make sure you know which one you plan to visit before putting it into your GPS. As suggested by the name, The Barn is Sloop's Dutch barn tasting room that originally served as the brewery's production facility. Anchoring a generational apple orchard, the barn doubles as a farm stand selling local products. Here, you can try Sloop's rotating lineup of beers that have helped earn the craft brewery its cult following, including flagship labels like Juice Bomb IPA, Disco Blastoff NE IPA, and Jam Razzle Dazzle sour ale. If you're more interested in trying some beers out in the country and don't need the full tour, this is a great stop-off. Otherwise, set your sights on their other tasting room at The Factory for a more immersive experience, right where it's made.

SLOOP BREWING @ THE FACTORY

755 East Drive, Hopewell Junction • sloopbrewing.com

You know a brewery is legit when it outgrows its building. In this case, Sloop expanded from their humble origins, producing inside a rustic barn, to taking over a 25,000-square-foot former IBM semiconductor plant in East Fishkill in only four years. Along with the extra room to produce their catalog of award-winning brews, the expansion allowed the crew to add a full kitchen serving creative bar food (everything from crispy ranch chickpeas and a peanut butter bacon burger to wood-fired pizzas, tacos, and dan dan noodles). Plus, free arcade games for the kids—or the adult who wants to feel like a kid again.

SUAREZ FAMILY BREWERY

2278 US 9, Hudson • 518-537-6464 • suarezfamilybrewery.com

Love craft beer, but kind of dislike the dude-centric vibe at most breweries and pubs? Suarez Family Brewery just might be your little slice of heaven. Craft beer fanatics know this label best for its award-winning lineup of delicate brews made with mixed fermentation methods and unfiltered lagers, often infusing New York farm-fresh ingredients like country-style beer with rhubarb, cherry, or honey. But its tasting room is truly unlike any other. Floor-to-ceiling windows stream natural daylight into the massive white-walled space backed by a woodland mural nodding to the Valley—it looks more like a beautiful art gallery than a brewery. Perhaps because of this, the tasting room tends to have a quieter vibe, even when it's at capacity. Taste their rotating tap list, then stock up on limited-release bottles, cans, and growlers to take home. Hardcore beer devotees, listen up: on Wednesdays and Sundays, the brewery serves selections from their vintage bottle list on-site.

>> **Know Before You Go:** Don't be fooled by the address—it's not in the Hudson you're thinking of. The brewery is located about 20 minutes south of the city of Hudson, so make sure to put the address in your GPS.

Western Hudson Valley

CLEMSON BROTHERS BREWERY

22 Cottage Street, Middletown • 845-775-4638 • clemsonbrewing.com

Just a few blocks down from Equilibrium Brewery (see below) is another stellar craft brewery, this one blessed with a full menu, no crazy lines, and a sizable outdoor area where you can kick it with a beer or three among a large group of friends. Keep an eye out for their frequently changing beer selection, which can include anything from approachable IPAs and session beers to experimental styles like chocolate peanut butter porter and mango pilsner.

>> **Know Before You Go:** Pardon the dust. Middletown is undergoing major redevelopment, with plans to extend the Heritage Trail bike path and polish up the downtown square. Breweries like Equilibrium and Clemson Brothers Brewery are helping to reinvigorate the area, but the rest of the town is admittedly still pretty rough. Expect that to change over the next few years, but this place is already worth visiting for the beer.

DEFIANT BREWING COMPANY

6 Dexter Plaza, Pearl River • 845-920-8602 • defiantbrewing.com

You never know what's going to be on tap at this microbrewery, and that's part of the charm. The production might be small, but the selection is huge: several kinds of IPAs, lagers, English porters, Belgian trippels, and the occasional experimental style (orange cream beer, anyone?). If you're playing designated driver, no need to twiddle your thumbs. The beer hall doubles as a smokehouse, serving up excellent barbecue and charcuterie, and it frequently hosts live music and other events.

>> **Know Before You Go:** Defiant Brewing is conveniently a two-minute walk from another local brewery (**Gentle Giant Brewing Company**), making it easy to squeeze two into one visit.

EQUILIBRIUM BREWERY

22 Henry Street, Middletown • eqbrew.com

The sleepy town of Middletown turns into a totally different scene on Saturdays, when hordes of craft beer collectors line up to get their hands on the latest can beer release. It's not too much of a shocker, considering this brewery's product was ranked the best craft beer in New York State and earned the prestigious 2018 Governor's Brewers' Cup award at the TAP New

York Craft Beer Festival. Just shy of three years old, Equilibrium's cult following has amassed so rapidly that they're pushing for more space, including plans to expand with a full beer garden near the Paramount Theatre a few blocks away. In the meantime, the retail store is mostly grab-and-go, but if you're the type who will go the extra mile for beer, this is one spot worth bragging about.

GETTING THERE: Unless you want to haul back some six packs, no need to worry about drinking and driving: Coach USA Shortline bus operates regular bus service between Port Authority and Middletown.

KUKA ANDEAN BREWING COMPANY

300 Corporate Drive, Blauvelt • 646-450-5852

Getting here is tricky without a car, and the tasting room hours are severely limited (Friday and Saturday), but true beer nerds appreciate a good challenge. These small-batch brews rarely make appearances in the five boroughs, so you'll have to go straight to the source if you want to taste the catalog. Kuka Andean's core lineup is pretty straightforward, but the seasonal and limited edition beers go wild (ginger mango IPA, banana nut brown, and Belgian plum witte have all made the rounds).

INDUSTRIAL ARTS BREWING COMPANY

55 West Railroad Avenue #25, Garnerville • 845-942-8776 • industrialartsbrewing.com

Making frequent cameos on the tap handles at New York City's finest craft beer bars, this cult favorite brewery ranks among the best in the state, which is why putting in the extra effort to get to its remote tasting room is a no-brainer. Batches are small and change frequently to ensure freshness and variety, but expect better-than-your-average brews with inventive combinations like New England IPA brewed with hibiscus and brut double IPA with cotton candy grapes. Like what you taste? The brewery has cans, crowlers, and growlers for sale, so you can take more home for later.

>> **What's on Tap?** Drafts change frequently at most of these small craft breweries, so check out BeerMenus.com if you want an idea of what you'll drink before you go.

Black Dirt Region

ARROWOOD FARM BREWERY

236 Lower Whitfield Road, Accord • 845-253-0389 • arrowoodfarms.com

About a half hour west of New Paltz is this acclaimed and certified organic farm brewery tucked away in the country. Everything that goes into the beer is local, from the water sourced from the limestone caves in Rosendale to the hops, yeast, herbs, fruits, and vegetables grown right on the farm. Arrowood even has its own apiary that produces honey for their honey porter.

>> **Make It a Double:** If you're without wheels to get to the farm brewery or just want to double up on your beers, head to New Paltz, where Arrowood Farm has an outpost tasting room conveniently located in the center of town (3B Church Street, New Paltz).

GLENMERE BREWING CO.

55 Maple Avenue, Florida • 845-651-1939 • glenmerebrewingco.com

Tucked away in the back of an industrial corridor of the tiny village of Florida is this microbrewery that's small in size but big on flavor. Serving only eight drafts within a tasting room the size of most New Yorkers' bedrooms, what Glenmere lacks in square footage they make up for with award-winning brews (two of which snagged gold medals from the 2018 New York State Craft Beer Competition). What differentiates this brewery from the rest is its commitment to buying local ingredients for its beers from farmers in the nearby Black Dirt Region for super-fresh pours that pack a punch.

LONG LOT FARM BREWERY

153 Johnson Road, Chester • 845-214-7033 • longlotfarmbrewery.com

There are so many craft breweries in New York State that you might even pass one without knowing. That's how this nanobrewery often gets overlooked. Housed within a fifth-generation farm, this lesser-known gem has an impressive selection on six taps, featuring beers made on-site with local ingredients straight from the farm and its neighbors around the nearby Black Dirt Region. Plus, there's the bonus of being able to brag to all your friends about the cool farm brewery you found that no one knows about.

RUSHING DUCK BREWERY

1 Battiato Lane, Chester • 845-610-5440 • rushingduck.com

Thanks to its frequent cameos at New York City's top craft beer bars, Rushing Duck becomes quite the scene on weekends when countless beer geeks from around the Tri-State Area pile in to load up on cans and growlers at their Duck Out retail shop and Duck In tasting room. Even if you're not a collector, there's certainly plenty to try among its 21 taps, making up for the schlep getting to its rural location. That also means an impressive lineup of everything from big IPAs and robust porters to experimental sours, barley wine, and nitro stouts. Order a pint from the bar and a plate from Bistro on the Go, a food truck parked outside that's run by local restaurant Christopher's Bistro.

// Order a flight and then stockpile award-winning bottles from Catskill Brewery

Western Catskills

CATSKILL BREWERY

672 Old Route 17, Livingston Manor • 845-439-1232 • catskillbrewery.com

There's no shortage of emerging breweries, but Catskill always has something interesting on tap that you won't find anywhere else. Think wild beer made with Brettanomyces yeast, whole flower dry-hopped IPA made with Simcoe and Sorachi Ace hops, and a beautiful barrel-aged Flanders-style red ale, all made using eco-friendly, sustainable brewing practices. The tasting room shares its floor space with the microbrewery so you can drink a flight where the magic happens and then take a growler, crowler, or limited-run 16-ounce can to go.

Northern Catskills

WEST KILL BREWING

2173 Spruceton Road, West Kill • 518-989-6001 • westkillbrewing.com

Seasonal brews with a dose of Catskill local flavor and foraged ingredients tucked away on a rural 127-acre historic dairy farm—what's not to love? Taps rotate regularly, but you can expect to find ingredient-forward beers like a Belgian pale ale aged with fresh, locally grown tulsi basil; an IPA brewed with Catskill Mountain wild honey; or a mixed culture saison with foraged creeping thyme and spruce tips. Check ahead to see if the taproom is hosting one of their many pop-up events ranging from oyster parties to live music. And don't forget to say hello to the West Kill Brewery cat, Teddy (he even has his own Instagram).

>> **Know Before You Go:** Like most Catskill businesses, hours are typically limited to weekends only. Children are welcome, and so are leashed dogs (as long as they stay outdoors). Feel free to bring your own food if you want anything beyond small snacks.

CIDER HOUSES

Black Dirt Region

ANGRY ORCHARD

2241 Albany Post Road, Walden • 888-845-3311 • angryorchard.com

Given that this name-brand hard cider is carried in nearly every bodega, Angry Orchard hardly needs an introduction. But its 60-acre orchard in Walden is where you can see the apples in action, tasting ciders exclusive to the property and drinking in their famous tree-house bar that overlooks the orchards and the Catskills. Along with year-round tours, they frequently host pairing events, game nights, and dinners. Just make sure to plan ahead during peak apple-picking season, when Angry Orchard's already popular tasting room becomes a total madhouse with crowds.

APPLEWOOD WINERY

82 Four Corners Road, Warwick • 845-988-9292 • applewoodwinery.com

If you haven't heard of this winery and cidery, chances are it's because they produce in small batches and only sell their product at their farm store. That limited distribution guarantees you're getting the freshest from the barrels of their award-winning wines and Naked Flock Hard Cider, which change frequently to include seasonal and experimental flavors like currant, pumpkin, and even espresso and gin.

>> **Know Before You Go:** Be careful when driving through the Black Dirt back roads that lead you here. GPS navigation is occasionally incorrect, so follow the marked signs instead of relying on Siri to avoid getting sent down an unpaved dirt road.

ORCHARD HILL CIDER MILL

29 Soons Circle, New Hampton • 845-374-2468 • orchardhillcidermill.com

This cider mill gives you a two-for-one outing, given that it's situated within the historic Soons Orchards, a family-owned U-Pick farm operating since 1910. Proximity to all those apples is a convenient perk for creating incredible heritage hard ciders and New York-style pommeau, a riff on the classic Normandy blend of apple juice and brandy. Orchard Hill's signature Ten66 is

// It's a kid-free zone at Pennings Farm Cidery, which means you can drink and eat wood-fired pizza in peace

aged in French oak barrels, giving it a beautifully refined and unique flavor showcased in New York's Michelin-rated restaurants. Afterward, pop into Soons' farm store, where you can load up on fruit, vegetables, house-made fudge, cool condiments, and other tasty snacks for the ride home.

PENNINGS FARM CIDERY

4 Warwick Turnpike, Warwick • 845-987-9922 • penningscidery.com

Pennings already had a longtime reputation among locals as the go-to place for U-Pick apples and the best seasonal apple cider doughnuts, but since adding a cidery in 2014, it's become a hot spot for super-fresh farmhouse hard ciders. These aren't your super-sweet variety, rather bone-dry, wild-fermented, honey-hopped, or infused with flavors like ginger-beet and maple-vanilla. Another unexpected bonus: the cider house is totally kid-free. That means you can feel free to kick back with some hard ciders, wood-fired pizza, and a beautiful backdrop of rolling orchards, carelessly dropping a bunch of f-bombs without offending the sensibilities of young families.

UPSTATE SHOPPING LIST

Not all Hudson Valley and Catskills producers have open doors for tours and shopping. Keep an eye out for these great foods and beverages to tote home.

AARON BURR CIDER · aaronburrcider.com

These are small production, Old World–style, effervescent farmhouse ciders made in Wurtsboro that have generated their own cult following in the five boroughs.

FJORD VINEYARDS · fjordvineyards.com

Until this up-and-coming indie vineyard opens their anticipated tasting room, you'll have to track them down at local wine shops and restaurants. It's worth the effort, though, as they're one of the only producers making Albariño in the Valley.

GRAFT CIDER · graftcidery.com

Old and New Worlds collide at this unique cider house that pulls a blend of classic techniques and unexpected flavors for its rotating roster (sour gose, fruited mochi cider, hopped tropical fruits).

HETTA GLÖGG · hettaglogg.com

Traditional Nordic mulled wine lovingly handcrafted in Kingston. Give it a try, along with local craft beers and bites, at their bar öl Beer and Bites (*85 Broadway, Kingston*).

THE HUDSON STANDARD · thehudsonstandard.com

Spruce up your home bar with unique shrubs and bitters like raspberry verbena spicy turmeric switchel.

PEONY VODKA BY THREE MEADOWS SPIRITS · peonyvodka.com

As the name suggests, it's flower-infused vodka, and the only one made with peonies (plus a handful of other botanicals). So if you haven't had peony vodka, this is the one to try.

SUNDSTRÖM CIDER · sundstromcider.com

This is a tough one to find, but if you love super-funky ciders made via spontaneous fermentation, make sure to grab it when you see it.

Shawangunk Ridge

BAD SEED CIDER CO.

43 Baileys Gap Road, Highland • 845-236-0956 • badseedhardcider.com

Making a name for themselves at New York City's weekly farmers' markets, Bad Seed finally made their foray into Brooklyn with their own tap house in 2018. If something is worth growing, you know it's gonna be good. For cider lovers, it's a particularly good destination, as they've got 23 rotating tap handles heavy on cider (plus a few beers) that include the arsenal of Bad Seed ciders (the bourbon barrel–aged cider is legendary) and some of their favorites from Hudson Valley and New York State. If you have time to make it a double, head out to their tiny outdoor farm bar (341 Pancake Hollow Road, Highland) where you can pick apples during peak season and enjoy cider doughnuts on the farm.

KETTLEBOROUGH CIDER HOUSE

277 Route 208, New Paltz • 845-255-7717 • kettleboroughciderhouse.com

Dressel Farms has been growing apples for four generations, cultivating a mix of dessert apples and hard cider varieties. They put their 450-acre apple orchard to good use in this coveted line of farmhouse-style ciders that you can taste under one roof. Many of the heirlooms grown on the property are revivals dating back to Prohibition, which pushed several types to the point of near extinction. Most of these small-batch ciders rarely make it out of New Paltz, so make sure to buy a growler to bring home.

TWIN STAR ORCHARDS

155 North Ohioville Road, New Paltz • 845-633-8657 • twinstarorchards.com

It's a bit of a backward story, but contrary to its name, Brooklyn Cider House actually got its start *outside of Brooklyn* on Twin Star's 50-acre orchard situated in the rural outskirts of New Paltz. Backdropped by a stunning view of the rolling tree-filled landscape and a serene pond, this producer is best known for the heirloom and rare apple varietals used to make its award-winning heritage ciders. Less sweet than commercially made ciders, these bottles lean toward dry, sour, funky, and raw-fermented flavors that are easy to crush during a hot summer day in its tasting room or pair with wood-fired pizzas made on-site every weekend on its pavilion. During fall harvest, the orchard opens as a U-Pick, so you stock up on apples during peak foliage season.

Upper Hudson Valley
TREASURY CIDER

9 Fishkill Farm Road, Hopewell Junction • 845-897-4377 • treasurycider.com

You know those crazy heritage-style artisanal ciders everyone in Brooklyn can't stop raving about? Yeah, this is one of those places. Thankfully so, because Treasury is among the top-rated producers reinventing the way we think about cider. Offering only a handful of traditional method bottles, Treasury showcases more than 80 varietals of heirloom, modern, and European apples from their 50-acre orchard within the 270-acre, third-generation Fishkill Farms. Vintage information is painstakingly documented, from year of planting and farming method to aging information and number of cases produced. That might sound excessive until you try it: delicate semi-dry, dry, effervescent, and unfiltered bottles produced in small batches that essentially taste like high-quality apple wine. Get a taste from June through October at their seasonal cider garden, with a sweeping view overlooking the Catskill Mountains, or cozy up in their indoor barn-turned-bar tasting room in November and December. If the tasting room is closed or off-season, you can still try a complimentary sample of their Homestead or Wiccopee ciders inside the farm store, which operates year-round.

Western Catskills
WAYSIDE CIDER

55 Redden Lane, Andes • 845-676-6002 • waysidecider.com

The tiny town of Andes is still an up-and-coming part of the Western Catskills, so don't beat yourself up if this incredible cider house isn't on your radar yet. Specializing in small-batch, high-quality ciders, Wayside leans on a combination of traditional and experimental styles geared toward methods like wild fermentation, barrel aging, mixed fruit blending, and fortification. Try them all at their elegant barn house tasting room, where their ciders are served alongside a fully stocked bar of New York beers, wines, and spirits. Because it's always better to have food on hand to pair with drinks, the cider house conveniently serves seasonally driven farmhouse comfort foods as well.

DISTILLERIES

Lower Hudson Valley
DENNING'S POINT DISTILLERY

10 North Chestnut Street, Beacon • 845-476-8413 • denningspointdistillery.com

It's easy to bypass this tiny distillery tucked away off the Main Street strip of Beacon, but then you'd be missing out on one of the top-rated bourbons from the 2017 San Francisco World Spirits Competition, and that would just be a travesty. Don't judge the distillery by its small size, either—they've got six unique spirits to taste through, made primarily from New York State ingredients. Along with their award-winning flagship Beacon Bourbon, Denning's has a gin, an apple brandy, a vodka, an American-style whiskey, and a wild herb- and honey-infused vodka called Maid of the Meadow. It's truly a "something for everyone" kind of distillery. If you're not one for taking liquor neat, no worries; they offer a handful of seasonal cocktails as well.

>> **Know Before You Go:** Tasting room hours vary from Friday through Sunday, with informal tours only available on Saturdays on a first-come, first-served basis. On the second and fourth Saturday of every month, the distillery hosts a live open blues jam session from 4 to 7 p.m., where instruments are provided and any musician can jump in.

Upper Hudson Valley

HILLROCK ESTATE DISTILLERY

408 Poole Hill Road, Ancram • 518-329-1023 • hillrockdistillery.com

Even if you're not a drinker, this is an incredibly beautiful place to spend an afternoon. Perched atop a hill overlooking the rolling landscape of the valley, the grounds of this historic Georgian estate offer incredible views (particularly during fall foliage season). But let's be real: the booze matters, and Hillrock doesn't disappoint. The key word here is whiskey, which comes in three different styles: a Solera-aged bourbon, a single malt, and a double cask rye— each earning local, national, and international awards of excellence. Tours are available daily by appointment, which take you through the grounds to see how everything moves from malt and grain to glass.

HUDSON VALLEY DISTILLERS

1727 US Route 9, Clermont • 518-537-6820 • hudsonvalleydistillers.com

With all the apple orchards scattered throughout the Hudson Valley, it was inevitable that someone would start making applejack. This farm distillery makes three of them, plus whiskey, vodka, and gin (because why not?). Book a tour and tasting, offered Fridays through Sundays, which includes three samples of their award-winning spirits. Or, if you just want a taste of the good stuff, try it in a cocktail at their bar that includes fresh, seasonal ingredients available for purchase at the market, along with recipes, so you can recreate it at home.

OLDE YORK FARM DISTILLERY

284 Route 23, Hudson • 518-721-8209 • oldeyorkfarm.com

Veer off the main strip of Hudson about 15 minutes east to find this woman-owned and family-operated distillery and cooperage continuing the tradition of area distillers dating to 1805. Unlike most distilleries, Olde York Farm is unique in that they actually hand-make their own oak barrels on-site, from sawing to toasting. Specializing in limited-release, seasonal batches brimming with local ingredients, this is definitely a food lover's distillery. Think: black walnut bourbon, lilac liqueur, ramp vodka, and mulled peach whiskey. Tasting room hours are limited to weekends, with free tours available of both the distillery and cooperage. Along with craft cocktails showcasing the spirits, the tasting room offers a handful of artisanal grilled cheeses and cheese boards to pair. Bonus: you can extend your visit by booking their two-bedroom Airbnb suite with private porch access and incredible waterfall and red barn views.

TACONIC DISTILLERY

179 Bowen Road, Stanfordville • 845-393-4583 • taconicdistillery.com

There's more than one way to make a whiskey, which is why this distillery makes five of them. From straight rye and bourbon to double barrel bourbon maple whiskey and private reserve, Taconic's portfolio is so solid that most of its selections have received a 90+ rating from the *Whisky Bible*. Unlike most whiskey producers, Taconic doesn't chill filter to impart more flavor. Learn more by visiting the distillery when it's open on Saturday afternoons and tasting through the lineup of whiskies. On a nice day, you can plop down in one of the Adirondack chairs outside with a craft cocktail, surrounded by the expanse of farmland.

Western Hudson Valley

BLACK DIRT DISTILLERY

114 Little York Road, Warwick • 845-258-6020 • blackdirtdistillery.com

Before you go down the rabbit hole of spirits at this farm distillery, you should probably brush up on the history of New York's Black Dirt Region, which it's named after. True to its name, the dirt is indeed a rich black color as a result of being the remnants of a 12,000-year-old shallow lake formed during a glacial period. This 5,500-acre pocket of land is renowned for its nutrient-rich soil that grows some of the region's most incredible produce—much of which is incorporated into this distillery's catalog of spirits. The 4,000-square-foot distillery churns out incredible bourbon, applejack, and rye, using locally grown corn and aged in American barrels. Its tasting room is located at Warwick Valley Winery and Distillery, where you can maximize your sampling of local spirits, ciders, and wines all under the same roof.

COPPERSEA DISTILLING

239 Springtown Road, New Paltz • 845-444-1044 • coppersea.com

Hudson Valley has no shortage of distilleries, but Coppersea stands out as one of the few malting distilleries in the world to use heritage methods like open fermentation, low-proof aging, and sustainable organic farming techniques to create their unique lineup of spirits. Think: oak-aged single malt whiskey made with unkilned barley malt; pear brandy and eau-de-vie made from local fruit and wild yeast; and the first bourbon using entirely state-sourced corn, rye, and barley, aged in New York American white oak. Coppersea's tasting room is open seasonally on weekends from noon to 5 p.m.

// The second floor of Orange County Distillery's Brown Barn Farms tasting room often screens movies and has a bird's eye view of live music below

ORANGE COUNTY DISTILLERY AT BROWN BARN FARMS

286 Maple Avenue, New Hampton • 845-374-2011 • orangecountydistillery.com

Something of an oasis within Orange County's iconic Black Dirt Region, this distillery's tasting room is literally in the middle of nowhere inside a converted barn on a farm surrounded by acres upon acres of rolling greenery. Okay, it's not *totally* in the middle of nowhere (it's about a 5-minute drive from Glenmere Brewing), but you'll never see bumper-to-bumper traffic along this stretch of country road, and there certainly aren't any sidewalks. Really, that's one of the many things that's so great about this incredible craft distillery and cocktail bar: it feels like a well-kept secret. Local is the key word here, which is where all of its ingredients come from for its dozen varieties of whiskies, gins, and vodkas, along with the herbs and produce for its cocktails. Plan to stick around, particularly in the evenings on Friday through Sunday, when there's live music, comedy, an on-site food truck, and the occasional bonfire.

>> **Make It a Double:** Want to get into the nitty-gritty of distilling? Black Dirt Distillery's production facility is located in nearby Goshen, for those who are super-geeky about distillery tours. But if you're just in it to sample booze, you're better off going to the cocktail bar at Brown Barn Farms.

// Taste small-batch whiskeys, vodka, and other artisan spirits at farm microdistillery Catskill Distilling Company

Western Catskills

CATSKILL DISTILLING COMPANY

2037 Route 178, Bethel • 845-583-3141 • dancingcatsaloon.com • catskilldistilling.com

Making the pilgrimage to Bethel Woods Center for the Arts to learn about the history of Woodstock Music Festival? Hitting up this distillery is an easy tack-on—it's stationed right across the street. An extension of the long-standing restaurant and bar Dancing Cat Saloon, this farm distillery pulls its water, grains, fruits, and botanicals only from New York State. Its tasting room, which is open daily for tastings and tours, is sprinkled with unique touches, like its custom-made copper stills and an authentic art deco bar from the 1939 World's Fair in Flushing, Queens. As for the booze, there's truly something for everyone, from the classics (straight rye whiskey and vodka made from whole wheat) to the esoteric (buckwheat American whiskey and a gin with a botanical profile so different they had to name it "Curious Gin").

PROHIBITION DISTILLERY

10 Union Street, Roscoe • 607-498-4511 • prohibitiondistillery.com

Roscoe is a hamlet best known for its fly-fishing (earning it the nickname Trout Town, USA), but over the past few years it has generated another reputation for its growing food and beverage scene, thanks to pioneers like this distillery that opened in 2013. As suggested, the distillery pays homage to New York's history during the Prohibition Era, crafting award-winning artisanal vodka, gin, and bourbon under the label "Bootlegger" that goes down smooth as silk. Their tasting room features tours of the microdistillery on-site, open year-round. During the summer, the back alley transforms into an outdoor bar for seasonal cocktails and local bites.

Northern Catskills

UNION GROVE DISTILLERY

43311 Route 28, Arkville • 845-586-6300 • uniongrovedistillery.com

Just at the northwest tip of the Catskills, this small farm distillery is slightly set apart from the major destinations along the well-worn weekender path. But if you have a car and the motivation to seek out unique spirits, this one is worth a visit for its local agriculture-focused liquors. Their award-winning flagship product, Vly Creek Vodka, leans on New York State apples and wheat, and Union Grove taps maple syrup from nearby Tree Juice Maple Syrup for its Catskill Mountain Maple Spirit and its maple-distilled version of Vly Creek Vodka. Every now and then, a limited edition will come out, like the Drie Brook Rye Whiskey, which uses local rye and malted barley; or FirGin, distilled with area balsam and Norway spruce trees, juniper, wild ginseng, lavender, freshly harvested horseradish, and other ingredients.

WINERIES

Shawangunk Ridge Wine Region

BENMARL WINERY AND VINEYARD

156 Highland Avenue, Marlboro • 845-236-4265 • benmarl.com

When winery-hopping through the farmlands of Marlboro, this multigenerational vineyard is a must for any bucket list. Its luscious 37-acre estate features sweeping views of the Hudson River and the Shawangunk Ridge, making this an excellent backdrop on its own. Throw in a lineup of award-winning wines, regularly scheduled thematic events (wine with your canine, anyone?), and a dash of history visiting America's oldest continually operating vineyard and the first licensed farm winery in New York State, and it's easy to understand why this coveted spot gets all the love.

// Discover your next favorite wine by trying a portfolio tasting at Millbrook Vineyards and Winery

BASHAKILL VINEYARDS

1131 South Road, Wurtsboro • 845-888-5858 • bashakillvineyards.com

Surprised to hear that Hudson Valley is packed with vineyards? Well, believe it or not, the Catskills has a winery worth visiting, too. Leveraging the microclimate of the Bashakill Wetlands, this 15-year-old winery uses organic viniculture methods to make unique wines like lavender-infused white and sparkling, chancellor grapes barrel-aged in oak for 18 months, and select batch oak-aged cabernet franc. Bonus: you can sample any four for free. Don't bother bringing your own food. Aside from the fact that it's not permitted, it's a better bet to order from their menu of scratch-made, farm-to-table Mexican and South American street food, build-your-own snack boards, and local artisanal ice cream. Along with food, drinks, and live music every weekend, the property is surrounded by incredible hiking trails and a nearby kayak boat launch, so that you can make a whole day out of wine drinking in the Catskills.

>> **Know Before You Go:** Hours operate seasonally from late April to late December. Leashed dogs and supervised children are both okay.

BROTHERHOOD WINERY

100 Brotherhood Plaza Drive, Washingtonville • 845-496-3661 • brotherhood-winery.com

Carrying the crown as America's oldest winery, Brotherhood has a fascinating backstory worthy of wine geeks and history nerds alike. Dating back to 1810, the winery is rooted in the Hudson Valley's French Huguenot upbringings, thanks to founder Jean Jaques, who owned and operated the vineyard until selling it to New York City wine merchants Jesse and Edward Emerson 60 years later. Brotherhood weathered Prohibition in the '20s under the control of Louis Farrell, who was able to sell wine legally under sacramental production. Even a disastrous fire in 1999 didn't stop the winery, now co-owned by the Baeza, Castro, and Chadwick Chilean winemaking families. More importantly: how's the wine? Taste is subjective, so that's up to you to decide. But the winery picked up three gold awards at the 2018 New York Wine Classic, so it's certainly got competitive chops. And learning the secrets of the winery's excavated caverns, containing more than 200 oak barrels and some of the oldest vintages in America, is a cool bonus.

>> **Know Before You Go:** Tasting room and tour hours operate seasonally, April through December. Check ahead for hours and ticket information.

ROBIBERO FAMILY VINEYARDS

714 Albany Post Road, New Paltz • 845-255-9463 • robiberofamilyvineyards.com

Somewhere between a happy accident and a labor of love, Robibero launched in 2010, eight years after Harry and Carole Robibero decided to purchase an existing 42-acre vineyard nestled in the farmlands of Shawangunk Ridge. Since then, the winery has flourished, with the production of everything from dry riesling and seyval blanc to petit verdot, cabernet franc, and baco noir. If you haven't heard of this independent, family-owned winery, that's because their wines are produced in small batches with extremely limited distribution. This means a trip to this winery earns you extra bragging rights among friends for finding a treasure right in New York City's backyard. Bring some blankets and cozy up next to the outdoor pit at their tasting room, which sells wood-fired pizzas on the weekend and other pairing snacks like meats, cheeses, and crackers.

>> **Know Before You Go:** Tasting room hours change seasonally. Robibero is also among the few dog-friendly spots, open to well-behaved pets kept on a short leash.

WHITECLIFF WINERY

331 Mckinstry Road, Gardiner • 845-255-4613 • whitecliffwine.com

New York's Finger Lakes region gets all the glory when it comes to wine, but sustainable wineries like Whitecliff are proving that Hudson Valley can tackle the grape, too. Producing more than 20 solid varietals, this is truly a "something-for-everyone" kind of winery. Taste through sparklings, whites, rosés, and reds running the gamut from seyval blanc and chardonnay to

// The afternoon views from Millbrook Vineyards and Winery are some of the Valley's best

cabernet franc, gamay noir, and traminette. Even if you're not a wine snob, you can't beat having a glass of the good stuff on the tasting room's back deck overlooking panoramic views of the Shawangunk Ridge—and you might find you learn a thing or two in the process.

Upper Hudson Valley

MILLBROOK VINEYARDS AND WINERY

26 Wing Road, Millbrook • 845-677-8383 • millbrookwine.com

Millbrook isn't the oldest winery in Hudson Valley, but a 30-year legacy still makes it a pioneer in recognizing the viniculture potential in the region. While New York State wines are still recovering from their tainted image of being overly sweet and fruity, Millbrook produces the kind of wines you actually want to drink: complex, bold varietals like cabernet franc and pinot noir; food-friendly whites like chardonnay and Riesling; and even a couple of good patio crushers like tocai friulano and rosé—best taken on an Adirondack chair outside the 1940s Dutch-style barn estate tasting room overlooking the rolling vineyard hills.

TOUSEY WINERY

1774 Route 9, Germantown • 518-567-5462 • touseywinery.com

With most great wineries, there's an interesting backstory. This one involves a couple falling in love in England, moving to Copenhagen, visiting the woman's father in the Hudson Valley who was a beekeeper making crème de cassis and who happened to have a license to produce more wine, deciding to throw caution to the wind, uprooting their lives to start a winery. Fortunately for everyone, the wines are pretty damn good, too. Inspired by their favorite European wines, Tousey produces top-notch bottles of riesling, chardonnay, cabernet franc, pinot noir, rosé, blanc de blanc, and even a select number of the original crème de cassis that started it all. All of these are priced so they won't break the bank, making them prone to sell out quickly. Their weekend tasting room has a modern, fun vibe with splashes of rustic accents that capture the current atmosphere of the Valley and a selection of local products you can stock up on for the trip home.

≡ Where To Drink and Pass Out

Eat, sleep, and start all over again by staying the weekend at these great boutique hotels with excellent on-site dining.

Western Hudson Valley

BENMARL WINERY AND VINEYARD

156 Highland Avenue, Marlboro • 845-236-4265 • benmarl.com

Ever dream of waking up with vineyard views? Now you can, at this popular winery nestled within the scenic Shawangunk Ridge with a little-known secret: it has its own two-room bed-and-breakfast. The first room includes a queen-sized bed, a balcony overlooking the Hudson River, and a fireplace, while the other is furnished with a double-sized bed and vineyard views; both rooms include a free wine tasting, a cheese plate, a 10% discount on wine purchases, and access to the owner's shared living room, which feels like a home away from home.

BUTTERMILK FALLS INN AND SPA

220 North Road, Milton • 845-795-1310 • buttermilkfallsinn.com

A cross between a bespoke mom-and-pop bed-and-breakfast, a farm-to-table restaurant, and a luxury day spa, Buttermilk Falls Inn and Spa has it all for the weekender who wants farm-to-table meals from their on-site restaurant Henry's at the Farm, luxe Red Flower body treatments, and eco-friendly, solar-powered spa facilities, all located on a bucolic farm just off the Hudson River. It's about a 10-minute drive from the Poughkeepsie Metro-North train station, making this an easy getaway without the overnight commitment for those who want a solid meal or day spa access (though the guest rooms outfitted with built-in fireplaces and whirlpool bathtubs aren't too shabby if you'd prefer to crash). Book an appointment, bring a bathing suit, and unwind, then explore Millstone Farm, Buttermilk's organic agricultural extension that includes an animal rescue, an aviary, a garden, a livestock barn, and an apiary.

THE GARRISON

2015 US 9, Garrison • 845-424-3604 • thegarrison.com

Wedged between Peekskill and Cold Spring, this insanely picturesque property has sweeping mountain views that make it a natural fit for the wedding circuit. But if you can squeeze in during a night that isn't booked, it's worth it for the cushy accommodations and on-site restaurant, The Valley, which has received glowing reviews across the board. The menu here changes weekly to keep up with the seasons, pulling fresh, local ingredients for delicately plated dishes worthy of the taste buds of discerning foodies.

STAGECOACH INN

268 Main Street, Goshen • 845-294-5526 • stagecoachny.com

Goshen is a Hudson Valley village best known for its rail trail and proximity to Schunnemunk Mountain, but it's starting to become a destination for the wedding and weekender circuits, thanks to this historic Colonial inn that got a major upgrade only a couple years ago. Originally built as a farm home in 1747, the property was converted into an inn in 1791, which accumulated a storied history over the next two centuries until its most recent renovation in 2014, after being acquired by its latest owners. Beloved by locals and travelers alike, the inn's white tablecloth, Spode-equipped dining room features dishes ranging from Hudson Valley ingredient upgrades to classic New American entrées and a tiny craft cocktail parlor. Its treasure lies in the solarium and patio, both featuring picturesque garden views. Staying overnight is even better than dining here, as the rooms are beautifully decorated with plush interiors (think: Pottery Barn chic) reflecting individual personas and luxe touches like an in-room fireplace, Molton Brown soaps, and down alternative bedding.

Upper Hudson Valley
HUDSON VALLEY DISTILLERS

1727 US Route 9, Clermont • 518-537-6820 • hudsonvalleydistillers.com

Who needs a designated driver when you can just stay at the distillery? Bring your crew to this massive four-bedroom renovated 19th-century farmhouse within stumbling distance of the popular distillery and surrounded by 10 acres of bucolic farmland. Hit up the tasting room for a flight and tour, then take the party back to one of the rooms, where there's plenty of space to spread out, including a full-sized tub (with a large soaking tub in one room).

HOTEL TIVOLI

53 Broadway, Tivoli • 845-757-2100 • hoteltivoli.org

A must-see for art lovers, this swanky and colorful inn belongs to famed artists Brice and Helen Marden, who have decked out the property with authentic works sprinkled casually

// Hotel Tivoli gets the most buzz for its high art décor, but the food is pretty damn good, too

around the house (one of the rooms has a signed Roy Lichtenstein). Downstairs, The Corner has an exceptional seasonally changing menu, as well as a drink list curated by coveted craft cocktail bar Employees Only from New York City. And if you're a fan of those beautiful ceramics at the restaurant, pop in next door at The Gallery Store to browse through curated handmade wares.

WM. FARMER & SONS

20 South Front Street, Hudson • 518-828-1635 • wmfarmerandsons.com

It feels like home—but probably better than the one you already have. Part restaurant, part boarding house, this historic property has become a hot ticket for city dwellers escaping to Hudson. Situated steps from the town's train station, the inn is split among three buildings, each with apartment-sized rooms and suites uniquely decorated with antiques and vintage-inspired knickknacks. Considering how stylish and in-demand the property is, the price is shockingly reasonable (particularly for groups willing to split the two-bedroom). Bonus: the ground floor restaurant is ridiculously good, with a seasonal menu boasting the best of Hudson Valley and an impressive bar menu developed by the late Sasha Petraske of renowned NYC craft cocktail bar Milk & Honey.

// Formerly a cinema, Rivertown Lodge is now a chic weekender destination

RIVERTOWN LODGE

731 Warren Street, Hudson • 518-512-0954 • rivertownlodge.com

Is it a movie theater or a motel? Well, in a former life, this renovated property has been both. Tucked away at the end of Hudson's Warren Street strip, the Rivertown Lodge is the latest iteration of a historic building that spent its first 30 years as a cinema (hence the Deco-style marquee), followed by another 40 years as the Warren Inn Motel (conveniently modeled into 27 catwalk-style rooms). Nodding to its colorful past, the hotel received a major face-lift in 2016 that includes a clean, whitewashed exterior, a custom mid-century modern–inspired interior, and a handsome tavern serving local ingredients, craft cocktails, and a handpicked natural wine list.

OLDE YORK FARM DISTILLERY

284 Route 23, Hudson • 518-721-8209 • oldeyorkfarm.com

Chances are good that you'll be so charmed by this woman-owned and family-operated distillery and cooperage that you'll want to extend your visit by booking their adjacent two-bedroom Airbnb suite. A short drive off the main strip of Hudson, this historic farmhouse has a relaxing country cottage vibe with plenty of space to spread out. There's no on-site spa, but the bathroom essentially feels like one, equipped with a rainfall shower, claw-foot tub, lavender and Himalayan pink bath salts, bath bombs, and plush bathrobes. Also, there's the major convenience of being situated right next to a craft distillery, which means you can order a bottle ahead for your room or hit the tasting room for drinks and buy to-go.

VANDERBILT LAKESIDE

161 Main Street, Philmont • 518-672-7070 • vanderbiltlakeside.com

Often overlooked by weekenders due to its location situated about 20 minutes east of the main Hudson strip, this is one of those perfect gems that most weekenders wish they knew about. It's got it all: the right blend of modern-meets-rustic comfort style, a peaceful and breathtaking lakeside view, nearby access to prime hiking trails, and a restaurant serving creative and healthy dishes loaded with local ingredients. On top of all that, the prices for all of this are much more affordable than you'd expect.

Eastern Catskills
FOXFIRE MOUNTAIN HOUSE

72 Andrew Lane, Mount Tremper • 845-688-2500 • foxfiremountainhouse.com

Ever wish you could steal a hotel's interior designer? You might start fantasizing about redoing your whole home after staying at this adorably Bohemian boutique property in the Catskills. Between the beautiful furnishings and the incredible seasonally driven menu at the hotel's restaurant, the idea of starting a new life up in the mountains doesn't sound so crazy. In the meantime, you'll have to settle for purchasing one of their signature handcrafted candles or soaps and a nice weekend dinner. And if you're into baths, make sure to ask if the room on the third floor is available; it has a deep soaking tub with excellent woodland views.

THE PINES

5327 Route 212, Mount Tremper • 845-688-7311 • catskillpines.com

"Hipster" is such a catchall phrase, but it sums up the aesthetic at this trendy shabby chic restaurant and inn located in the up-and-coming town of Mount Tremper, neighbor to the popular town of Phoenicia. Weathered wood-paneled walls and rooms furnished with reclaimed interiors and antiques set the backdrop for rock 'n' roll and honky-tonk live music nights and upscale Catskills farm-to-table and local artisanal drinks in the restaurant. Upstairs, five rooms are available, modestly decorated with an upscale rustic-minimalist approach.

SCRIBNER'S CATSKILL LODGE

13 Scribner Hollow Road, Hunter • 518-628-5130 • scribnerslodge.com

A resort relic that survived from the Catskills' Borscht Belt days of the 1960s, the property freshened up with modern renovation in 2016, reflective of its surrounding area's current design-focused digs. There's rarely a bad view; most of its 38 rooms have private balconies

// The Arnold House merges mid-century modern chic and vintage rustic Catskills design

and large windows overlooking its 20-acre mountainous landscape and expansive pool. Even if you aren't shacking up here, it's worth stopping for dinner at the lodge's acclaimed restaurant, Prospect, offering upscale takes on seasonal local ingredients.

Western Catskills

THE ARNOLD HOUSE

839 Shandelee Road, Livingston Manor • 845-439-5070 • thearnoldhouse.com

Beyond the highly Instagrammable vintage mid-century-modern-meets-rustic-Catskills cabin, the on-site tavern is pretty damn good, too. Think: ravioli from nearby Northern Farm-house with brown butter and seasonal vegetables, local Beaverkill trout with purple potatoes and grilled ramps, and a spin on mozzarella sticks using local Tonjes halloumi and tomato coulis. In fact, you can find great dining at all the sister properties owned by this hospitality group, Foster Supply, which has built its own stylish mini-empire within the Catskills at North Branch Inn, Nine River Road, and The DeBruce—each with its own personality and incredible farm-to-table menus. This 13-room property overlooks seven acres of scenic landscape for a secluded weekend hiking through the woods or on the river, exploring the local sights, or a relaxing staycation hibernating indoors.

// If you've ever wondered what it's like to stay in those gorgeous farmhouse mansions, you can make a whole weekend of it at The DeBruce

NORTH BRANCH INN

869 North Branch Road, North Branch • 845-482-2339 • northbranchinn.com

With only one road and a population under 500, the hamlet of North Branch is so tiny that this revitalized boutique boarding house is its main feature. Divided among three properties (including a former post office) along a small rural strip in the hamlet of North Branch, each of its 14 renovated rooms has a cozy, bespoke vintage feel that's better than your run-of-the-mill bed-and-breakfast. Despite its secluded location, the property is blessed with an incredible restaurant where chefs often pull vegetables and herbs straight from North Branch's garden for farm-to-table dinners. Bonus: the main house is home to an authentic turn-of-the-century wooden bowling alley where you can still play.

THE DeBRUCE

982 Debruce Road, Livingston Manor • 845-439-3900 • thedebruce.com

Like the outdoors but not interested in roughin' it? Clearly you're not alone, as this upscale bed-and-breakfast is perpetually booked by New York City weekenders. Earning national acclaim from *Esquire* and *Condé Nast Traveler* as one of the top Catskills destinations proba-bly doesn't hurt, either. The DeBruce isn't a full-service hotel (it offers no room service, in-room televisions, or special perks, for example, and Wi-Fi is spotty at best), but the rooms are thoughtfully curated with crisp linens and fluffy comforters, design-centric furnishings and priceless natural views of the Catskills. Dining here is a little unusual—the kind of fine dining you'd find in the city or at another upscale destination: an intimate 28-seat dining room and nine-course tasting menu for dinner and an à la carte breakfast menu that runs on the pricier side for outside guests (it's tweezer food, after all) and included for overnight guests. Which means that if tasting the local bounty, kicking around nature, lounging by a pool, or reading a book are your weekend objectives, it's a pretty reasonable inclusive overnight package (particularly during midweek and off-season when you can grab the best deals).

Northern Catskills

BRUSHLAND EATING HOUSE

1927 County Highway 6, Bovina Center • 607-832-4861 • brushlandeatinghouse.com

If you really want to get off the beaten path, the Western Catskills are much less developed compared with weekender-friendly areas closer to public transit. That said, you're more likely to score a better deal at places like Brushland, which doubles as a farm-to-table restaurant and a shabby chic bed-and-breakfast. So if taking advantage of nature is the primary goal, but you want a solid meal and a cozy place to rest your head, this is a great destination boarding house that will get you both. Four Airbnb properties are available, with spacious two- and three-bedroom full-size apartments and cottages for a fraction of what you'd pay in Hudson or other popular destinations.

5

Flash from the Past

Weekend Escapes for History Geeks

If eating up history is your idea of a perfect weekend, it truly doesn't take much to find some form of antiquity within Hudson Valley and the Catskills. Just pick an era—each town has seen it all.

As one of the early Colonial settled areas during the New World expansion of the 1600s, the whole area is rooted in American history and proud of it (in fact, there are about a dozen inns that still brag about their connection to President George Washington). Early Dutch settlements still stand in the historic districts of places like New Paltz, Kingston, and Newburgh. Stately Victorian mansions and estates occupied by the Vanderbilts, Roosevelts, and other aristocratic dynasties line the Hudson River, preserved like time capsules complete with luscious gardens. Those breathtaking landscapes were put to good use during the inception of the Hudson River School, which shaped early American art. Some of the homes of the school's most distinguished founders, like Thomas Cole, Frederic Edwin Church, and successors like American realist painter Edward Hopper, have been transformed into gallery estates, where you can view period artwork in authentic settings.

// See relics from the legendary 1969 Woodstock music festival at the Museum at Bethel Woods

Ornate turn-of-the-century theaters continue to operate as cinemas and music halls in places like Kingston, Poughkeepsie, and Middletown (some with original Wurlitzer pipe organs and other authentic features). Many of the original Catskills resorts of the 1950s and '60s Borscht Belt have long since been shuttered and closed, but a new generation of boutique hotels and getaways inspired by the campy, vintage aesthetic have begun to surface that make for a perfect *Dirty Dancing*–inspired throwback weekend (despite the fact the 1987 movie was actually shot in Virginia—but same drift).

The town of Bethel became the epicenter for the 1969 Summer of Love when a humble farm held the first-ever Woodstock Music Festival. Little did the farm family know that a half century later their festival would inspire countless copycat music festivals around the world. The original festival grounds are preserved as a natural landscape at the Bethel Woods Center for the Arts, a performing arts venue and immersive rock history museum that honors its hippie pioneers with frequent concerts and events. Celebrating its 50th anniversary, Bethel Woods has become somewhat of an annual pilgrimage for veteran rockers and music aficionados.

Guided tours can be interesting, but for the true history nerd, it's worth making this an authentic overnighter. Believe it or not, you can actually stay in a romantic castle, a grand mansion, a landmark lodge, or a cozy inn with a fascinating past (some of which are notoriously haunted). Make some history of your own by checking out these aging relics.

≡ *Best Towns for History Geeks*

HYDE PARK

Hardcore history geeks should plan to dedicate a full weekend to this hotbed of National Historic Sites. Legacy families like the Roosevelts and Vanderbilts all hung their hats along this estate trail, which includes the **home, presidential library,** and **museum of Franklin D. Roosevelt**; the **Eleanor Roosevelt National Historic Site**; the **Vanderbilt Mansion National Historic Site**; and the **Staatsburgh State Historic Site**. See the full itinerary on page 238.

TARRYTOWN

As one of the first Dutch settlements along the Hudson River, Tarrytown is a central point for several major landmarks, including elegant mansions and old Dutch churches. It's the home of **Lyndhurst Mansion**, a Gothic Revival estate whose former inhabitants include railroad tycoon Jay Gould and former New York City mayor William Paulding.

Tarrytown borders **Sleepy Hollow**, the town written about by iconic author Washington Irving (whose estate, **Washington Irving's Sunnyside**, is actually down the way from Lyndhurst in the village of Irvington). In Sleepy Hollow, you can take a tour at **Kykuit**, a 40-room estate belonging to four generations of the Rockefeller family before being turned into a historic site. Of course, the Dutch colonies weren't all glitz and glamor throughout the ages; **Philipsburg Manor**, a colonial-era farming, milling, and trading center, tells the stories of the two dozen African slaves that lived within its walls.

History and art collide at the **Union Church of Pocantico Hills**, home to the last work of famed artist Henri Matisse and nine contributions from fellow French master Marc Chagall. And in a pinch, honestly there's just so much history in this area you'll probably stumble upon something simply walking down one of the villages' main streets.

Getting There

One hour by car or train. This is an easy day trip to make without a car as many historic destinations are situated directly off the Metro-North Railroad Hudson Line (Irvington, Tarrytown, Philipsburg Manor) and typically have inclusive, discounted getaway packages you can purchase in advance or from Grand Central Terminal in Manhattan.

Getting Around

Most estates are within walking distance of the closest train station or a quick taxi/bus. If you want to hit a few stops in one day or make a weekend of it, it might be worth renting a car to save time. Many train stations now have Zipcar parking spaces, or car rental companies will happily pick you up if you plan to rent from them.

Highlights

KYKUIT, THE ROCKEFELLER ESTATE

381 North Broadway, Sleepy Hollow • open seasonally from May 2 through November 10, with tours operating Thursday to Sunday (October: daily except Tuesday) • depending on the tour and the day of the week, tickets range between $15 and $40

If it wasn't evident from seeing their names plastered all over New York institutions, the Rockefeller family is such an ingrained part of early American royalty that their estate is now a historic site of the National Trust for Historic Preservation. Furnished with all the authentic luxuries reflective of the four generations that lived there, tours allow a unique opportunity to explore the fascinating history, architecture, gardens, and priceless art of this landmark estate.

LYNDHURST MANSION

635 South Broadway, Tarrytown • 914-631-4481 • lyndhurst.org • hours change seasonally, but the house is typically open Thursday to Monday from 10 a.m. to 4 p.m. • ticket prices vary, depending on the tour and event (classic mansion tours and specialty gardens and grounds tours are $18; events are roughly $20–45); buy tickets online ahead of time as tours are prone to selling out

They just don't make them like they used to. Like many of the historic estates scattered along the Hudson River, Lyndhurst is nothing short of stunning. The European-inspired architecture at this 19th-century Gothic Revival mansion has been turning heads since it was built, drawing several notable residents over the years, including former New York City mayor William Paulding, merchant George Merritt, and railroad tycoon Jay Gould. Today, it's a well-preserved museum filled with enviable art, antiques, and furnishings. Its grounds maintain landscape design suggestive of the times, with a labyrinth-like path and flowering rose garden and fernery. Don't be surprised if you feel pangs of disappointment knowing you'll have to return to your cramped apartment.

>> **Know Before You Go:** Keep an eye out for special events and tours when Lyndhurst gets glitzed up for holidays like Halloween and Christmas or hosts an annual flower and antique show.

PHILIPSBURG MANOR

381 North Broadway, Sleepy Hollow • open seasonally May 1 to November 10 from Wednesday through Sunday • adults, $12; seniors 65+ and students 18-25, $10; children 3-17, $6; members and children under 3, free

Among all the magnificent estates lining the Hudson River, it's easy to overlook the history impacting the lives of the non-aristocratic members of Colonial America. Specifically, the enslaved populations whose histories are virtually unseen. Philipsburg Manor, a former thriving gristmill and trading complex, is unique in that it provides a look into the Philips family from the perspective of the 23 enslaved Africans who lived and toiled there. While you're here, plan to tack on a tour of Kykuit, starting at Philipsburg Manor. Guests are taken to the estate via shuttle bus.

WASHINGTON IRVING'S SUNNYSIDE

3 West Sunnyside Lane, Irvington • open seasonally May 1 through November 10, Wednesday to Sunday • adults, $12; seniors 65+ and students 18–25, $10; children 3–17, $6; members and children under 3, free

Even if you never read Washington Irving's "The Legend of Sleepy Hollow," you're probably familiar with its famously spooky villain, the Headless Horseman. He's the reason so many people make the trek to the eponymous lower Hudson Valley town every year on Halloween. But the Founding Father of American Literature who inspired a generation of writers like Nathaniel Hawthorne and Edgar Allan Poe lived a bit farther south, in Irvington, in an estate called Sunnyside, an interesting architectural mash-up of Gothic Revival, Scottish Gothic, and Tudor Revival styles that Irving added as expansions of an original two-room stone Dutch farmhouse. Though the house stayed within Irving's family for many years, it was historically preserved after being acquired by John D. Rockefeller and then was turned into a landmark and museum, which you can visit and tour today.

UNION CHURCH OF POCANTICO HILLS

555 Bedford Road, Tarrytown • 914-631-2069 • upch.org • tours run seasonally April 3 through December 3, open Wednesday through Monday • $7

Another Rockefeller connection, this Gothic Revival church was built by John D. Rockefeller after his Kykuit estate. Aside from its historic architectural importance, the church is most famously known for its stained glass, which includes Henri Matisse's final piece, the Rose Window, and nine windows by Marc Chagall. Because of the church's small size, this is an easy one to tackle on your own, but guided tours also run roughly every 30 minutes.

☰ *Historic Homes and Gardens*

Lower Hudson Valley

ROSEN HOUSE AT CARAMOOR CENTER FOR THE MUSIC AND ARTS

149 Girdle Ridge Road, Katonah • 914-232-1252 • caramoor.org • seasonally, August through mid-June, by advance appointment Monday to Friday • adults, $10; members and children, free

Furnished with an eclectic hodgepodge of fine and decorative Asian and Renaissance art, this Mediterranean-style house situated within the Caramoor Center for the Music and Arts was built in the 1930s by Walter Rosen and is unique for more than just its luxe treasures. In addition to its sumptuous European aesthetic with an extravagance second only to Liberace, the Rosen House is one of the few estates where you can enjoy the property beyond a tour. Afternoon tea is served daily in the open-air summer dining room, which overlooks the Spanish Courtyard, which frequently hosts chamber music, jazz, recitals, and other music. The Music Room, a tapestry-covered and Renaissance-inspired acoustic hall, hosts its own set of music events on the regular.

Western Hudson Valley

BOSCOBEL HOUSE AND GARDENS

1601 Route 90, Garrison • 845-265-3638 • boscobel.org • seasonally, mid-April through December, Wednesday to Monday 9:30 a.m.–5 p.m. • ticket prices range $6–18 for individuals (free for children under 6) or a family price for up to four is $35 ($45 if seeing the house in addition to the gardens and grounds)

Like most other notable Hudson Valley estates, this Neoclassical mansion is filled with its share of decorative arts and historic treasures. But specifically to those who prize Federalist-style arts, Boscobel is best known for its enviable collection of this particular era. The estate is nice and all, but the gardens and grounds are the real reason to visit: a sprawling landscape facing the Hudson River and the mountains surrounding the US Military Academy at West Point. Shady maple trees and apple orchards line the pathways, connecting to sunny meadows, a formal English rose garden, a sculpture garden commemorating the Hudson River School artists, panoramic valley views, and woodland trails. Boscobel is also the backdrop for the Hudson Valley Shakespeare Festival, which is the best time to experience the property.

MOHONK MOUNTAIN HOUSE

1000 Mountain Rest Road, New Paltz • 845-765-3286 • mohonk.com

The most obvious feature about this sprawling castle resort and National Historic Landmark is that it looks like it was pulled out of Wes Anderson's film *The Grand Budapest Hotel*. It's down-right visually stunning. The Victorian jewel of Shawangunk Ridge, this 150-year-old lakeside property nestled in the outskirts of New Paltz is filled with historic artifacts and surrounded by 1,200 acres of natural beauty. Naturally, this means that it's not only a pricey luxury property, but it has had its fair share of famous guests. Among them are five former presidents of the United States. So even if you can't afford to stay here, you can still learn about the history of the property by taking one of the daily house tours, which includes a detailed background on its authentic Victorian décor, vintage artwork, and a look into a-day-in-the-rural-life at Mohonk during the 19th century, including antique carriages and antique farm and kitchen equipment.

Upper Hudson Valley

INNISFREE

362 Tyrrel Road, Millbrook • 845-677-8000 • innisfreegarden.org • Wednesday to Sunday and holidays, 10 a.m.–5 p.m. • adults, $10; seniors (65+) and children (ages 4–12), $5

World-renowned for its stunning landscape design, Innisfree is more than a garden: it's a whimsical wonderland. Inspired by Chinese and Japanese naturalistic design, the 150 acres of sprawling gardens, meadows, streams, terraces, and woodlands took more than 50 years to complete. Dreamed up as a private garden for owners Walter and Marion Beck, the garden was opened to the public in 1960 under the direction of landscape architect Lester Collins. Though Innisfree is internationally celebrated, like many Hudson Valley attractions, it's one of those incredible fixtures worth seeing that somehow remains a hidden treasure.

LOCUST GROVE ESTATE

2683 South Road, Poughkeepsie • 845-454-4500 • lgny.org • visitor center is open 10 a.m.–5 p.m. weekdays from January through March, and daily April through December, with access to the mansion via a group tour (check the website for the most up-to-date schedule); access to the garden and grounds is open daily 8 a.m. to dusk • adults, $12; youth (ages 6–18), $6

Every historic estate in the Valley has a fascinating story and architectural features, but Locust Grove is somewhat unique in both its design and history, compared with the others. First, there's the style, which is Italianate as opposed to the classic Dutch barn houses and Colonialist manors common throughout the region. Then there's its owner: artist and inventor Samuel F. B. Morse, most famously known for codeveloping Morse code and the single-wire telegraph system. Beyond an intimate look inside the daily life of this interesting historical personage, the estate has nearly 200 acres of immaculately maintained gardens, grounds, and woodland hiking trails to explore (spring and fall are the most romantic times to visit).

MARTIN VAN BUREN NATIONAL HISTORIC SITE

1013 Old Post Road, Kinderhook • 581-758-9689 x2040 • nps.gov.mava • grounds are open daily from sunrise to sunset; visitor center is open Saturday and Sunday 9 a.m.–4:30 p.m., with tours at 10 a.m., 12 p.m., and 2 p.m. • free

Lindenwald, the Kinderhook home of America's eighth president, Martin Van Buren, doesn't get nearly as much love as the Roosevelts' two estates in Hyde Park. But if you're really into American presidential history, this is one of the few tours you should add to the list. It was here that Van Buren ran his two presidential campaigns. The site provides an interesting look at the life of one of America's earliest leaders.

☰ *Historic Hideaways and Revamped Rooms*

Ever wonder what it's like to sleep in a castle or a historic mansion? Prefer the character of a well-worn home over a cookie-cutter chain hotel? There are more historic bed-and-breakfasts scattered throughout the Hudson Valley and Catskills than can fit into one book, but here are a few long-standing abodes worth checking out.

Lower Hudson Valley

CASTLE HOTEL & SPA

400 Benedict Avenue, Tarrytown • 914-631-1980 • castlehotelandspa.com

When life hands you the opportunity to sleep in a castle with incredible sweeping views of the Hudson River, it's probably the smart choice to just do it. Originally built at the turn of the century under the moniker Carrollcliffe Castle, this historic estate is now a top-rated luxury hotel, spa, and restaurant. It shouldn't come as much of a shocker that rooms don't run cheap (or that the property is often booked early for weddings and events), but should you want to make it a special getaway, opt for summer, when you can take advantage of the seasonal outdoor swimming pool, whirlpool, and mile-long strip of landscaped jogging trail.

Upper Hudson Valley

THE 1850 HOUSE INN

435 Main Street, Rosendale • 845-658-7800 • the1850house.com

As suggested by the name, this inn and tavern has a storied history that dates back to 1850. Though the property has shifted hands a few times, it retains an authentic, aging charm with comfortable, modern updates. It's also a solid weekender destination for those hitting the Wallkill Valley Rail Trail, given that Rosendale is a midway point between New Paltz and Kingston, adjacent to the Rondout Creek and a few miles from the Minnewaska and Mohonk Preserves. Its tavern continues to operate on the first floor, serving seasonal menus, local beers, and craft cocktails.

THE BEEKMAN ARMS

6387 Mill Street, Rhinebeck • 845-876-7077 • beekmandelamaterinn.com

Proudly claiming to be the oldest inn in America, The Beekman Arms certainly has receipts to back it up. Dating to 1766, the inn and tavern has actual documentation of its check-in records from the American Revolution. Given its lengthy tenure and reputation, The Beekman Arms has hosted countless famous guests, including former presidents George Washington, Franklin

D. Roosevelt, and Bill Clinton. The property may be old, but the accommodations have fortunately received a modern upgrade with plush bedding and air conditioning. Bonus: as a nice gesture, the property stocks each room with a complimentary decanter of sherry.

TIGER HOUSE

317 Allen Street, Hudson • 518-828-1321 • tigerhousehudson.com

A former hunting lodge dating to 1901, this unique Dutch Jacobian-style property is now a haven for stylish New York City weekenders escaping to Hudson. *Ornate* is an understatement—common areas are brimming with stunning original woodwork and authentic fixtures that give this location a timeless elegance many places can only try to replicate (the plant-filled solarium is a great place to take your morning coffee or read a book). Each of the five spacious rooms is furnished with fine details, like antique four-poster beds, gas fireplaces, large soaking tubs, and private terraces.

Western Hudson Valley
HASBROUCK HOUSE

3805 Main Street, Stone Ridge • 845-687-0736 • hasbrouckhouseny.com

This romantic little getaway consists of three renovated 19th-century boutique properties—a main inn, a carriage house, and a country cottage—each outfitted with modern luxury amenities like goose down pillows, a claw-foot soaking tub, Frette linens, Aesop soaps, and Nespresso machines (after all, not every part of the experience needs to be historic, right?). On the main floor, its elegant farm-to-table restaurant Butterfield serves a seasonally changing menu of contemporary Hudson Valley cuisine like house-smoked wild salmon tartare, local artisanal cheeses, and cabernet-braised short ribs.

Eastern Catskills
SCRIBNER'S CATSKILL LODGE

13 Scribner Hollow Road, Hunter • 518-628-5130 • scribnerslodge.com

A resort relic surviving the Catskills' Borscht Belt days of the 1960s, this property received a nice upgrade in 2016 to catch up with the area's rustic-chic revival. Aside from the nice furnishings, nature is really the big draw. There are no bad views, given that most of its 38 rooms have private balconies and large windows overlooking its 20-acre mountainous landscape and expansive pool. Even if you aren't shacking up here, it's worth stopping for dinner at the lodge's acclaimed restaurant, Prospect, which offers upscale takes on seasonal, local ingredients.

>> **Transit Pro-Tip:** Luxury charter shuttle **Line** offers drop-off service to Scribner's from Manhattan Thursday through Monday (646-798-8116; ridewithline.com).

WASHINGTON IRVING INN

6629 Route 23A, Tannersville • 518-589-5560 • washingtonirving.com

Hudson Valley's most prolific writer, Washington Irving, never actually stayed at this 19th-century Victorian-style inn in the Catskills. Nonetheless, it maintains a writerly charm with plenty of original fixtures, like its ornate library with built-in wooden shelving, old-fashioned touches like afternoon tea service, and guest rooms inspired by and named after local legends like Candace Wheeler, Thomas Cole, and Maude Adams. Tucked away in the Catskill State Park near Hunter Mountain, this historic property benefits from its convenient access to nature and the outdoors, along with a serene atmosphere perfect for a writing sabbatical or winter hibernation.

Western Catskills

BEAVERKILL VALLEY INN

7 Barnhart Road, Lew Beach • 845-439-4844 • beaverkillvalleyinn.com

In the late 19th century, the Catskills were teeming with fishing lodges, inns, and boarding houses geared toward city weekenders in search of natural refuge and anglers taking advantage of the Beaverkill Valley's trout fishing. Funny how some things never change. A relic of a bygone era in the Catskills, this inn has a unique history and careful preservation that earned it a spot on the National Register of Historic Places. Original features are peppered throughout, like fireplaces with hand-cut key stones and ornate woodwork, along with modern amenities like an indoor pool, air conditioning, and Wi-Fi—plus a few unique additions, like an incredible farm-to-table restaurant and a self-service ice cream parlor. Outdoor adventure remains the biggest draw, given the inn's ideal location adjacent to the Beaverkill River. Everything from fly-fishing and tennis to 40 miles of private hiking and biking trails, an ice skating rink, and cross-country skiing are accessible from the property.

BURN BRAE MANSION

573 High Road, Glen Spey • 845-856-3335 • burnbraemansion.com

Burn Brae Mansion isn't just historic, it's also haunted. At least according to the show *Ghost Hunters*, actress Linda Blair of *The Exorcist*, and nearly every person who has ever slept there. But that's part of the territory with old estates. This turn-of-the-century mansion originally belonged to former Singer Sewing Machine company president George Ross MacKenzie and now is best known for its paranormal activity and annual haunted Halloween trail. Whether or not you believe in ghosts, the mansion is filled with all sorts of interesting details like original Tiffany glasswork and a guided tour of the "Attic of Curiosities," a strange collection of antiques, costumes, dolls, and all sorts of niche items you'd never think would become collectibles. Plus, there's a pool, which is always a nice perk to have for a weekend escape.

6

Hurry Up and Relax

Weekend Escapes for Spas and Retreats

There are a million reasons to love living in New York City—and about a million more that make leaving it a downright necessity: riding shoulder-to-shoulder on your oppressive daily commute, loud neighbors, constant traffic, and even skirting around those beloved scrappy street rats surviving on pizza crusts. Getting away requires more than physically removing yourself; you want to disconnect entirely. Good news: you're only a few hours away from turning down the volume and going totally offline.

Blame it on the holistic holdover from the crunchy hippies of the late '60s and early '70s, or the expanse of untouched forests that make it easy to go off the grid, but the result is the same: a surplus of health and wellness retreats scattered throughout the Hudson Valley and Catskill Mountains. From bougie day spas to minimalist weeklong spiritual retreats, there is a huge range of options for resetting the clock and dipping into some deserved self-care.

Unlike the spa treatments in New York City, you don't have to worry about being shoved into the dirty, loud streets after a relaxing (and probably monumentally pricey) treatment. Think: crisp mountain air, lounging next to serene ponds in a plush robe, strolling through quiet forested paths, and refueling your body with beautiful, organic produce from local farms. Admit it—sounds pretty good, doesn't it?

Want to recharge your batteries doing something a little more invigorating? Learn the practice of mindful meditation at places like Kadampa Meditation Center and Menla. Brush up on Reiki or take a sound bath at Maha Rose. Get fully pampered with a CBD massage and a premium facial at Copperhood Spa or Emerson Resort. Drop in for a yoga session or take a weekend retreat at Ananda Ashram. Or completely reset your diet and habits at places like Yo1 Wellness Center and Sanivan Holistic Retreat.

In fact, Hudson Valley produce is so fresh and flavorful that even meat-eaters might succumb to the healthy ways of plant-based living. It makes sense, considering there's no shortage of trendy farm-to-table spots that have paved the way for inventive vegetarian and vegan restaurants. Along with making the most of local greens and grains, you can find house-made nut cheeses and meat substitutes using all-natural ingredients, so that you can leave feeling good inside and out.

Detox, cleanse your chakras, or just work out the kinks at these spas and retreats that take relaxation seriously.

≡ *Relaxing Highlights*

Upper Hudson Valley

BODHI HOLISTIC SPA

543 Warren Street, Hudson • 518-828-2233 • bodhiholisticspa.com

Want the spa experience but your schedule is too packed to make a full weekend of it? This service-oriented holistic spa centered in the Warren Street strip of Hudson just might be your speed. Services don't run cheap, but they're on par with any upscale spa. Think: drop-in yoga classes, Naturopathica facials, acupuncture, scrubs and wraps, waxing and salon services, and specialized massage treatments like Himalayan salt stone, myofascial release, energizing blue eucalyptus and aromatherapy, and classic Swedish, Thai, and deep tissue. If you're looking to detox your mind as well as your body, they even offer tarot card readings, Reiki and chakra therapy, craniosacral therapy, and hypnosis. Even if you don't take a course here, the shop is well worth a visit for picking up palo santo sticks, bath salts, essential oils, candles, and other curated spa gifts.

>> **Secret Airbnb Alert:** The three-bedroom apartment located on the third floor is available to rent on Airbnb. It includes a claw-foot tub in the master bath, a rainfall shower, a spacious living room and rooftop deck, a full kitchen, and plush bedding, at a price that won't break the bank.

BUTTERMILK FALLS INN AND SPA

220 North Road, Milton • 845-795-1310 • buttermilkfallsinn.com

As far as spas that embody the essence of modern Hudson Valley go, Buttermilk Falls is where it's at. Farm-to-table lunches, Red Flower body treatments, Swedish-style massage using fresh lavender grown on-site, plus an eco-friendly solar-powered dry sauna, a eucalyptus steam room, and a geothermally heated endless pool—all located on a bucolic farm just off the Hudson River. It's about a 10-minute drive from the Poughkeepsie Metro-North train station, making this an easy getaway without the overnight commitment (though the guest rooms outfitted with built-in fireplace and whirlpool bathtub aren't too shabby if you'd prefer to crash). Book an appointment, bring a bathing suit, and unwind, then explore Millstone Farm, Buttermilk's organic agricultural extension that includes an animal rescue, an aviary, a garden, a livestock barn, and an apiary.

MAHA ROSE NORTH

130 Morgan Hill Road, Hurley • 929-600-3200 • maharose.com

If the name of this holistic retreat center sounds familiar, it's because you might have come across its original location in Brooklyn. Combining a multitude of ancient holistic practices with contemporary applications, think of it as new age wellness workshops and retreats for hipsters. Think: past life regression and sound bath therapy led by a Celtic pagan, full moon rituals, and breathwork healing with a Reiki master, plus crystals, tarot card readings, and astrology, all taught by experienced and licensed practitioners.

Western Hudson Valley
ANANDA ASHRAM

13 Sapphire Road, Monroe • 845-782-5575 • anandaashram.org

Part of the Yoga Society of New York, this retreat and spiritual center focuses on practices developed by founder Shri Brahmananda Sarasvati. Yoga classes geared toward students of all levels are taught here—from restorative and gentle flow to Hatha and advanced Vinyasa—along with workshops like Sanskrit courses, dance, music, and Ayurvedic studies. Drop-in classes are affordable ($15), and so are weekend retreat packages (albeit with humble shared dorm and semi-private lodgings, so if you want something cushier, opt for somewhere else).

MOHONK MOUNTAIN HOUSE

1000 Mountain Rest Road, New Paltz • 845-765-3286 • mohonk.com

The most obvious feature about this historic castle resort is that it looks like it was pulled out of Wes Anderson's film *The Grand Budapest Hotel*. It's downright visually stunning. Mohonk is the Victorian jewel of Shawangunk Ridge, a 150-year-old lakeside property in the out-skirts of New Paltz that's filled with historic artifacts and surrounded by 1,200 acres of natural beauty. Unsurprisingly, that makes this one of the pricier destinations that's better experienced by taking a day trip for a bougie afternoon at the spa. The indoor heated pool and fitness center are reserved for overnight guests only and services are subject to availability (book in advance), but snagging a day spa package grants you access to its luxe eucalyptus steam room, dry rock sauna, and outdoor heated mineral pool (don't forget to bring a bathing suit!). Afterward, chill out on one of the property's two glass-enclosed verandas overlooking an incredible panoramic mountain view, or its solarium outfitted with a stone fireplace and complimentary tea bar.

Eastern Catskills

EMERSON RESORT AND SPA

5340 Route 28, Mount Tremper • 845-688-2828 • emersonresort.com

Luxury doesn't come cheap, but it will get you pretty much whatever you want. Emerson is among the high-end spas in the Catskills, offering essentially every kind of spa treatment imaginable: all the classic massages (Swedish, Thai, prenatal, sports medicine, aromatherapy, hot stone, shiatsu, Reiki); experimental massages (CBD treatment, Ayurvedic); body treatments like mud wraps, scrubs, and hydrotherapy soaks; fancy state-of-the-art facials; and even signature customizable services. While you're there, don't miss the world's largest kaleidoscope, housed in a converted silo on the property.

MENLA

375 Pantherkill Road, Phoenicia • 845-688-6897 • menla.us

A vast landscape of serenity, the Catskills have become a popular outpost for Eastern spirituality retreats like this renowned cultural center teaching the practices of Tibetan Buddhism from the Dalai Lama. Its 4,000-square-foot Dewa spa features luxe amenities like traditional wooden Finnish-style and contemporary far infrared light saunas, steam rooms, and herbal bath therapy in deep soaking tubs, Ayurvedic steam box therapy, and rain showers (a day pass is a relative steal at $35 off-peak/$45 peak pricing). Services lean toward traditional Tibetan and Ayurvedic medicine, though a variety of Western-style spa services are also available. The spa is lovely, but the big draw is the range of holistic retreats, which include programs like shamanic dreaming and yoga, forage hikes with mushroom cultivation, Ayurvedic cleanses, and even focused psychotherapies such as PTSD healing. If you're somewhere in between, Menla offers personalized weekend getaways with a number of comfy lodging options.

THE WINDHAM SPA

16 Mitchell Hollow Road, Windham • 518-734-9617 • thewindhamspa.com

This boutique spa has somewhat of an unusual backdrop: a classic farmhouse complete with a wraparound front porch. Don't be fooled by the homey bed-and-breakfast look—inside is

// The Kadampa Meditation Center in Glen Spey is one of only three temples of its kind in the world

a luxe getaway perfect for a spa day with friends. Think: marble soaking basins for pedicures using palo santo or grapefruit and pine, customized massages, mangosteen facials, and micro-dermabrasion treatments.

Western Catskills

KADAMPA MEDITATION CENTER

47 Sweeney Road, Glen Spey • 845-856-9000 • kadampanewyork.org

One of only three Kadampa Meditation Center temples in the world, this unique spiritual destination attracts visitors from around the globe who come to learn and practice this contemporary form of Buddhism. Of course, you don't have to be a Buddhist or even a spiritual person to come visit and decompress. All are welcome to drop in for a guided tour of the temple and property, with an introduction to meditation and a 15-minute guided practice. After, take a stroll through the serene walking trails surrounding the temple and grab a snack at the World Peace Café. If you enjoy the practice and want to continue, the center hosts a number of affordable classes and weekend retreats for all levels.

≡ *All-In-One Weekend Retreats*

Lower Hudson Valley

INN AND SPA AT BEACON

151 Main Street, Beacon • 845-205-2900 • innspabeacon.com

Situated conveniently on Beacon's main strip, just a short walk from the Metro-North train station, this boutique hydrotherapy spa has all the deluxe services for an easy day trip or a cozy weekend. A day pass scores access to their thermotherapy spa, which includes a Bullfrog Spa JetPak Therapy System (a fancy hot tub with about 16 jet massage options). Additional services include facials, Swedish and deep tissue massage, hydrating hair and lip treatments, waxing, and private yoga and personal training sessions. As suggested by the name, the property is both a spa and an inn, if you want to walk around in your slippers for an overnighter or weekend getaway. Inclusive spa packages are frequently available, often tacking on a thematic experience like a private plein-air painting session or tickets to The Shakespeare Festival at Boscobel Gardens.

APOTHECARY SHOPPING LIST

2 NOTE HUDSON • 2notehudson.com

Handcrafted natural, organic bath and body products developed by two musicians who blend unique fragrances inspired by compositions.

COLD SPRING APOTHECARY • coldspringapothecary.com

Small-batch botanicals for the body and home using natural healing properties of essential oils, herbs, and extracts.

FAT OF THE LAND APOTHECARY • fatofthelandapothecary.com

Healing oils, tinctures, and elixirs made from wild harvested and home-grown ingredients in Hudson Valley.

HUDSON MADE • hudsonmadeny.com

Independent bath and body product company that sources ingredients within a 200-mile radius of Hudson, New York.

VILLAGE COMMON MERCANTILE • thevillagecommon.com

Herbaceous and woodsy natural candles and room sprays inspired by the American landscape and gardens, made in Catskill.

Upper Hudson Valley
WON DHARMA CENTER

361 Route 23, Claverack • 518-851-2581 • wondharmacenter.org

Searching for an excuse to totally disconnect? This Buddhist retreat is a cellphone- and laptop-free zone, ensuring ultimate Zen for practicing mindful meditation in its stunning 1,800-square-foot meditation hall. In fact, anything considered a distraction from noble silence and peaceful meditation is off-limits, right down to a neutral-colored clothing dress code. Because spiritual meditation is the core of the program, rooms are modest and clean, with twin beds in a shared dormitory, single, or double room. So if you're looking to be pampered, opt for a spa.

Eastern Catskills
COPPERHOOD RETREAT AND SPA

7039 Route 28, Shandaken • 845-688-2460 • copperhood.com

This is a resort and retreat for people who are serious about spas. It's for when you want to be pampered, steamed, scrubbed, shoved in a sauna, massaged with luxurious aromatherapy oils, and given a personalized detox diet; when you want to get a glowing facial or body wrap and stretch out with a little yoga or a brisk walk through the Catskills, followed by more hot tubbing until you are officially *relaxed*. Wait, it's time to leave? You really have to go back to the weekday grind? Ugh. Copperhood has gotten pretty good at the restorative spa experience after 36 years, offering everything from day spa treatments and access to the facilities (a steal at $40) to weekend getaways with full detox meal plans (the rooms are pretty dated and it's definitely pricey, but the spa facilities are excellent). Plus, direct access to hiking trails, tennis courts, fly-fishing on the Esopus Creek, and all the other coveted Catskills outdoor activities.

Western Catskills
SANIVAN HOLISTIC RETREAT AND SPA

12 Columbia Drive, Hurleyville • 845-434-1849 • sanivan.com

Go off-the-grid at this independently-owned retreat and spa in the Catskills that combines the comfort of a bed-and-breakfast with rejuvenating holistic practices. Because of its small size, the property is able to provide personalized services from therapeutic massage, sound work, and holistic facials to extended wellness retreats focusing on organic meals and cleanses. Plush furnishings give this a welcoming home-away-from-home vibe, but with luxe amenities like a heated indoor saltwater pool, sauna, and steam room that are likely much, much better than your home. Pack comfy clothes, a bathing suit, and your toiletries, then let the staff at Sanivan do the rest.

// Hit the reset button at Yo1 Wellness Center, a newly opened Ayurvedic retreat in the Catskills

YO1 WELLNESS CENTER

420 Anawana Lake Road, Monticello • 855-256-8851 • yo1.com

More of a retreat than a spa, Yo1 is a niche, pricey, holistic wellness concept that draws older-skewing clientele and isn't on the cool Catskills getaways circuit. If you're looking to get a massage and sit in a hot tub, this is not for you. But it's also an incredibly unique, highly structured, and totally transformative concept that you should know exists. While some yoga classes might casually drop terms like "namaste" into a short 30-minute session, Yo1 teaches legit Ayurvedic and naturopathic therapies used by Indian holistic practitioners for 5,000 years. That means committing to an all-inclusive, customized program tackling bodily issues ranging from a full detox, stress relief, and physical therapy to reshaping your entire diet and lifestyle, running anywhere from a day package to 10-day stay. Just shy of a year old, the brand new 1,300-acre secured property has 68,000 square feet of therapy areas inside a jarringly sterile, futuristic atmosphere that's somehow completely calm and inviting. Generously sized suites overlook sweeping views of pine forests and serene lakes. Menus are personalized to fit your health goals, with cooking classes where you can learn how to continue the practices you pick up here in your daily life. A combination of massage, meditation practice, herbal remedies, and oil therapies are tailored to each person, and inclusive of the stay rate, so you can schvitz, stretch, sleep, and snack, and then walk out feeling right as rain.

☰ *Healthy Eats*

Lower Hudson Valley

CARIBREEZE VEGAN DELIGHT

42 North Main Street, Spring Valley • 845-426-2600 • caribreeze.com • $

This might be one of the only places where you can order both jerk seitan and lasagna from the same menu. The Caribbean-Italian hybrid takeout concept is unusual, but there's no sense in knocking something delicious. Especially when it's a no-frills, family-owned vegan restaurant dedicated to using entirely healthy oils and natural ingredients. Dig into guilt-free dishes like mac and cheese, chana masala, batata, and callaloo.

SKINNY BUDDHA ORGANIC KITCHEN

159 Lexington Avenue, Mount Kisco • 914-358-1666 • myskinnybuddha.com • $

Whether you're trying to hit the reset button on your system or happen to be riddled with food allergies and restrictions, this organic, vegan, and gluten-free restaurant offers flavorful, nutritious, and filling options that feel approachable, not restrictive. Favorites like loaded nachos, penne Bolognese, and even a lox bagel with cream cheese are all free of dairy, meat, and gluten, but so tasty that chances are you won't even notice the lack of meat.

Upper Hudson Valley

THE ROSENDALE CAFE

434 Main Street, Rosendale • 845-658-9048 • rosendalecafe.com • $

This crunchy little local favorite consistently earns the top spot as the Valley's best vegetarian restaurant. A mainstay for more than 25 years, its constantly changing menu features eclectic and hearty meat-free dishes ranging from a tempeh Reuben and mushroom tofu stroganoff to a sweet potato burrito and ravioli of the day. In the evening, the restaurant features weekly salsa dancing lessons and a monthly art reception with local artists.

Western Hudson Valley

CONSCIOUS FORK

14 Railroad Avenue, Warwick • 845-988-5253 • consciousfork.com • $$

Recharge your batteries at this casual vegan café and juice bar, featuring made-from-scratch healthy sandwiches, grain bowls, smoothies, fresh-pressed juices, and house-made kombucha using non-GMO and organic produce from area farmers.

LAGUSTA'S LUSCIOUS COMMISSARY

11 Church Street, New Paltz • 845-288-3426 • lagustasluscious.com • $

The café offshoot of popular vegan chocolatier Lagusta's Luscious Confectionery, this inventive plant-based kitchen whips up everything from scratch for dishes like baked mac and cheese casserole with cashew béchamel and their socialist sliding scale soup special featuring locally sourced farm greens, shiitake mushrooms, tofu, wide rice noodles, and miso broth, spiced with shichimi togarashi. They even have a whole cheese board using house-made nut cheeses and seasonal pickles.

PURE CITY

100 Main Street, Pine Bush • 845-744-8888 • purecityny.com • $$

Vegans and vegetarians tired of choosing between a side salad and "Earth Mother"–style cafés should appreciate this entirely plant-based Chinese restaurant, where everything is low sodium and cholesterol, using all-natural ingredients. Which means limitless options for vegetarian riffs on orange chicken, General Tso's, spicy soft tofu hot pot, and crispy seitan with dipping sauce and steamed asparagus.

Eastern Catskills
GARDEN CAFE

6 Old Forge Road, Woodstock • 845-679-3600 • thegardencafewoodstock.com • $$

It shouldn't come as too much of a shocker that the hippie-centric village of Woodstock would have a sunny vegan café. What it lacks in meat, it makes up in choice: a true "something for everyone" place where you can find everything from black-and-white-peppercorn-crusted tofu with polenta and avocado mousse to Indian red lentil vegetable enchiladas in coconut tomato sauce.

7

The Great Outdoors

Weekend Escapes for Tree Huggers

Something that will always blow your mind: realizing how quickly the overwhelming sense of New York City's urban congestion completely disappears just an hour outside city limits. It's like having the volume turned down on your life. Coasting along the Hudson River while riding the Metro-North or Amtrak train, you'll see the landscape shift with the rising mountainous, forested peaks. Mobile service will begin to fade out as you pass secluded, winding roads. And then it suddenly hits you: "Oh, right. We're in the country."

The endless hustle-and-bustle of city living makes it easy forget that the great outdoors are just sitting there, right in our own backyard, only an hour away. There are endless miles of camping, hiking, biking trails, water sports, ziplining, skiing, and fishing, all open year-round. Easy hiking trails loop around serene lakes, shady forests, and beautiful waterfalls, where the only traffic you'll encounter is a rare hiker or the rustling of wildlife scampering by. The expanse of open land has made it possible for large-scale art to break out of the museum and into several sculpture parks. Wandering through the wild landscapes of places like Storm King and Art Omi can easily fill up a whole day otherwise spent indoors at large-scale museums. If

// There's a reason why the Upper Delaware River is dubbed a scenic byway: the views are downright breathtaking year-round

you'd rather skip the walk, many scenic outlooks can be reached through a quick drive, or you can rent a bike and tackle the many rail trails throughout the Hudson Valley and Catskills.

Countless tents pack into campsites along the Upper Delaware River throughout summer weekends for cookouts and sleeping under the stars. Playing in the water is more fun than looking at it, which is why so many kayaks, tubes, canoes, and rafts are available to rent. Not into roughin' it? Go glamping in a myriad of alternative rustic lodgings like a yurt, airstream trailer, cabin, geodome, or Scandinavian-style Lushna.

When fall foliage hits, you can take it all in from above in a hot-air balloon, a nail-biting skydiving trip, or flying through the multi-colored trees on a zipline. Cooler temperatures in spring and fall are also prime for mushroom foraging or fly-fishing for salmon and stillwater trout—or just reaping the benefits of someone else's hard work at a local restaurant. Winter is all about hitting the mountains: skiing, snowboarding, snowshoeing, and sledding. Caravans frequently run urban snow bunnies from the city to places like Hunter Mountain, Belleayre Mountain, Holiday Mountain, and Windham Mountain. And even if you don't have the coordination to dip into winter sports, rest assured there's bound to be a roaring fire with spiked hot cocoa or mulled wine within reach for hibernating.

>> **Know Before You Go:** Check local park service websites for the most up-to-date information on trail conditions and closures, which change regularly.

≡ *Best Towns to Get Outdoors*

NARROWSBURG

Narrowsburg isn't in the heart of camping territory, but it's an excellent gateway where you can set your compass to find campgrounds, hiking, and scenic outlooks along the Catskills' Upper Delaware River. Consider it the last main drag for the comforts of civilization before diving into a weekend of outdoor adventures like mountain hiking, kayaking and tubing, campfires, a big sky of stars, and no cell phone reception. Hit the river with a kayak, canoe, tube, or monster 20-person party raft through Reber River Trips, Lander's River Trips, and Kittatinny Canoes (which also has paintball and zipline courses).

If you don't want to go off the grid entirely, check out Narrowsburg's Main Street strip of up-and-coming boutiques, galleries, and restaurants like One Grand Books, Sunny's Pop, The Velvet Maple, MayerWasner, and The Heron. Theaters NACL and Forestburgh Playhouse are both within a 20-minute drive of each other for a taste of local performing arts culture. And if you just want a few hours of peaceful meditation in the woods, recharge your batteries at Kadampa Meditation Retreat, a Buddhist temple in nearby Glen Spey.

>> **Know Before You Go:** Among the countless city dwellers without camping supplies? Make sure to hit up an outfitter before you leave town (find a list of camping gear rentals on page 171). Lighten the travel by renting an inclusive permanent setup like platform tents on Tentrr or cabins, yurts, airstream trailers, and other alternative rustic lodging via Hipcamp or Glamping Hub.

Getting There

2 hours 20 minutes via car from New York City. Don't even bother trying this without a car. Make sure to have GPS directions available for offline, or at least the courage necessary to ask a local for directions in a pinch.

Outdoorsy Highlights

KITTATINNY CANOES AND CAMPGROUND

3846 Route 97, Barryville • 800-356-2852 • kittatinny.com

Pop a tent and spend an action-packed weekend in nature or just hit the water at this campsite and outdoor adventure outfitter on the Upper Delaware Scenic and Recreational River. This is definitely a bare-bones BYO equipment place where you're renting campgrounds, so if you want a permanent platform tent or cabin experience, look elsewhere. Whether you want to explore nature through a leisurely canoe trip, commandeer a solo or tandem kayak, spend a lazy afternoon tubing, or hit the rapids white-water rafting, Kittatinny has it all (plus a dual zipline and paintball course, if you want to tack that on). Depending on your paddle skill level

// Grab a canoe, kayak, or raft from Lander's River Trips, with locations along the Delaware River

and how much time you want to spend on the river, there are options for everyone. Kittatinny even offers primitive overnight camping trips along the Delaware Water Gap National Recreation Area.

LANDER'S RIVER TRIPS

5961 Route 97, Narrowsburg • 800-252-3925 • landersrivertrips.com

Kayak, canoe, tube, or raft your way down the Upper Delaware River, and then make a camping weekend out of it at this outdoor adventure outfitter with riverfront locations in Narrowsburg and Barryville. Overnight packages offer decent deals (though you'll need to factor in bringing your own equipment from home or renting from an outfitter), but even regular day-trip prices make this a solid budget-friendly option. Bonus: even during peak season, there's no need for reservations. So if you happen to be in the Catskills on the perfect afternoon, it's easy to take an impromptu 4–6 hour river trip.

REBER RIVER TRIPS

3351 Route 97, Barryville • 844-525-3086 • reberrivertrips.com

If it floats, chances are this indie river outfitter has it: rafts, canoes, single and double kayaks, tubes, and Reber's claim to fame: a 20-person party raft. Reber doesn't have its own campgrounds for an inclusive weekend on the river, but their rates tend to be on the cheaper side ($22–45 per person for an all-day rate).

While You're Near Narrowsburg . . .

See a Performance:

THE FORESTBURGH PLAYHOUSE

39 Forestburgh Road, Forestburgh • 845-794-1194 • fbplayhouse.org

If you consider yourself a Broadway geek, if you loved *Glee*, or if you just appreciate really campy early bird specials while watching cabaret, this playhouse is New York State's oldest continuously operating professional summer theater and only a 40-minute drive from Narrowsburg if you want to see a live show from accredited NYC actors in the woods.

NACL THEATRE

110 Highland Lake Road, Highland Lake • 845-557-0694 • nacl.org

Short for North American Cultural Laboratory, this nonprofit theater hosts a rotating event calendar featuring thought-provoking stage work from actors, playwrights, musicians, and other performers. Catch everything from experimental theater tackling controversial topics to dinner-dance parties and burlesque.

Practice Mindful Meditation:

KADAMPA MEDITATION CENTER

47 Sweeney Road • Glen Spey • 845-856-9000 • kadampanewyork.org

One of three Kadampa Meditation Center temples in the world—all are welcome to drop into this unique Buddhist spiritual destination that attracts visitors from around the globe. Get a quick 15-minute introduction to meditation and guided practice, then stroll through the serene walking trails surrounding the temple and grab a snack at the World Peace Café. If you enjoy the practice and want to continue, the center hosts a number of affordable classes and weekend retreats for all levels.

Have a GOOP-Approved Shopping Trip:

MAYERWASNER

55 Main Street, Narrowsburg • 845-252-3828 • mayerwasner.com

Are you the kind of person who envies art professor chic? Get all those draping architectural cuts and fine hand-dyed textiles at this designer boutique. If the price tag shocks you, rest easy that you get what you pay for: every item is manufactured locally in upstate New York and Pennsylvania using ethical design and providing living wages to employees.

ONE GRAND BOOKS

60 Main Street, Narrowsburg • 845-252-3541 • onegrandbooks.com

It's rare that a bookstore has a cult following, but that's something worth getting behind. Best known for its celebrity-curated book collections, One Grand lets popular writers, artists, and other creative types like author Ta-Nehisi Coates, chef René Redzepi, and comedian Chelsea Handler pick their favorite titles to grace their shelves, à la Oprah's Book Club–meets–staff picks.

SUNNY'S POP

76 Main Street, Narrowsburg • 845-252-5090 • sunnyspop.com

If you're low on cash and prone to impulse purchases, avoid this store at all costs because Sunny's Pop is the kind of boutique that you kind of want to hate, but where you also want to buy everything (and it won't come cheap). This is your GOOP-friendly boutique, featuring everyday objets d'art like fancy housewares, bath and body products, stationery, and other curated items.

THE VELVET MAPLE

22 Main Street, Narrowsburg • 646-266-0205 • thevelvetmaple.com

Find something old and something new at this lifestyle boutique and interior design studio that features fashion, furnishings, and knickknacks handpicked by indie designers and fresh vintage finds at prices that won't kill your wallet.

Where to Stay
For Something Close to Nature Without Sleeping Outside
NORTH BRANCH INN

869 North Branch Road, North Branch • 845-482-2339 • northbranchinn.com

Divided among three properties (including a former post office) along the small rural strip in the hamlet of North Branch, each of this boarding house's 14 renovated rooms has a cozy, bespoke vintage feel that's better than your run-of-the-mill bed-and-breakfast. Despite its secluded location, the property is blessed with an incredible restaurant where chefs often pull vegetables and herbs straight from North Branch's garden for farm-to-table dinners. Bonus: The main house is home to an authentic turn-of-the-century wooden bowling alley where you can still play.

STICKETT INN

3380 Route 97, Barryville • 845-557-0913 • stickettinn.com

Yes, the name is intentional, and it's the kind of tongue-in-cheek welcome you should expect from its incredibly charming husband-owners Roswell Hamrick and Johnny Pizzolato. An intimate property with only five suites, each stylish space is dressed with locally made Shibori bedding and themed by interest: "Eat" is outfitted with a kitchen and geared toward the traveler who wants to cook local farm-fresh produce; "Steam" is equipped with a private steam shower and cold plunge basin. In the courtyard, there's a four-seat jacuzzi with disco light options for hot-tubbing under the stars. Pick up a cup of coffee in the morning or have a drink with Johnny and Roswell in the evening at their bar and welcome center, where they have a custom-made cider (aptly named Stickett Inn Cider Dry and Hard) and great swag worth toting home.

Where to Eat and Drink

Shop ahead for food if you're going to rough it in the Catskills or along the Upper Delaware River. But you can always stock up at these spots:

For When Artisanal Snacks Are a Last-Minute Necessity

FORESTBURGH GENERAL STORE

2841 NY-42, Forestburgh • 845-707-4862 • forestburghgeneral.com

On the way to town, swing by this general store that features all the items you actually want to stock up on for a weekend in the Catskills: craft beers and ciders, fresh-made sandwiches, jewelry, clothing, and bath bombs.

For Something Better Than a Campfire Cookout

THE HERON

40 Main Street, Narrowsburg • 845-252-3333 • theheronrestaurant.com

The love child of two New York City culinary vets, this charming New American restaurant is among the hot spots putting the tiny hamlet of Narrowsburg on the map as a premier Catskills culinary destination. Dig into comforting, feel-good New American dishes with local ingredients and inventive tweaks like baked Malpeque oysters, caramelized onion mac and cheese, and Tonjes blue cheese ice cream (don't be freaked out—it's great!). After dinner, take advantage of the restaurant's prime location along the Upper Delaware River, which twinkles with outdoor lights at night.

// On a nice day, The Laundrette has the best views of the Delaware River

THE LAUNDRETTE

20 5th Street, Narrowsburg • 845-588-2004 • thelaundrette.xyz

Another trendy restaurant adding to Narrowsburg's growing dining scene, this wood-fired pizza joint serves up more than your run-of-the-mill margherita. Local ingredients are put to work with inventive, global riffs like a Korean bulgogi pizza with corn, olives, mozzarella, mushrooms, and kimchi; and Indian saag paneer pizza. Even if you don't have an appetite, it's worth swinging by to grab a drink and take advantage of their incredible patio overlooking the Upper Delaware River.

PHOENICIA

Despite its tiny population of roughly 300 residents within an even smaller half-square mile footprint, the main strip of this Catskills hamlet seems practically metropolitan next to its rustic backdrop of rolling mountains and the Esopus Creek. Ex-city dwellers are becoming full-on transplants, setting up shop with all the boutique shops, restaurants, and hotels overworked travelers love. It's the best of the outdoors with a craft cocktail always in reach—what's not to love?

Outdoor adventures are accessible right off Phoenicia's Main Street, such as the Tanbark Loop, a moderately challenging hiking trail, or Esopus Creek, where you can learn to fly-fish with an outfitter like Esopus Creek or rent tubes from local mainstay Town Tinker Tube for legit white-water rapid tubing. More challenging hiking trails can be found in the nearby town of Big Indian, including landmarks like Giant Ledge and Panther Mountain Trail, a strenuous hike worth the climb for its sweeping scenic views. Mountain activities run year-round at places like Hunter Mountain and Belleayre Mountain, which both offer zipline courses in the summer and premium skiing trails in the winter. Check out New York State's highest waterfall at Kaaterskill Falls or cool off during the summer with a dip at Belleayre Beach at Pine Hill Lake.

Before you head home, spend a few hours bouncing around Woodstock, a cutesy small town best known for sharing the name with the legendary 1969 local rock music festival (which was actually hosted in the other Catskills town of Bethel). Still, the village hams up the hippie vibes for the floods of tourists that frequently make the pilgrimage by mistake, featuring an array of rock 'n' roll hotels and friendly Bohemian tourist boutiques decorated with peace signs and doves. Woodstock's dining scene is one of the most robust in the area, so there are plenty of food options to choose from (see page 63 for a food weekend in Woodstock).

Getting There

BY CAR | 2 hours via I-87 from New York City. Unless you plan to stay put in the main strip of Phoenicia, rent a car. Part of the fun exploring the Catskills is getting lost in the vast rural landscape, which means traveling long distances between destinations.

BY BUS | 3 hours 15 minutes via Trailways NY ($25–65 each way). If you want to lower the weekend budget or are fine staying in town, Trailways NY offers daily round-trip service to Phoenicia from Port Authority. Luxury charter bus Line also offers direct service from NYC to popular boutique hotels in Phoenicia, Hunter, and Woodstock ($39 each way).

Outdoorsy Highlights

BELLEAYRE MOUNTAIN SKI CENTER

181 Galli Curci Road, Highmount • 845-254-5600 • belleayre.com

Belleayre is kind of the Goldilocks of Catskills ski resorts. It's year-round, making it a good visit for ziplining in the warmer months or snow sports in the winter. Slightly smaller than Hunter Mountain, it has just the right amount of options for all levels (50 trails, 8 chairlifts, and a vertical drop of 1,404 feet) and just a tiny bit less foot traffic, so you can enjoy the slopes without the crowds. The majority of slopes are geared toward intermediate challenging trails, though there are also easier and more difficult trails to try, plus 5.7 miles of cross-country trails. It's just as easy to plan a day trip (Trailways NY has an inclusive round-trip ski package), and because more charter buses are headed toward Hunter, you can count on fewer

// Sullivan County is home to some of the best fly-fishing areas in the country

New Yorkers competing to get tickets. The Catskill Thunder gondola is worth revisiting off-season, too, when it turns into a scenic mountain ride in midsummer.

ESOPUS CREEL

Phoenicia • 845-303-9466 • esopuscreel.com

Book a half- or full-day outing with two local experts who provide everything you'll need for fly-fishing on the Esopus Creek in Phoenicia, from wader rentals and gear to the requisite fishing licenses. Lessons should be booked in advance, and can be tailored from fly-fishing basics for newbies to expert-level expeditions. Water and snacks are provided, but make sure to bring extra food, just in case.

HUNTER MOUNTAIN

64 Klein Avenue, Hunter • 800-486-8376 • huntermtn.com

Hunter Mountain certainly isn't the cheapest option (a half day for two will cost you $260 for a guide and doesn't include lunch), but it's the most convenient choice if you're trying to book for larger groups without equipment or access to a car (several coach bus operators run daily direct service from Manhattan). Depending on the stream report, trips go to the Esopus River or Schoharie River. Like most fly-fishing courses, you'll need to book ahead with a 50% deposit and secure a New York State Fishing License. And if you want to make a weekend of it, Hunter has an inclusive property on-site that features an outdoor pool, spa, and access to their year-round ziplining course (with decent off-season pricing, too).

KAATERSKILL FALLS

Route 23A, Haines Falls

It's a moderate 1.4-mile round-trip hike to catch views of this 260-foot-tall dual-tiered waterfall on Spruce Creek in the Catskill Mountains. The highest cascading waterfall in New York State, it's quite the looker, which is why it was captured in many landscape paintings from artists of the Hudson River School. That also makes it an incredibly well-known and popular hike year-round, so expect to share the trail.

TOWN TINKER TUBE

10 Bridge Street, Phoenicia • 845-688-5553 • towntinker.com

Open Memorial Day through Labor Day, Town Tinker Tube is one of the most popular seasonal tubing outfitters on the Esopus Creek, easy to drop in on without a reservation. Its convenient location squarely in walking distance of everything in Phoenicia and reasonable day rates ($40) don't hurt, either. Don't expect a lazy river—this is white-water territory.

Where to Eat and Drink
For Something More Refined Than Your Campfire Cookout
PEEKAMOOSE RESTAURANT

8373 Route 28, Big Indian • 845-254-6500 • peekamooserestaurant.com

It's only a 12-minute drive to the small town of Big Indian for a rustic Catskills meal in the heart of it all. Think: fisherman's stew with pan-seared scallops, golden snapper, and charred tomato broth; wild mushroom risotto laced with pecorino and white truffle oil; and local rainbow trout with spaghetti squash.

For a Better-Than-Average Diner Experience
PHOENICIA DINER

5681 Route 28, Phoenicia • 845-688-9957 • phoeniciadiner.com

Ending up at the Phoenicia Diner is sort of a requirement of going to Phoenicia. It's a Route 28 institution that still manages to make everyone feel like they've landed on something crazy special. With the exception of the menu, not much has changed about its 1962 façade, so it has the genuine, dated charm of the old Catskills. Expect modern riffs on classic Catskills diner food (get the pan-fried trout!), plus a selection of craft cocktails. Attached to the restaurant is a head-turning vintage airstream trailer that serves as the kitchen for their seasonal outdoor pop-up bar, The Lot, which serves food and hosts a weekly lineup of live music. Don't bypass the cool gift shop swag, which has retro-inspired shirts, totes, key rings, and other souvenirs.

For a Little Brooklyn in the Back Woods
THE PINES

5327 Route 212, Mount Tremper • 845-688-7311 • catskillpines.com

"Hipster" is such a catchall phrase, but it sums up the aesthetic at this trendy shabby chic restaurant and inn located in the up-and-coming town of Mount Tremper near its popular neighbor, Phoenicia. Weathered wood-paneled walls and rooms furnished with reclaimed interiors and antiques set the backdrop for rock 'n' roll and honky-tonk live music nights and upscale Catskills farm-to-table and local artisanal drinks in the restaurant. Upstairs, five rooms are available, modestly decorated with an upscale rustic-minimalist approach.

Where to Stay
For Catching Summer Camp Vibes
SIMPLER TIMES CABINS

5973 Route 28, Phoenicia • 845-688-5410 • simplertimescabins.net

This mom-and-pop rustic cabin community is conveniently in walking distance of the main strip of Phoenicia so that you and your friends can roll in for an impromptu summer camp weekend of outdoor activities like hiking, white-water rapids tubing on the Esopus Creek, and hanging by the firepit. But when the mood strikes, you can easily grab a nice meal or cocktails at popular nearby spots like The Graham & Co. and Phoenicia Diner. Cabins are modestly furnished with beds and bathrooms, with some equipped with efficiency kitchens and televisions. Because of its low-key amenities, this is an excellent value for budget-conscious travelers and groups.

For Something Boutique and Bougie
THE GRAHAM & CO.

80 Route 214, Phoenicia • 845-688-7871 • thegrahamandco.com

If you like the party vibe of Montauk but would rather hit the mountains than the beach, you'll find your people at this boutique Catskills hotel. A big draw for New York's fashionable creatives, the 20-room property has all the Instagram-worthy backdrops: a firepit, a pool, a badminton court, vintage-inspired design, and enough cutesy swag for days. Steps away from Stony Clove Creek and Esopus Creek, it's easy to venture out into nature and get back in time to hang around the campfire.

For Something Cute and Quirky
KATE'S LAZY MEADOW

5191 Route 28, Mount Tremper • 845-688-7200 • lazymeadow.com

There's no shortage of swanky new spots dripping with modest mid-century design, but this campy Catskills destination is all about groovy vibes. That's because its owner is none other than Kate Pierson of the B-52s and her partner, Monica Coleman, who have built a veritable "love shack" appropriately situated just outside Woodstock. Each cabin is outfitted with its own bespoke retro interior, bursting with wild colors reminiscent of *Pee-wee's Playhouse* and plenty of space to spread out in for group weekends. And for the fine art geek, look into snagging one of the two suites designed by artist Phillip Maberry.

FRIENDLY GUIDES

Hey, we can't all be nature experts. Ride along with these experienced explorers on your next outdoor adventure.

THE OUTSIDE INSTITUTE • theoutsideinstitute.org

From plant walks and foraging to beekeeping and botany, Catskills outdoor expert Laura Silverman offers frequent group events and curated private tours across the board.

FREESTONE EXPEDITIONS • freestoneexp.com

Whether you want to embark on a day fly-fishing trip, a gourmet foraging adventure, or a survivalist weekend in the woods, this outfitter will curate your small custom trip for up to four.

CATSKILL FUNGI • catskillfungi.com

Love mushrooms? Sign up for a foraging walk or weekend retreat where you can scout for wild medicinal mushrooms like reishi, chaga, and maitake.

MORGAN OUTDOORS • morgan-outdoors.com

Before you hit the trails, swing by this outdoor store to pick up equipment rentals and get insider tips on the best spots to hike, along with updated trail condition information.

CATSKILL MOUNTAIN WILD • catskillmountainwild.com

Hike, fish, or paddle your way through the Catskills with local native and experienced outdoorsman Jeff Vincent.

☰ *Take a Hike*

EASY HIKES

Lower Hudson Valley

BLUE MOUNTAIN RESERVATION

435 Welcher Avenue, Peekskill

For a seasoned New Yorker who regularly pounds the pavement, it's a manageable mile-long walk from the Peekskill Metro-North train station to reach this 1,500-acre park within the 12-mile Briarcliff-Peekskill Trailway. Roughly 20 hiking and biking trails of all levels are here (the Dickey Brook Trail and Boundary Trail are easier; climbing to the summits of more challenging peaks like Mount Spitzenberg or Blue Mountain will earn you excellent views).

CROTON GORGE PARK

35 Yorktown Road, Cortlandt

Grab your camera, because the views at this waterfall dam are downright gorge-ous (really, though, the gorge is quite stunning). This is where the trailhead for the Old Croton Aqueduct picks up, a 26.2-mile scenic path that stretches to the edge of Yonkers. Access to the gorge itself is an easy walk (the parking lot is only a few feet away if you want to skip the hike entirely), and it's a low-impact stroll through the wooded Aqueduct Trail to reach the apex of the dam that has even more impressive eagle-eye views.

HUDSON HIGHLANDS STATE PARK PRESERVE

3011 Route 9D, Cold Spring

Stretching from Annsville Creek in Peekskill to Dennings Point in Beacon, this 8,000-acre state park includes trails of all levels and easy access points from Metro-North train stops in Cold Spring, Breakneck Ridge, and Beacon. In addition to incredible sweeping views of the Hudson River, there are three different ruin sites to explore (Bannerman Castle, Dennings Point Ruins, and Cornish Estate). Check out page 178 for where to find these secret stop-offs.

Western Hudson Valley

HARRIMAN STATE PARK

Seven Lakes Drive, Ramapo • parks.ny.gov/parks/145

With more than 200 miles of hiking trails, 31 lakes and reservoirs, a couple of beaches, and several camping areas, you'll have your pick of options here for a solid hike. Pine Swamp Loop (slightly longer than 3 miles) and Tom Jones Mountain Loop (4.6 miles) are among the easier hikes, with decent overlooks and a shelter at Tom Jones for making a firepit. Trails are marked by the level of difficulty, with conditions updated regularly through the park service website. Check out the website ahead of time to determine which path you'd like to take (there are plenty!) and to find access points, parking locations, and other important information.

MANITOGA TRAILS

584 Route 9D, Garrison • visitmanitoga.org • suggested donation of $5

Design nerds and crunchy hikers converge at the studio and home of modernist industrial designer Russel Wright. Dubbed "Dragon Rock," the stunning, experimental, glass-walled estate was built into the site of an abandoned quarry overlooking a 30-foot waterfall, pool, and 75 acres of natural woodland landscape. Take a tour of Wright's architectural home or hit the hiking trails that wind throughout the property and connect to extensions of the Osborn Loop Trail and Appalachian Trail.

>> **Transit Pro-Tip:** Get $5 off by purchasing the Metro-North Ticket option via the Manitoga website, then purchase train tickets through Metro-North. For Saturday and Sunday 11 a.m. tours, you can catch a $4 round-trip trolley from the Cold Spring train station to Manitoga.

Upper Hudson Valley

BASH BISH FALLS

Route 344, Taconic State Park, Copake Falls

Technically there are two ways to access this beautiful 200-foot waterfall and gorge: Taconic State Park in New York or Bash Bish Falls State Park in Massachusetts. Either way, you're crossing the state line into the Berkshires for this hike, which means hitting up two scenic locations in one weekend. Nice work. The New York side is much easier, about a quarter-mile from the trailhead to the falls and much flatter than the other side. Be prepared to encounter plenty of other hikers; this is a popular trail for both destinations.

HIGH FALLS CONSERVATION AREA

540 Roxbury Road, Hudson

This incredibly easy 1.2-mile trail situated roughly 20 minutes east of Hudson is a fast and beautiful hike to add on to a weekend upstate. Three trails lead through the conservation area, with gentle climbs through shady woodlands, ending with incredible views of a 150-foot cascading waterfall.

// Getting to this beautiful waterfall inside the High Falls Conservation Area is an easy hike

POETS' WALK

776 River Road, Red Hook

More of a romantic stroll than a brisk hike, this picturesque 2.2-mile Hudson Valley trail lets you meander through grassy meadows, thick forests, river views, and several reflection and scenic outlook points, featuring handcrafted benches and a gazebo. If you're hoping for some privacy, opt for a weekday; this trail gets a lot of foot traffic during the weekends.

WALKWAY OVER THE HUDSON STATE HISTORIC PARK

61 Parker Avenue, Poughkeepsie • walkway.org

Technically, this is more of a pedestrian pathway than a straight-up hike (the longest elevated pedestrian bridge in the world, actually), but you really can't beat the views from 200 feet above the Hudson River, connecting the towns of Poughkeepsie and Lloyd. Plus, it's a 1.28-mile walk across, so it's still pretty good exercise. This is also a great option for those with mobility issues, because there are ADA handicapped accessible entrances. Check ahead for the latest updates on hours and closures—these change frequently.

Western Catskills

FRICK POND

Rockland

Flat and short, the 2.2-mile hike around Frick Pond within the Willowemoc Wild Forest is among the easiest trail loops in the Catskill State Park. The trail winds through shady forests, wrapping around the pond and connecting to nearby loops around Mongaup Pond and Hodge Pond. Mongaup Pond is a little longer (3.1 miles), but about the same level of difficulty and with peaceful woodland trails that loop around the pond.

GETTING THERE: Set your GPS to Catskill State Fish Hatchery (402 Mongaup Road, Livingston Manor), then follow Mongaup Road about 1.5 miles toward Frick Pond Trail.

MONGAUP RIVER TRAILS

703 Route 97, Sparrow Bush

It's all beautiful tree-lined river views on this 1.7-mile, mostly flat trail that picks up at the intersection between the Upper Delaware Scenic and Recreational River on Route 97 and the Mongaup River. The trail gains only slightly in elevation, but it has a handful of interesting landmarks along the way, like original stone walls and a historic cemetery dating back to the early 1800s.

SLIGHTLY MORE CHALLENGING HIKES

Lower Hudson Valley

ANTHONY'S NOSE

171-143 Bear Mountain-Beacon Highway, Garrison

Did you know that the Appalachian Trail (AT) runs through Hudson Valley? Indeed, and no special equipment is needed for this 1.9-mile hike that that connects with the AT via the Camp Smith Trail. Rocky and steep, yet fairly quick, once you get past the strenuous first half mile, the climb is well worth the effort for its breathtaking views of the Purple Heart Memorial Bridge and the Valley. To get here without renting a car, take the Metro-North to the nearby Manitou train station (about 2 miles away), then call a Lyft/Uber to drop you off at the Anthony's Nose/Appalachian Trail trailhead at Bear Mountain-Beacon Highway.

MOUNT BEACON PARK

788 Wolcott Avenue, Beacon

One of the most popular hikes that's easy to access without a car, the trailhead to Mount Beacon picks up about 2 miles east of the Metro-North Beacon train station (cut the walk to the trail by taking a cab). Getting to the fire tower at the top, however, requires a bit more effort. The beginning has a steep incline that reaches 2,000 feet in elevation, followed by several flights of stairs. But the payoff is worth the trek for some of the most incredible views stretching across the valley.

HIKING RESOURCES

Before you hit the trail, check out these sites for in-depth information.

HIKE THE HUDSON VALLEY · hikethehudsonvalley.com

Hudson Valley's comprehensive hiking website features countless trails with details like photos, difficulty levels, and insider tips.

ALLTRAILS · alltrails.com

Check out user-submitted reviews on this website and mobile app that features tips about every trail under the sun.

SAM'S POINT

400 Sam's Point Road, Cragsmoor

Pretty much every hike in Hudson Valley and the Catskills has some beautiful scenery, but not every trail can boast having a 180-foot waterfall, ice caves, and a dwarf pine forest all in one place. Along with its breathtaking peaks, the hiking trails at this popular Minnewaska State Park Preserve wind through Verkeerderkill Falls and ice caves, which stay cold enough to keep ice and snow frozen through midsummer. Along the way, you might encounter wild blueberries, huckleberries, and a dwarf pine forest, with trees only about a foot high. Depending on how far you want to trek, hikes average between 3.8 and 11 miles, making this a more challenging day trip.

Eastern Catskills

KAATERSKILL FALLS

NY-23A, Haines Falls

It's a moderate 1.4-mile round-trip hike to catch views of this 260-foot-tall dual-tiered waterfall on Spruce Creek in the Catskill Mountains. The highest cascading waterfall in New York State, it's quite the looker, which is why it was captured in many landscape paintings from artists of the Hudson River School. That also makes it an incredibly well-known and popular hike year-round, so expect to share the trail.

DIAMOND NOTCH FALLS

443 Diamond Notch Road, Lanesville

The reward of seeing these double falls at the end of this moderate 2.2-mile hike near the Westkill Creek makes this a popular weekender trail. Diamond Notch's falls don't have the impressive vertical drop of the Kaaterskills, but its wide, cascading waters over sturdy rock formations are a beautiful backdrop for a relatively short hike.

≡ Scenic Outlooks Without the Schlep

Lower Hudson Valley

BEAR MOUNTAIN STATE PARK

Route 9W North, Bear Mountain • $10 per vehicle

For a novice hiker, the stair-heavy, 3.9-mile Bear Mountain trail loop to the Perkins Memorial Tower lookout is totally doable. But if you don't have a couple of hours to devote to a leisurely hike, the scenic drive is ranked among the area's best. On a clear day, the unobstructed panoramic views stretch far enough to see the Manhattan skyline and Catskills mountains. While you're there, you can continue the drive to the historic Bear Mountain Inn, which has its own overlook, restaurant, café, trading post, and spa. Or you can take in the state park's seasonal outdoor pool, ice skating rink, and other park attractions.

GETTING THERE: Plan to drive for this one, taking the Palisades Interstate Parkway to Exit 19 toward Perkins Memorial Drive, and follow to the top of the hill.

Upper Hudson Valley

SAUGERTIES LIGHTHOUSE

168 Lighthouse Drive, Saugerties • saugertieslighthouse.com

This converted historic lighthouse now operates as a lovely bed-and-breakfast, but you don't have to stay overnight to take in the waterfront views open free of charge from sunrise to sunset. Most come for the picturesque location along the Hudson River, but the property is nestled within 17 acres of wooded grounds that include a half-mile trail for a light stroll. All that nature where land meets water makes for great snapshots of area wildlife and romantic sunsets.

GETTING THERE: Tack this on for a car rental weekend driving through nearby towns like Kingston and Rhinebeck.

TIVOLI BAYS

Cruger Island Road, Tivoli • dec.ny.gov/lands/92370.html

You don't have to scale a mountain to find a great view in Hudson Valley. In fact, you might want to head down a few levels to this bay tucked away inside a Tivoli forest preserve and hiking trail. Less trafficked than some of the more popular preserves, often it's just you and the birds, snapping turtles, and other wildlife that usually hang around these parts (not to mention

// Tivoli Bays is an intimate, lesser-known spot for catching excellent sunset views

plenty of bugs). But around sunset, you might run into a few locals when the marshy wet-land looks downright magical, glowing against its mountainous backdrop, as the sky turns to darkness.

GETTING THERE: This is definitely a destination that requires a car, best done while spending the weekend anywhere between Saugerties and Kingston/Rhinebeck.

Western Hudson Valley
SHAWANGUNK MOUNTAINS SCENIC BYWAY

mtnscenicbyway.org

Unlike the Upper Delaware Scenic Byway, the Shawangunk Byway is somewhat of a cluster of routes encircling the Shawangunk Range. There are four carved-out routes—all roughly 20 minutes each and a worthwhile drive. The northern loop passes through the Mohonk Pre-serve, Minnewaska State Park Preserve, Rondout Creek, and Wallkill River. Cut the drive in half by taking Routes 44 and 45 from Gardiner to Kerhonkson, with the bonus of passing a handful of notable stop-offs like Tuthilltown Spirits Distillery, Whitecliff Vineyard and Winery, Kettleborough Cider House, and Yard Owl Craft Brewery. The southern route swings past Cragsmoor, where you can access Sam's Point at Minnewaska State Park Preserve (which also includes the path to the ice caves, Verkeerderkill Falls, and a dwarf pine forest) and Pine Bush (a short distance away from Angry Orchard's tasting room). And the Wallkill Valley route fills in the gaps on the eastern side of the mountain range and Wallkill River, heading from New Paltz south toward Gardiner, through Wallkill, and west toward Pine Bush.

GETTING THERE: **The northern loop** traverses Route 299 from New Paltz west to Route 55 through the Mohonk Preserve and Minnewaska State Park Preserve, then north on Route 209 from Kerhonkson to Route 213 through High Falls and Rosendale before looping back south to New Paltz on Route 32. **Route 55** picks up in Gardiner, passing over the Wallkill River and connecting with Route 44 at the Mohonk Preserve, then follows the same route through the Minnewaska State Park Preserve to Kerhonkson as the northern loop. **The southern route** begins where the northern loop and Route 55 leave off in Kerhonkson, following Route 209 south through Ellenville to Route 52 along the Rondout Valley to Cragsmoor and the hamlet of Pine Bush, with a tail extension on 302 through the farmland to Bullville. **The Wallkill Valley route** starts in New Paltz, taking Route 208 south toward Wallkill and Walden, then west on Route 52 to Pine Bush.

Eastern Catskills

HUNTER MOUNTAIN SCENIC SKYRIDE

64 Klein Avenue, Hunter • 800-486-8376 • huntermtn.com

When you don't want to drive, but you don't want to walk either, there's always the scenic skyride. After the winter snow melts off, Hunter Mountain turns its six-passenger chairlift into an aerial ride that transports riders to the summit of the 3,200-foot mountain. Fall foliage is the best time of year to take a ride, albeit a popular one. From the top, you can catch views stretching across the northern Catskills to as far as the Berkshire Mountains in Massachusetts and Green Mountains in Vermont.

GETTING THERE: Carless like most New Yorkers? No problem. Taking the bus will likely save you money; a handful of bus operators offer round-trip service and inclusive tour pricing to Hunter Mountain, including Sourced Adventures, Urban Sherpa, Paragon Sports, NYC Snow Bus, and OvRride, for $45–250.

Western Catskills

UPPER DELAWARE SCENIC BYWAY

upperdelawarescenicbyway.org

Think of it as the Big Sur of New York. Curving along the upper portion of the Delaware River, which runs between New York and Pennsylvania, Route 97 holds up to its original tagline from 1939 of being "The Most Scenic Highway in the East." About 50 miles of road twist and turn from Port Jervis to Hancock, with plenty of marked outlooks and stop-offs along the way for breathtaking views sweeping across the mountainous landscape. Find the best photo opportunities at places like Hawk's Nest, Roebling's Delaware Aqueduct, and the towns of Barryville and Narrowsburg. The drive itself is stunning, but there are tons of attractions worth exploring. Campsites like Kittatinny Canoes, Reber River Trips, and Lander's River Trips offer tubes, canoes, kayaks, and rafts for rent. Find great dining and boutiques in Narrowsburg (if the weather is nice, try to grab a riverside table at The Laundrette), and dip into the up-and-coming town of Callicoon to check out Callicoon Brewing Company and the historic Callicoon Theater.

GETTING THERE: This is definitely a driving tour. Access to the byway picks up at NYS Route 97 just outside of Port Jervis and continues north along two lanes.

≡ On a Roll

Lower Hudson Valley
OLD CROTON AQUEDUCT TRAIL

For a quick trip out of the city, hit this historic waterway that was transformed into a 26.2-mile bike path that follows east of the Hudson River and Palisades from Yonkers to Croton-on-Hudson. The most level path is on the south end on the South County Trailway, about 14 miles between Yonkers and Mount Pleasant, whereas the trail can become muddier and more uneven with gravel and dirt as you head north (you're better off renting a mountain bike). If you do end up taking the whole trail, you can find several cool stops along the way, like Washington Irving's Sunnyside, Lyndhurst Mansion, Kykuit Rockefeller Estate, and the Tappan Zee Bridge. At the tail end is Croton Gorge Park, where you can stop off to see the 200-foot Croton Dam along the reservoir.

>> **Where to Rent a Bike:** Pick up a rental at **Hastings Velo**, which is about a 5-minute walk from the Hastings-on-Hudson Metro-North train station.

>> **Deal Alert:** Purchase a Metro-North Getaway weekend package for discounts on round-trip train fare and a one-day bike rental with a helmet from **Endless Trail Bikeworx**, located a couple blocks from the Dobbs Ferry station.

Upper Hudson Valley
HARLEM VALLEY RAIL TRAIL

hvrt.org

A work in process, there are roughly 16 miles of trail completed of the anticipated 46-mile project that will eventually connect the towns of Wassaic and Chatham. Because it's so new, the biking path is paved and even for a smoother ride. However, Wassaic is also the last stop on the Metro-North train line to New York. So if you're traveling without a car, you'll want to build up enough energy for a round-trip instead of a station-to-station trip. If you're able to handle a longer ride, it's about 11.6 miles to the village of Millerton, where you'll find fun stop-offs like The Moviehouse, Oblong Books and Music, The Millerton Inn, and an Irving Farm coffeehouse.

>> **Where to Rent a Bike:** BYOB. You'll have to bring your own bike if you're traveling by train, because there are no bike shops near the train station. Another option (if you plan to drive) is to head to Bash Bish Falls near Copake Falls and rent a bike from **Bash Bish Bicycle** (247 Route 344, Copake Falls) to head south on the trail.

Western Hudson Valley
WALLKILL VALLEY RAIL TRAIL

Running roughly 21 miles between Gardiner and Kingston, this former railroad corridor-turned-bike path is a great route that has plenty of worthwhile stops along the way. Unpaved with dirt and gravel, it's a mostly flat—albeit bumpy—and easily navigable road lined with shady trees that offer some reprieve from the harsh summer sun. The first six miles between New Paltz and Gardiner will take you along a beautiful backdrop of the Shawangunk Range, with stops at tasting rooms like Whitecliff Vineyard and Winery and Tuthilltown Spirits Distillery, and farm stands including Dressel Farms, Taliaferro Farms, and the Phillies Bridge Farm Project. In New Paltz, there are tons of great restaurants to discover (see page 212), along with the Samuel Dorsky Museum of Art at SUNY New Paltz. Continuing north, you'll pass the Wallkill River and Rondout Creek, go through long stretches of pastoral landscape, and finally reach the reward of landing in Kingston, a town stocked with enough food, shopping, art, and night-life attractions to fill up a whole weekend.

Novice bike riders may want to stick to the 6-mile route between Gardiner and New Paltz, which is easier to do round-trip. If you are traveling without a car, start in New Paltz—which has bus service from the city—and head south toward Gardiner. Experienced bikers who want to tackle the full ride should definitely have a car available at either end, unless you're able to do 22 miles each way.

>> **Know Before You Go:** Despite the large size of both places, transit to New Paltz and Kingston can be pretty complicated. When planning your trip, consider the following to determine your

route: Do you have a car? How far can you realistically bike round-trip? Are you more interested in the bike ride itself, or are you using it as a scenic vehicle to access other attractions?

>> **Where to Rent a Bike:** If you're heading out from Gardiner, reserve a bike at **Lightsey Cycles**. In New Paltz, check out **Bicycle Depot**. Midway between New Paltz and Kingston is **TRT Bicycles** in Rosendale, a bike shop that specializes in off-road rentals.

Black Dirt Region
HERITAGE TRAIL

It's pretty smooth sailing on this forest-lined 14-mile trail that stretches straight through Orange County, from Goshen to Harriman. The road is well-paved with asphalt, making it a popular trail for bikers and pedestrians. Along the way, you can stop off in towns like Chester, where you'll find popular brewery Rushing Duck Brewing and incredible Middle Eastern food at Allan's Falafel, and New Hampton, home to Soons Orchard, where you can go apple picking or try their excellent hard cider brand, Orchard Hill.

>> **Where to Rent a Bike: Joe Fix Its** has about 30 bike rentals available and is located conveniently about two blocks away from the trail entrance on St. James Place (where you can grab an ice cream cone at **Trailside Treats Creamery**).

// Rent a bike in Goshen and hit the 14-mile Heritage Trail, lined with local breweries and distilleries

Upper Catskills

CATSKILL SCENIC TRAIL

catskillscenictrail.org

Stretching 26 miles along the west branch of the Delaware River, this multiuse trail is a beautiful tree-lined pathway for biking, hiking, cross-country skiing, and horseback riding. Opt for a hybrid or mountain bike for these trails; the terrain fluctuates between hard-packed cinder and unpaved dirt and crushed stone roads that might prove too challenging for a classic road bike. This rail trail doesn't bypass as many small town stop-offs as some of the other scenic trails, so plan to start on the Roxbury side, where you can stay at places like thematic motel resort The Roxbury, shop at cute boutiques like Roxbury General, or visit nearby attractions like the Roxbury Mountain Maple sugar shack in Hobart and Union Grove Distillery in Arkville.

>>   **Where to Rent a Bike:** In Roxbury, rent bikes from the general store, **Roxbury General**, or head to the nearby **Plattekill Mountain** resort, which not only rents mountain bikes but has a special bike park with trails cut specifically for riding.

≡ *Get Your Feet Wet*

Lower Hudson Valley

HUDSON RIVER EXPEDITIONS

14 Market Street, Cold Spring • 845-809-5935 • hudsonriverexpeditions.com

Take your pick of kayak, canoe, or standing paddleboard rentals with departures from locations in Cold Spring and Peekskill (both conveniently off the Metro-North Railroad). Or, if you'd rather travel with a group, Hudson River Expeditions offers regular thematic tours, like kayaking and hiking through Bannerman Castle with a historian, twilight yoga and kayaking through Cold Spring, and paint-and-paddle on the Hudson River. Check ahead to find out about availability of route access points and equipment availability, with updates routinely posted on their website.

MOUNTAIN TOPS OUTFITTERS

144 Main Street, Beacon • 845-831-1997 • mountaintopsoutfitters.com

Launching from Beacon's Long Dock Park (23 Long Dock Road, Beacon), this local outfitter offers hourly kayak rentals and scheduled group paddle tours of Dennings Point and Bannerman Castle from June through October. Given its close proximity to the Beacon Metro-

North train station, this is a great option for a quick day trip without a car (plus you can save extra money by snagging an all-inclusive Metro-North Getaway package for round-trip train fare and a 2-hour kayak rental for the price of a 1-hour rental). Reservations are highly recommended during peak season; you can make a reservation by calling ahead.

MOUNTAIN VALLEY GUIDES

845-661-1923 • mountainvalleyguides.com

With locations docked at the Newburgh Waterfront, Hastings-on-Hudson, and Cornwall-on-Hudson, this seasonal all-inclusive outfitter provides everything you need for a guided kayak river trip—right down to the beer, if you choose their Paddles and Pints tour, which takes you to two different local breweries. After all, kayaking on the Hudson is an activity in itself, but throw in a three-hour paddle to a waterfall at Fishkill Creek, kayaking to a private sandbar BBQ, or being able to paddle with your dog in tow to a remote stretch of beach, and the adventure gets a lot more fun. Reserve in advance on their website to ensure you get a spot (a smart move for most bookings during peak season).

STORM KING ADVENTURE TOURS

4 Duncan Avenue, Cornwall-On-Hudson • 845-534-7800 • stormkingadventuretours.com

Don't plan to take this kayaking trip *and* hit up Storm King Art Center in the same day. That's just not going to happen. But if you're going to make a weekend of it, this is a great way to continue soaking up the sun. Storm King Adventure Tours offers about a dozen kayak tours that run roughly 3 to 4 hours each, including trips along Bannerman Castle, Hidden Cove, Plum Point Beach, and even sunset and moonlight themed tours. Plan to have a car for this one or factor in extra money for a taxi; the meeting location isn't conducive to public transit. Make sure to call ahead—this is one spot that doesn't take reservations online.

Upper Hudson Valley
ATLANTIC KAYAK TOURS

845-246-2187 • atlantickayaktours.com

Situated along the upper Hudson River, Atlantic Kayak Tours has a handful of locations scattered among Norrie Point Environmental Center, Saugerties, Tivoli Bays, and the town of Catskill. If you're short on time or want to spend the whole day on the water, there are options for both—but you'll need to register and pay in advance. Consider this your go-to option when you're making a weekend in the Kingston, Rhinebeck, or Hudson area, but if you want to book a trip on the fly, it can be trickier. You'll do well to call in advance to explore programs and book a reservation.

// Grab an oar and get paddling at Mills Norrie State Park

Eastern Catskills

TINKER TOWN TUBE RENTALS

10 Bridge Street, Phoenicia • 845-688-5553 • towntinker.com

If you're not hiking in the Catskills, then you should be on the river. Along with boasting excel-lent fishing conditions, Esopus Creek is prime for tubing and rafting adventures. Tubes are the main attraction (though they rent kayaks as well), but don't expect a leisurely lazy river experience—this is white-water territory. You'll need to be an experienced swimmer to take part, as the rapids have tough natural obstacles like waves, rocks, and trees to navigate around. Dangerous as it is exhilarating, this is an insanely popular summer activity that's best tacked onto a weekend visiting Phoenicia, Mount Tremper, and Woodstock.

Upper Delaware Scenic and Recreational River

KITTATINNY CANOES AND CAMPGROUND

3846 State Route 97, Barryville • 800-356-2852 • kittatinny.com

Pop a tent and spend an action-packed weekend in nature or just hit the water at this camp-site and outdoor adventure outfitter on the Upper Delaware Scenic and Recreational River. Whether you want to explore nature through a leisurely canoe trip, commandeer a solo or tandem kayak, spend a lazy afternoon tubing, or hit the rapids white-water rafting, Kittatinny has it all (plus a dual zipline and paintball course, if you want to tack that on). Depending on your paddle skill level and how much time you want to spend on the river, there are options for everyone. Kittatinny even offers primitive overnight camping trips along the Delaware Water Gap National Recreation Area.

LANDER'S RIVER TRIPS

5961 Route 97, Narrowsburg • 800-252-3925 • landersrivertrips.com

Kayak, canoe, tube, or raft your way down the Upper Delaware River, and then make a camping weekend out of it at this outdoor adventure outfitter with riverfront locations in Narrowsburg and Barryville. Overnight packages offer decent deals (though you'll need to factor in bringing your own equipment from home or renting from an outfitter), but even regular day-trip prices make this a solid budget-friendly option. Bonus: even during peak season, there's no need for reservations. So if you happen to be in the Catskills on the perfect afternoon, it's easy to take an impromptu 4- to 6-hour river trip.

REBER RIVER TRIPS

3351 Route 97 • Barryville • 844-525-3086 • reberrivertrips.com

If it floats, chances are this indie river outfitter has it: rafts, canoes, single and double kayaks, tubes, and Reber's claim to fame: a 20-person party raft. Reber doesn't have its own campgrounds for an inclusive weekend on the river, but their rates tend to be on the cheaper side ($22–45 per person for an all-day rate).

FLY-FISHING

Upper Hudson Valley
KENCO OUTFITTERS

1000 Hurley Road, Kingston • 845-340-0552 • atkenco.com

If Kingston is the most convenient town for your upstate weekender, you can't beat the fly-fishing deal at this popular outfitter. March through November, Kenco offers a fly-fishing basics class every Saturday for the dirt-cheap price of only $15 (and that includes gear, too). Make sure to sign up in advance for the two-hour session via their website; these tend to fill up fast during peak season. For those already versed in fly-fishing, Kenco offers a smaller, more advanced course for groups of four that costs $75 per person (a relative steal compared to most private guides).

Eastern Catskills

ESOPUS CREEL

Phoenicia • 845-303-9466 • esopuscreel.com

Book a half- or full-day outing with two local experts who provide everything you'll need for fly-fishing on the Esopus Creek in Phoenicia, from wader rentals and gear to the requisite fishing licenses. Lessons should be booked in advance, and can be tailored from fly-fishing basics for newbies to expert-level expeditions. Water and snacks are provided, but make sure to bring extra food, just in case.

HUNTER MOUNTAIN

64 Klein Avenue, Hunter • 800-486-8376 • huntermtn.com

Hunter Mountain certainly isn't the cheapest option (a half day for two will cost you $260 for a guide and doesn't include lunch), but it's the most convenient choice if you're trying to book for larger groups without equipment or access to a car (several coach bus operators run daily direct service from Manhattan). Depending on the stream report, trips go to the Esopus River or Schoharie River. Like most fly-fishing courses, you'll need to book ahead with a 50% deposit and secure a New York State Fishing License. And if you want to make a weekend of it, Hunter has an inclusive property on-site that features an outdoor pool, a spa, and access to their year-round ziplining course (with decent off-season pricing, too).

Western Catskills

CATSKILL FLIES

6 Stewart Avenue, Roscoe • 607-498-6146 • catskillflies.com

Upper Beaverkill Valley is the Catskills' fly-fishing country, and within the heart of it is the town of Roscoe, lovingly dubbed Trout Town. So if a day of hanging out in waist-high waders on the river trying to catch trout sounds up your alley, reserve a day learning how to cast, tie knots, and other basics of fly-fishing with a private instructor. Fly-fishing, in general, tends to run on the pricier side, but Catskill Flies is on the cheaper end of the spectrum (rates run about $120 for a half day; $200 for a full day, which includes the instructor, equipment, and lunch).

☰ *Aerial Adventures*

ZIPLINING

Upper Hudson Valley

CATAMOUNT SKI/AERIAL ADVENTURE PARK

17 Nicholson Road, South Egremont, MA • 413-528-1262 • catamounttrees.com

Yes, this skiing and aerial adventure just barely crosses the Massachusetts line into the Berkshires, so it's technically not "Hudson Valley" anymore. But if you happen to spend a weekend near Hudson or are passing through Taconic State Park in Copake Falls, there's no reason to bypass this excellent zipline course that will give you the best of both worlds with its sky-high views. While Hunter Mountain lays claim to the longest, fastest, and highest zipline, Catamount boasts the largest number of courses and the largest park, so you can climb and soar for hours on a self-guided adventure.

Eastern Catskills

NEW YORK ZIPLINE CANOPY TOURS AT HUNTER MOUNTAIN

7740 Main Street, Hunter • 518-263-4388 • ziplinenewyork.com

Flying through fall foliage sounds so much cooler than taking a few snapshots from the ground, doesn't it? Spring, summer, or fall are the best times to visit this zipline company that operates three courses at Hunter Mountain: an adventure tower, a mid-mountain canopy tour, and the SkyRider: the longest, fastest, and highest zipline in North America, spanning 4.6 miles in length and going at speeds up to 50 miles per hour. On Saturdays throughout the summer, you can book a three-hour nighttime tour on the mid-mountain course, where you can sail across six ziplines, four rope bridges, and nine tree platforms under the stars.

Upper Delaware Scenic and Recreational River

KITTATINNY CANOES AND CAMPGROUNDS

3846 Route 97, Barryville • 800-356-2852 • kittatinny.com

Kittatinny doesn't have as many adventure courses or ziplines as do other operators, but you'll be hard-pressed to find more outdoor activities in one place. In addition to being the only zipline on the Delaware River (a great place to hit up during peak fall foliage season), it's also home to activities like canoeing, kayaking, rafting, tubing, paintball, and camping. Kittatinny's ziplines operate on a classic dual racing drop line (no adventure course), sailing down a half mile to drops of 3,000 feet at speeds of up to 60 miles per hour.

SKYDIVING

Lower Hudson Valley

IFLY INDOOR SKYDIVING

849 Ridge Hill Boulevard, Yonkers • 914-449-4359 • iflyworld.com

Like the idea of flying, but not ready to jump out of a plane? This national indoor skydiving facility has a location in Westchester County that just might fit your bill, teaching you all the skills and maneuvers of skydiving in a safe, controlled wind tunnel.

SKYDIVE THE RANCH

55 Sand Hill Road, Gardiner • 845-255-4033 • skydivetheranch.com

Stationed in Gardiner Airport, this longtime skydiving company is a licensed USPA (United States Parachute Association) instruction school that arranges jump programs for all experience levels, dropping from 13,000 feet in the air. First-timers can take tandem jumps with experienced skydivers, or, if you're ready to move up, you can learn how to free-fall with instructor assistance. Fell in love with skydiving and want to make it a hobby? Check out specialty events like wingsuit skills, night diving, and other thematic jumps.

HOT-AIR BALLOONS

Sailing in a hot-air balloon is not a budget-friendly activity by any means, but there's a reason why it's on so many bucket lists: it's downright breathtaking. Whether it's a romantic weekend or you want to see fall foliage from 3,000 feet in the air, these three balloon operators can take you there.

Western Hudson Valley

ABOVE THE CLOUDS • Randall Airport, 100 Airport Road, Middletown • 845-360-5594 • abovethecloudsinc.com

FANTASY BALLOON FLIGHTS • Randall Airport, 100 Airport Road, Middletown • 845-856-7103 • fantasyfliers.com

Upper Hudson Valley

BALLOON NY • Columbia County Airport, 1142 Route 9H, Ghent • 607-435-9839 • balloonny.com

≡ *Winter Sports*

Lower Hudson Valley

THUNDER RIDGE SKI AREA

137 Birch Hill Road, Patterson • 845-878-4100 • thunderridgeski.com

Not only is this the closest ski resort to New York City, but it's also one of the easiest day trips to make without a car. Metro-North offers a seasonal Getaway package, allowing you to purchase an inclusive discounted round-trip train fare and lift ticket, plus discounts on rental equipment when you arrive. Throughout the winter season, Thunder Ridge offers a free shuttle that picks up and drops off at the Patterson train station. The ski area splits its runs primarily between beginner and intermediate levels, which might disappoint some skiers (30 trails, 90 skiable acres, 600-foot vertical drop and 1,250-foot peak elevation). But it is also one of the few places that offers twilight and night skiing, which comes in handy for a full weekend on the slopes.

// Not into high speed ziplines? Catamount Ski Resort has the largest adventure course in New York State

Western Hudson Valley

MOUNT PETER SKI AREA

51 Old Mount Peter Road, Warwick • 845-986-4940 • mtpeter.com

Easily accessible just 1.5 hours outside of New York City in Orange County, this modestly sized resort features an even split among beginner, intermediate, and expert courses on its combined 14 ski trails, making this a great option for groups of different experience levels. Beginners can take a free ski and snowboard group lesson with the purchase of a lift ticket, or they can skip the slopes entirely and hit the 600-foot tubing run. And Mount Peter's nighttime ski hours are a fun perk that should sit well with everyone. Getting there without a car is possible, but not direct. Plan to drive or take a bus to Warwick and transfer through Lyft/Uber.

Eastern Catskills

HUNTER MOUNTAIN

64 Klein Avenue, Hunter • 800-486-8376 • huntermtn.com

Skiing, snowboarding, tubing, ice climbing, and snowcat tours are only a few of the activities you can do at this year-round Catskills mountain resort that also offers zipline courses, hiking trails, 4x4 off-road adventures, fly-fishing, rock climbing, and about a dozen seasonal festivals. But if you just want to hit the trails in winter, their Empire Terrain Parks are split between three mountain areas (Hunter East, Hunter West, and Hunter North) with a total of 320 skiable acres, 13 lifts, and 67 trails. Beginners can rent equipment and take lessons at Hunter East, which includes a state-of-the-art Learning Center at its base for introductory lessons geared toward skiers of all ages. The bulk of the trails are in Hunter West; the latest Hunter North expansion brought 80 acres of skiable terrain, five new trails, and a high-speed six-passenger chairlift.

MOUNTAIN TRAILS CROSS COUNTRY SKI CENTER

6198 Main Street, Tannersville • 518-589-5361 • mtntrails.com

Most people are acquainted with area downhill ski resorts, but the Catskills have ample terrain for other winter sports like snowshoeing and cross-country skiing. Winding through snow-covered woodland forests, meadows, and reservoirs, Mountain Trails boasts 35 kilometers of skiable trails for all levels and terrains. Tickets and rentals are also a steal compared to classic downhill ski resorts, making this a more affordable test drive for those inexperienced with winter mountain sports. The only potential downside is transit, for which you'll definitely need to rent a car. Unlike other popular destinations, Mountain Trails doesn't have direct bus operator service from Manhattan.

WINDHAM MOUNTAIN

19 Resort Drive, Windham • 518-734-4300 • windhammountain.com

Just a touch smaller than Hunter Mountain, Windham is another top year-round mountain resort destination in the Catskills. The slopes are similar, with 54 trails stretching across 285 skiable acres, six terrain parks, 12 lifts, and a vertical rise of 1,600 feet. Slightly pricier than Hunter, it has some upscale perks worth coughing up a few extra bucks, like night skiing on nine trails, specialty ski programs (off-piste and alpine touring classes; conquering mountain fear workshops), more robust on-site dining options, and a luxury spa. Because it's slightly pricier, it tends to have smaller crowds during peak season (always a plus on the slopes).

>> **Transit Pro-Tip:** Hunter Mountain and Windham Mountain both have easy day-trip access with many direct round-trip shuttle service options departing from Manhattan, along with organized group tours and inclusive weekend ski trip packages. Find a list of charter bus operators on page 32.

Western Catskills

HOLIDAY MOUNTAIN SKI AND FUN PARK

99 Holiday Mountain Road, Monticello • 845-796-3161 • holidaymtn.com

Holiday Mountain doesn't have as many slopes and trails as some of its flashier neighbors (only six), but if you're looking for a bargain or you're a novice skier, lift tickets and equipment rentals cost half the price of other resorts. That said, there are fewer bus operators offering direct service, so you'll have to rent a car or get creative with the Short Line bus to Monticello and Lyft/Uber from there.

// Hit the slopes at Holiday Mountain in Monticello

Upper Catskills

BELLEAYRE MOUNTAIN SKI CENTER

181 Galli Curci Road, Highmount • 845-254-5600 • belleayre.com

Belleayre is kind of the Goldilocks of Catskills ski resorts. Slightly smaller than Hunter Mountain, it has just the right amount of options for all levels (50 trails, 8 chairlifts, and a vertical drop of 1,404 feet) and just a tiny bit less foot traffic so you can enjoy the slopes without the crowds. The majority of the slopes are geared toward intermediate challenging trails, though there are also easier and more difficult trails to try, plus 5.7 miles of cross-country trails. It's just as easy to plan a day trip (Trailways NY has an inclusive round-trip ski package), and since more charter buses are headed toward Hunter, you can count on fewer New Yorkers competing to get tickets. The Catskill Thunder gondola is worth revisiting off-season, too, when it turns into a scenic mountain ride midsummer.

PLATTEKILL MOUNTAIN

469 Plattekill Road, Roxbury • 607-326-3500 • plattekill.com

Offering just the right mix of 38 multilevel trails and four lifts across two summits (peaking at an 1,100-foot vertical drop), this northwestern Catskills ski resort has a number of options for everyone. Independently owned and operated, the lodge has a homier vibe for an apres-ski than some of its neighbors, including live music on weekends. Plan to drive for this one and make a weekend of it, as its location is best suited for longer stays in the northern Catskills destinations like Andes, Bovina Center, Arkville, and Hobart.

Nighttime with Nature

POP A TENT

Lower Hudson Valley

MALOUF'S MOUNTAIN CAMPGROUND

Beacon • 845-831-6767 • maloufsmountain.com

If you want to camp without a car, this unique hike-in/hike-out camping experience was basically built for it. Hop on the Metro-North train to Beacon and a complimentary shuttle will take you to the campground. More rustic than your average campground, Malouf's has two options: a tarped platform that provides just enough coverage for bringing your own sleeping bag and mat, or a bare-bones, primitive-style camping site where you'll need to rent equipment from an outfitter. Clean bathroom facilities are on-site, so you don't have to be a totally crusty camper. Platform sites conveniently come equipped with a grill for fire, a gas stove, and a chow kit for cooking and cleaning essentials, while primitive camping sites have a firepit, a picnic bench, and a garbage can. If you don't want to lug in a heavy cooler stocked with your own food, you can order everything from eggs and coffee to country-style ribs, steak, and veggie burgers to be delivered to your campsite.

Eastern Catskills

NORTH-SOUTH LAKE CAMPGROUND

874 North Lake Road, Haines Falls • 518-589-5058

Tucked away in the heart of the Catskill Forest Preserve, this popular lakeside campground puts campers directly within hiking distance of scenic landmarks like Kaaterskill Falls and the Overlook Mountain House ruins for the dirt cheap price of $22 per night (you'll need to BYO transit and equipment). Despite being surrounded by wooded forests, you won't be totally going off the grid. As the largest area campground in the state, it features seven camping loops with a combined 219 tent and trailer sites, plus water, restrooms, and shower access.

Western Catskills

FROST VALLEY YMCA

2000 Frost Valley Road, Claryville • 845-985-2291 • frostvalley.org

Best known for its children's summer camp programming, the Frost Valley YMCA also offers personalized Catskills retreats for groups and families with virtually every kind of lodging. Whether in a cabin, a platform tent, a dorm-style lodge, or a yurt, you can choose to be as connected or disconnected to modern conveniences as you see fit. That said, because of the organization's size and family-friendly camping, if you want to have a kid-free weekend, it's best to stay elsewhere.

HAPPY DAYS CAMPGROUND

454 Horseshoe Lake Road, Swan Lake • 845-583-6575 • happydayscampground.com

If you're heading out to Bethel Woods for a weekend, why not turn it into a throwback summer camping trip? Tent and RV campsites are both available to rent, but a cool lesser-known feature is that you can rent a two-bed vintage camper for only $75/night. Because it's authentic vintage, expect to forgo conveniences like a bathroom, cooking equipment, air conditioning, or TV. But you'll have the ability to brag about staying in a vintage camper to all of your friends, and that's something you just can't put a price on.

ROSCOE CAMPSITE PARK

2179 Old Route 17, Roscoe • 607-498-5264 • roscoecampsite.com

Located directly next to the Beaverkill River in the Catskills, this might seem like your run-of-the-mill campground at first glance. But there are a few interesting options beyond popping a tent (though you can do that, too). In addition to its three cabin options that include river-front woodland cabins, barn-style bunk cabins, and deluxe lofted cabins, Roscoe also rents a handful of covered wagons outfitted with glamping amenities, like space heaters and beds with linens. While you're there, the campground can help coordinate popular outdoor activities like fly-fishing, moderate hiking, tubing, kayaking and canoeing on nearby Lake Wanita, biking through the Catskill Scenic Trail, and more.

Upper Delaware Scenic and Recreational River

KITTATINNY CANOES AND CAMPGROUND

3846 Route 97, Barryville • 800-356-2852 • kittatinny.com

Pop a tent and spend an action-packed weekend in nature or just hit the water at this campsite and outdoor adventure outfitter on the Upper Delaware Scenic and Recreational River. This is definitely a bare-bones BYO equipment place where you're renting campgrounds, so if you want a permanent platform tent or cabin experience, look elsewhere. Whether you want to take a leisurely canoe trip, commandeer a solo or tandem kayak, spend a lazy afternoon tubing, or hit the rapids white-water rafting, Kittatinny has it all (plus a dual zipline and paintball course, if you want to tack that on). Depending on your paddle skill level and how much time you want to spend on the river, there are options for everyone. Kittatinny even offers primitive overnight camping trips along the Delaware Water Gap National Recreation Area.

LANDER'S RIVER TRIPS

5961 Route 97, Narrowsburg • 800-252-3925 • landersrivertrips.com

Kayak, canoe, tube, or raft your way down the Upper Delaware River, and then make a camping weekend out of it at this outdoor adventure outfitter with riverfront locations in Narrowsburg and Barryville. Overnight packages offer decent deals (though you'll need to factor in bringing your own equipment from home or renting from an outfitter), but even regular day-trip prices make this a solid budget-friendly option. Bonus: even during peak season, there's no need for reservations. So if you happen to be in the Catskills on the perfect afternoon, it's easy to take an impromptu 4- to 6-hour river trip.

RENT-A-TENT

No tent, no problem. These outfitters deliver everything you need for a weekend in the woods.

DUFFLE OUT · duffle-out.com

Tents aren't the only expense that factors into a camping weekend. There's all the other stuff, like lanterns and headlamps, sleeping pads, stove and fuel, cookware, a wash bin, soap, and a stick lighter. Fortunately, this smart equipment rental company figured out how to shove it all into one handy duffle bag, plus have it delivered and picked up from your New York City doorstep.

GEAR TO GO OUTFITTERS · geartogooutfitters.com

Rent equipment that fits your outdoor weekend needs from this national outfitter that ships directly to your house or camping destination. Find everything from standards like tents, sleeping pads, and backpacks to snowshoes, trekking poles, and backpacking chairs.

LOWERGEAR OUTDOORS · lowergear.com

Whether you just need a tent for a campground lot or want to go full primitive mode out in the woods, this Arizona-based outfitter can deliver whatever you need, where you need it. From one-person backpacking tents to eight-person family tents for car camping, they have name-brand rentals of all sizes and prices, depending on what you're doing during the weekend.

OUTDOORS GEEK · outdoorsgeek.com

Find all your standard name-brand camping equipment plus DIY glamping options at this Colorado-based outfitter that ships nationwide. Try out new and gently used equipment, and at the end of your trip, send it back with a prepackaged return label—or if you like it, you can buy it.

CUTESY CABINS

Eastern Catskills

SIMPLER TIMES CABINS

5973 Route 28, Phoenicia • 845-688-5410 • simplertimescabins.net

This mom-and-pop rustic cabin community is within walking distance of the main strip of Phoenicia so that you and your friends can roll in for an impromptu summer camp weekend of outdoor activities like hiking, white-water rapids tubing on the Esopus Creek, and hanging by the firepit. But when the mood strikes, you can easily grab a nice meal or cocktails at popular nearby spots like The Graham & Co. and Phoenicia Diner. Cabins are modestly furnished with beds and bathrooms, and some are equipped with efficiency kitchens and televisions. Because of its low-key amenities, this is an excellent value for budget-conscious travelers and groups.

PHOENICIA LODGE

5987 Route 28, Phoenicia • 845-688-7772 • phoenicialodge.com

Offering a mix of cozy cottages and simple rooms, this cluster of rustic red-and-white lodges outfitted with wood-paneled walls gives off major vintage Catskills vibes. Neighboring with Simpler Times along the Esopus Creek, it's within walking distance of the main strip of Phoenicia and all the Catskills' famous outdoor attractions, so you can swing in for a semi-rustic and budget-friendly weekend in the woods without having to worry about renting special equipment or transit (premium charter bus operator Line offers daily round-trip service to nearby destinations The Graham & Co. and Sweet Sue's; 646-798-8116; ridewithline.com). The cottages are modest but equipped with a few choice modern conveniences like private bathrooms, air conditioning and heating, an efficiency kitchen, TV, Wi-Fi, and gas fireplaces in some units.

Western Catskills

THE GLEN WILDE

44 Church Road, Mountain Dale • 917-676-6228 • theglenwilde.com

The precursor to the tiny house trend, this revamped bungalow community from the Catskills' Borscht Belt era retains its cool mid-century vibe with architectural details like vaulted ceilings along with vintage furnishings. Modern upgrades like the addition of sturdy bedding lofts and refinished bathrooms bring a touch of luxury to an otherwise rustic setting, ideal for a weekend in the woods or a writing sabbatical. Of note: these bungalows don't have air conditioning, so plan wisely when booking during steamy midsummer.

Upper Catskills
COLD SPRING LODGE & CABINS

530 Oliverea Road, Big Indian • 845-254-5711 • coldspringlodge.com

Nestled along the Esopus Creek within the Catskill Forest Preserve, this rustic cabin community is just secluded enough for a weekend in the woods, hitting up hiking trails, outdoor sports, and landmarks such as Kaaterskill Falls without being totally removed from society (it's only a 15-minute drive to towns like Phoenicia and Mount Tremper). Six furnished two- and three-bedroom cabins are modestly decorated but outfitted with better-than-expected amenities like wood-burning fireplaces, efficiency kitchens, Wi-Fi, private bathrooms, and basic linens, towels, and kitchenware for easy in-and-out trips. Cold Spring Lodge isn't as cute and modern as nearby modern boutique hotels, but it's a super-affordable option and a great value for splitting among tightly budgeted group trips. In addition to hiking trails and natural swimming hole access, the property has a pool on-site (always a nice bonus).

>> **Transit Pro-Tip:** This is one of the few woodland cabin destinations you can get to without a car. Cold Spring Lodge now offers shuttle transport between Trailways NY bus stops in Big Indian and Pine Hill, and you can prearrange transit to nearby attractions like Belleayre Mountain, grocery stores, bars, and restaurants.

EASTWIND HOTEL & BAR

5088 Route 23, Windham • 518-734-0553 • eastwindny.com

Channeling the trendy rustic-meets-minimalist chic aesthetic of Scandinavia, this hip Catskills lodge just outside Windham Mountain is outfitted with mid-century modern furnishings and boasts a unique addition: three Lushna-style cabins (an intimate 220-square-foot enclosed triangular hut, essentially a form of glamping you'd most likely hear about from your coolest friend) with sauna access. If you prefer to keep things indoors, opt for a suite or the writer's room, both of which have sweeping mountainside views. There's no in-house restaurant, but the property has a weekend High Spirits craft cocktail bar that pops up Friday through Sunday.

THE WOODHOUSE LODGE

3807 County Route 26, Greenville • 518-893-1511 • thewoodhouselodge.com

So stylishly mid-century modern, yet so deliciously rustic Catskills—exactly the kind of thing that makes designers swoon. This 10-room cabin lodge is all about the details, like handmade custom felt-and-leather headboards, Brooklinen bedding, down alternative pillows, and luxe natural bathroom amenities. Tucked away in the northern Catskills about 30 minutes northwest of Hudson, it's just country enough to disconnect for a weekend in nature, but with all the modern conveniences so you don't come home with a funky hiking smell.

ALTERNATIVE LODGING

Upper Hudson Valley

COLLECTIVE RETREATS AT LIBERTY FARMS

129 Ostrander Road, Ghent • 970-445-2033 • collectiveretreats.com/retreat/collective-hudson
-valley

Like the idea of staying on a working organic farm, but too much of a city dweller to give up
luxuries like electricity and a cozy bed? This Hudson Valley retreat offers the best of both
worlds, featuring spacious platform-style tents outfitted with plush bedding and linens, electricity and heat, and private bathrooms with rainfall showers. When you can't be bothered to
draft up a weekend itinerary (ahem!), you can easily tack on activities like an in-tent massage,
private fly-fishing lesson, farm-to-table in-tent dining, sailing with Tivoli Sailing Company, or a
kayaking adventure. Be warned: inclusive fancy concierge services will typically cost you more
than a DIY itinerary.

GATHER GREENE

176 Levett Road, Coxsackie • 262-448-3683 • gathergreene.com

Dying to stay in one of those minimalist tiny homes you keep seeing in architectural design
magazines? This northwestern Hudson Valley commune has 17 of them, each miniature cabin
outfitted with a king bed, premium Brooklinen bedding, a private bathroom stocked with toiletries from local apothecary 2 Note Hudson, mini fridge, outside deck, chargers, pour-over
coffee, and a floor-to-ceiling view of the woods. Sounds awesome, right? You're not alone. This
is a super-popular wedding weekend destination spot, but they open up seven summer weekends to individual stays (book well in advance).

GATHERWILD RANCH

331 Roundtop Road, Germantown • 203-807-1462 • gatherwild.com

Stretching across 15 acres of bucolic farmland including a former apple orchard and chicken
coop, this rustic glamping concept puts you in unique, semi-outdoor setups like modern yurts,
a tepee, or a van converted into a bedroom at a reasonable price that won't break the bank.
However, part of the reason it's cheaper: no electricity. Amenities are all outdoors, including a
composting toilet, solar shower, outdoor kitchen, and charcoal grill. After all, if you're going to
stay outdoors, you might as well make it count.

Western Catskills

GEODOME AT THE OUTLIER INN

Woodridge • outlierinn.com

Between its collection of tiny houses, bungalows, vintage 1950s Spartenette trailer, and classic cottages, you'll want to stay in all the rooms at this eclectic, alternative lodging concept in the southern Catskills. Its true gem is a geodome that lets you sleep in a bubble under the stars. The caveat, however, is you need to BYO bed (air mattress or otherwise), and it's not particularly budget-friendly for such a bare-bones overnight experience that doesn't include breakfast (you'll want to bring your own food, too). Whether you get to fulfill a lifelong dream of staying in a geodome or opt for one of their other colorfully decorated rooms, it's certainly a unique 12-acre property featuring a variety of quirky amenities you really won't find anywhere else (an animal farm with bunnies, sheep, and goats; a double outdoor shower; a recording studio for musicians; a fiber arts workshop; and an on-site vintage shop).

WILLOWEMOC WILD FOREST YURT

60 Browns Road, Livingston Manor • 845-439-4367 • willowemocwildforestyurt.com

Not as rustic as a standard tent, yet not as polished as a luxury retreat, this shabby chic yurt and safari tent nestled within the Catskill Forest Preserve offers a unique and peaceful getaway for communing with nature. Unlike other campground resorts, the property is a mom-and-pop spot with limited lodging that feels truly disconnected from the regular world. Accommodations are cushier than your average sleeping bag and mat experience, but if you're looking for glamping luxury, this is definitely on the crunchier side (eco-friendly lights are solar-powered and there are no electric outlets or heating options as in more modern, upscale yurts and safari tents).

Only in Upstate New York

Weekend Escapes for Eccentrics

Don't be fooled by the upswing in fancy galleries, hip restaurants, and cool boutique getaways. The Hudson Valley and Catskills region is very much still a place for weirdos, by weirdos. It makes sense, given its expansive history and landscape, that there are plenty of hidden enclaves for artist communities, fascinating ruins, bizarre celebrations, and unique stays to enhance any weekender trip with a few strange stopovers.

Even as a new generation of trendy properties reinvigorates rural communities, it's somewhat of a relief to know that upstate New York still has an abundance of eclectic, authentic attractions, as opposed to the repetitive, homogenous chain stores and modern developments everywhere else. This is still a place where you can explore abandoned hotels and castles, lingering relics of the dawn of American history, where it's only an hour drive between the world's largest kaleidoscope hiding inside a converted silo and a town so proud of its trout population that it hosts an entire parade devoted to it.

Perhaps that's why there are so many unique destinations hiding in the mountains—it's

// Along with tours, Bannerman Castle hosts regular events like evening movie screenings and concerts

always been a place where creatives and outside thinkers can disconnect from city life. Artist retreats pave the way for hidden sculptural gardens and galleries, attracting enterprising bed-and-breakfast owners to develop their own ideas of vacationing paradise, like staying in a room designed to look like a groovy 1960s acid trip. It's all there.

Maybe you want to get in a hike, but reaching the summit isn't as interesting as trying to discover an abandoned hotel. You'd balk at the idea of attending a music festival, but the idea of going to the largest celebration of experimental Russian, Slavic, Balkan, and other eastern European music sounds too insane to miss. Or perhaps you're dead set on visiting the original site where Woodstock happened, at the Bethel Woods Center for the Arts, so why not try to stay at the legendary Big Pink House, where Bob Dylan wrote and recorded music? This is a chapter that covers all those little hidden quirks to enhance your weekend trip.

≡ Ruins

Lower Hudson Valley

BANNERMAN CASTLE

Pollepel Island • bannermancastle.org

Explore the fascinating ruins of Bannerman Castle, situated on Pollepel Island between the cities of Beacon and Newburgh, directly on the Hudson River. Now abandoned and deteriorating, this Scottish-style fortress originally existed as an arsenal that was built around 1900. After a bizarre and lengthy series of events, the island experienced a massive fire in the late 1960s and is now under the stewardship of the Bannerman Castle Trust, which operates tours via kayak and boat. Because it's more fun to experience the island beyond a walking tour, keep an eye out for specialty events like live theater performances, concerts, and movie screenings throughout the summer.

GETTING THERE: 1 hour 28 minutes via Metro-North to Beacon. The island is accessible by boat and kayak tours conducted through the Bannerman Castle Trust, departing from Beacon and Newburgh. Don't try to do this on your own; there are dangerous currents running along the island that tour guides know how to navigate around.

>> **Know Before You Go:** Tours operate seasonally from May through October. While the grounds have stairs and carved paths, walking around the property can be challenging for non-able-bodied persons. Plan to wear comfortable shoes and bring items for spending the day or evening in nature (sunscreen, bug spray, hat, water, etc.).

CORNISH ESTATE RUINS

Cold Spring

As beautiful as it is tragic, this withering estate was originally built in 1917 for Edward and Selina Cornish, who famously died within two weeks of each other in 1938. A fire in 1958 destroyed much of the property, and the rest of it fell into disrepair by the 1960s. Remnants of their once-beautiful mansion have been overtaken by the natural elements, now consisting of partially formed stone frames that signal a past life.

GETTING THERE: 1 hour 30 minutes via Metro-North to Breakneck Ridge. Access to the Hudson Highlands State Park is about a mile hike via the Undercliff Trail to the Cornish Estate ruins. Flat and well-paved, this is an easy trail for novice hikers.

DENNINGS POINT RUINS

210 Dennings Avenue, Beacon

Beacon is actually home to several ruins, including this abandoned brick factory that has become a popular hiking destination for weekenders. Throughout history, the Hudson River has been used as a primary waterway for transporting building materials and goods, which is why there are so many aging industrial and manufacturing buildings in towns bordering it. The Dennings Point Ruins are the remains of what used to be Dennings Point Brick Works, which operated from the late 19th century until 1939. Two other companies operated from the property until it was purchased by New York State in 1988 to turn into a state park. Today, the building stands vacated, but not alone—it gets plenty of weekend visitors stopping by.

GETTING THERE: 1 hour 28 minutes via Metro-North to Beacon. It's about a mile walk from Long Dock Park (just outside the Beacon train station) along the scenic Riverfront Trail to reach the Dennings Point Ruins inside Dennings Point State Park. From there, you can explore the trails in the park or head to nearby Madam Brett Park—both are easy hikes for beginners.

LETCHWORTH VILLAGE

Letchworth Village Road, Thiells

When a building is abandoned and turns to ruins, there's a strong possibility that something terrible happened. In the case of Letchworth Village, it was a notoriously terrifying mental institution with abysmal conditions, considered entirely unethical by modern practices, that operated from the turn of the century until 1996, when it closed. Sounds creepy, doesn't it? Naturally, ghost hunters and paranormal fanatics are obsessed with this place, supposedly prone to orb sightings and other indications of ghost activity. Building remnants are littered with graffiti and crumbling infrastructure—all the makings of a place no one should want to visit but can't help seeing anyway.

GETTING THERE: 45 minutes via car from New York City. Do you really want to visit a super-creepy abandoned mental asylum without a car? Thought so. Because Letchworth hasn't been in operation for more than 20 years, it no longer has an address (put in Fieldstone Middle School into your GPS). But the property is easily accessible off the main Letchworth Village Road.

Eastern Catskills

OVERLOOK MOUNTAIN HOUSE RUINS

Woodstock

In the endless fight between nature and human development, this abandoned hotel proves that nature always wins. Situated at the top of Overlook Mountain Wild Forest, this scenic hike takes you to the remnants of the skeletal remains of the former Overlook Hotel, now eroded and bare-boned, the remaining portions entangled by a web of overgrown plants. In a past life, this luxury hotel was a haven for upscale New York City weekenders before shifting ownership multiple times, burning down twice, and finally being abandoned during its third rebuild. It's an invigorating hike to climb to the ruins (2,900 feet), but continue on and you'll be rewarded with incredible views from the fire tower at the summit (3,150 feet).

GETTING THERE: 2 hours via car from New York City. A new .7-mile trailhead was added in 2018, connecting from Macdaniel Road in Woodstock to the original Overlook Mountain Trailhead that leads to the Overlook Mountain House and Fire Tower. Set your GPS to the KTD Tibetan Buddhist Bookstore, located across the street, to find the entrance (352 Meads Mountain Road, Woodstock).

☰ *Esoterica*

Lower Hudson Valley

MOTORCYCLEPEDIA

250 Lake Street, Newburgh • 845-569-9065 • motorcyclepediamuseum.org • adults, $15; seniors 65+, military and veterans, $12; students (ages 12–18), $10; youth (ages 7–11), $5; children 6 and under, free; ticket price grants access to both Motorcyclepedia and The Velocipede

Boasting more than 85,000 square feet of space with 600 motorcycles and three full-sized motordomes, this museum often slips under the radar, even among motorcycle fanatics and locals. So when you tell everyone that you saw the oldest working motorcycle (dating to 1897) and other elusive hogs, you might be the only one of your friends in the know. Even if you're not a seasoned rider, the museum is undoubtedly impressive and allows a rare chance to see a motordome used by Evel Knievel (and wonder how he had the nerve to ride a motorcycle through that thing).

THE VELOCIPEDE

109 Liberty Street, Newburgh • motorcyclepediamuseum.org • adults, $15; seniors 65+, military and veterans, $12; students (ages 12–18), $10; youth (ages 7–11), $5; children 6 and under, free; ticket price grants access to both the Motorcyclepedia Museum and The Velocipede

The sister to Motorcyclepedia, this esoteric exhibit in downtown Newburgh features an unusual collection of 19th- and early 20th-century velocipedes (the forerunner to the bicycle), including high wheelers, tricycles, a motorized bicycle, and other antiquities.

Upper Hudson Valley

KINGSTON ARTIST SOAPBOX DERBY

Kingston • kingstonartistsoapboxderby.com

Once a year, it's not uncommon to see a giant Ms. Pacman head rolling down the Broadway strip in Kingston. Most likely, it's Kingston Artist Soapbox Derby Day, the annual community event in which dozens of people race elaborate, DIY sculptures on nonmotorized wheels. Going 23 years strong, the spectacle grows bigger each time and is something to be seen.

Eastern Catskills

EMERSON KALEIDOSCOPE

5340 Route 28, Mount Tremper • 845-688-5800 • emersonresort.com/worlds-largest-kaleidoscope • $5 per person; children 11 and under are free

Leave it to the Catskills to have the world's largest kaleidoscope, a multisensory collaboration between kaleidoscope artist Charles Karadimos, psychedelic art pioneer Isaac Abrams, and his son Raphael, a computer artist. Housed within a converted silo, the 56-foot-long theater uses video installation and a three-dimensional, three-mirror system to project a trippy light show. The only thing more bizarre than its existence in the middle of the Catskill Mountains is its location at Emerson Resort & Spa, a luxury hotel.

Western Catskills

LIVINGSTON MANOR TROUT PARADE

Livingston Manor • catskillartsociety.org/troutparade

No, really. It's actually a trout-themed parade. One where people dress up with makeshift fish heads and costumes, then march down Livingston Manor's Main Street with elaborate floats, puppets, and banners. As cool as it is weird, you kind of have to respect the town's dedication to surrealist whimsy. Plus, at the end, everyone parties at local spots like Catskill Brewing and the Kaatskeller, so you can only imagine how much funnier an entire town dressed like trout looks after a couple of drinks.

// A parade dedicated entirely to trout is one of the many attractions you'll only find in the Catskills

Upper Catskills

JETLAG FESTIVAL

Downsville • jetlagfestival.com

There's no shortage of esoteric festivals in Hudson Valley, but this one is really . . . specific. For whatever reason, the Peaceful Valley Campsite in Downsville has become the location of choice for the largest festival of Russian, Slavic, Balkan, and other eastern European music in the United States. It's as weird as it sounds, and incredibly popular, so if you want tickets, you'll have to fight for them in advance.

☰ *Quirky Stays*

Upper Hudson Valley

THE BIG PINK HOUSE

56 Parnassus Lane, Saugerties • bigpinkbasement.com

If you're a hardcore Bob Dylan fan, an overnight stay at this legendary location where he and The Band recorded *The Basement Tapes* and wrote the album *Music from Big Pink* is a priceless experience. For everyone else, it's an incredibly expensive stay for a pretty average-looking property in the middle of the country that you could probably get for a much better value elsewhere. Either way: the entire 1,850-square-foot, three-bedroom house is available for rent (minus the basement). Superfans consistently rank the experience as near-spiritual; the house remains decorated with much of the original furnishings and photos, so that it's a some-what well-preserved step back into the 1960s (the owners are more than happy to give tours, with an overview of the history).

WING'S CASTLE

717 Bangall Road, Millbrook • 845-677-9085 • wingscastle.com

An architectural anomaly, Wing's Castle is one of Hudson Valley's most bizarre and fascinat-ing bed-and-breakfasts. Constructed mostly out of scavenged and recycled materials, this hodgepodge estate that looks like a Jim Henson or J. R. R. Tolkien fantasy is the 47-year living art and dream home project of artists Peter and Toni Ann Wing. In 1970, the Wings sought to build a grand castle on a hill. After being turned down by contractors who found the project too complicated, they decided to take matters into their own hands and have made the proj-ect a continuous lifelong project. What has resulted is an incredible Gothic-inspired fairy-tale castle and Hobbit-like country cottage containing a myriad of intricate details like hand-tiled mosaic art, a cauldron bathtub in the Dungeon basement suite, a "Stonehenge" sunset ter-race, and a pool "moat."

// This eclectic mansion was built by local artists Peter and Toni Ann Wing, and features salvaged materials from around the Hudson Valley

Upper Delaware Scenic and Recreational River

STICKETT INN

3380 Route 97, Barryville • 845-557-0913 • stickettinn.com

Yes, the name is intentional, and it's the kind of tongue-in-cheek welcome you should expect from incredibly charming husband-owners Roswell Hamrick and Johnny Pizzolato. An intimate property with only five suites, each stylish space is dressed with locally made Shibori bedding and themed by interest: "Eat" is outfitted with a kitchen and geared toward the traveler who wants to cook local farm-fresh produce; "Steam" is equipped with a private steam shower and cold plunge basin. In the courtyard, there's a four-seat jacuzzi with disco light options for hot tubbing under the stars. Pick up a cup of coffee in the morning or have a drink with Johnny and Roswell in the evening at their bar and welcome center, where they have custom-made cider (aptly named Stickett Inn Cider Dry and Hard) and great swag worth toting home.

Eastern Catskills

KATE'S LAZY MEADOW

5191 Route 28 • Mount Tremper • 845-688-7200 • lazymeadow.com

There's no shortage of swanky new spots dripping with modest mid-century design, but this campy Catskills destination is all about groovy vibes. That's because its owner is none other than Kate Pierson of the B-52s and her partner, Monica Coleman, who have built a veritable "love shack" appropriately situated just outside Woodstock. Each cabin is outfitted with its own bespoke retro interior bursting with wild colors reminiscent of *Pee-wee's Playhouse*, along with plenty of space to spread out for group weekends.

Western Catskills

GEODOME AT THE OUTLIER INN

Woodridge • outlierinn.com

Between its collection of tiny houses, bungalows, vintage 1950s Spartenette trailer, and classic cottages, you'll want to stay in all the rooms at this eclectic, alternative lodging concept in the southern Catskills. Its true gem is a geodome that lets you sleep in a bubble under the stars. The caveat, however, is that you need to BYO bed (air mattress or otherwise), and it's not particularly budget-friendly for such a bare bones overnight experience that doesn't include breakfast (you'll want to bring your own food, too). Whether you get to fulfill a life-long dream of staying in a geodome or opt for one of their other colorfully decorated rooms, it's certainly a unique 12-acre property featuring a variety of quirky amenities you really won't find anywhere else (an animal farm with bunnies, sheep, and goats; a double outdoor shower; a recording studio for musicians; a fiber arts workshop; and an on-site vintage shop).

Upper Catskills

THE ROXBURY MOTEL

2258 County Road 41, Roxbury • 607-326-7200 • theroxburymotel.com

Maybe the thought of sleeping in a room decorated like a coconut cream pie never occurred to you, but if the idea sounds appealing, you can actually do that at The Roxbury Motel. Despite the unassuming exterior, each of the rooms at this Catskills lodge are notoriously kitschy and thematic, from the Fred Flintstone-inspired caveman room to an over-the-top baroque suite that would have made Liberace proud. On-site is the property's co-ed Shimmer Spa, where you can use the hot tub and sweat lodge for only $20 per day.

9

Festivals and Seasonal Stops

Limitless nature, incredible art, excellent food, hundreds of artisanal beverage producers, and year-round scenic conditions are just a handful of the reasons to celebrate upstate New York. But leave it to locals to put together whimsical full-scale festivals that provide an extra incentive to head north.

Short on time, but still want to taste everything? There's no shortage of food and beverage festivals (including several niche ones, like the Hudson Valley Garlic Festival). Hunter Mountain fills to capacity every spring with craft beer fanatics ready to fill their glasses at the state competition and tasting festival called TAP New York. You'd think autumn would be the best time to have a cider celebration, but fall foliage tourism is so wildly popular that the locals raise their glasses to its cider makers in June for Hudson Valley Cider Week.

Woodstock inspired a whole generation of rock music festivals around the world, but the tradition has transformed so that there's space for all kinds of genres throughout the year. Bethel Woods, the original site of Woodstock, has a modern amphitheater that can play host to events like Mountain Jam, inviting more than 40 acts, including Willie Nelson, The Avett

// See performers like Blondie and Alice Cooper at Bethel Woods Center for the Arts

Brothers, and Dispatch, to perform among three stages, plus yoga and a craft beer tap house, because why not? For something a little more esoteric, Basilica Hudson has made a name for itself hosting experimental music festivals like 24-Hour Drone and Basilica Soundscape, where noise artists like Miho Hatori (of Cibo Matto), Lightning Bolt, and The Haxan Cloak have all headlined. But you're also likely to find anything from country and bluegrass to chamber music weekenders all over the region.

Autumn is a celebration of its own, as Hudson Valley and the Catskills turn into an endless colorful expanse for fall foliage, apple cider doughnuts, and seasonal festivities. Given its lengthy history and abundance of preserved properties, it's no shocker that the region is also a major Halloween destination for haunted getaways. Every year, the backwoods at Burn Brae Mansion transform into an eerie haunted trail staffed by costumed actors. But the mansion has another reputation as one of the most haunted inns in America, with paranormal activity flying off the charts on shows like *Ghost Hunters*.

Back-to-back festivals definitely pick up throughout the summer and fall, but like most things in the region, you can always stumble upon something cool happening year-round—including a handful of eccentric events you'll only find upstate (don't miss the Trout Parade, JetLag Festival, or Soapbox Derby on page 181).

 **Spring**

APRIL

24-HOUR DRONE AT BASILICA HUDSON

basilicahudson.org

More of an immersive art experience than a classic music festival, you have to love that something so esoteric can exist in Hudson Valley. As suggested by the name, the annual 24-hour festival features avant-garde drone and experimental noise artists. Unlike most music festivals, guests are allowed to come and go as they please during this prolonged event. But if you end up staying, no need to worry about food—the event usually has food from local restaurants available for purchase.

TAP NEW YORK AT HUNTER MOUNTAIN

tap-ny.com

TAP New York is the two-day craft beer and food festival of beer nerd dreams. The largest craft beer festival in New York, this wildly popular event grows exponentially every year, reflecting the enormous presence and love of solid brews throughout the state. This means that attending the event grants access to not only the best beers in Hudson Valley and the

Catskills, but everything you've wanted to try from Long Island to Buffalo. There's tons of food, too, including an entire selection of creative, handheld wraps to snack on the go, like the muffaletta vegan wrap and the cochinita pibil wrap.

MAY

HUDSON-BERKSHIRE WINE AND FOOD FESTIVAL

hudsonberkshirewinefestival.com

Wine, food, and the best of two legendary agricultural destinations wrapped up in one weekend? It's hard to find a reason not to go. This event tends to be more family-friendly than events like TAP New York (a blessing or a curse, depending on how you feel about drinking around children), but tickets are super-reasonably priced at only $10/day in advance or $25 at the door to try samples from local producers like Berkshire Mountain Distillers, Hudson Valley Distillers, Clermont Vineyards and Winery, and Hillrock Estate Distillery. Food producers, crafters, and jewelry makers are also on-site at the Columbia County Fairgrounds event, selling wares to take home.

 **Summer**

JUNE

DEEP WATER LITERARY FESTIVAL

deepwaterfestival.com

Considered one of the country's best bookstores, One Grand Books in Narrowsburg began working with the Delaware Valley Arts Alliance to launch this new three-day literary festival that brings in top local and national talent in all literary genres. Headliners have included Booker Prize winner Marlon James, journalist Masha Gessen, and readings by actors Mark Ruffalo and Dylan Baker.

HUDSON VALLEY SHAKESPEARE FESTIVAL

hvshakespeare.org

Now in its 33rd year, this annual theater festival brings classic Shakespeare plays to life at the Boscobel House and Gardens outdoor theater tent. Proximity to New York City's world-renowned theater scene is a bonus, bringing in new and upcoming talent from major Broadway, off-Broadway, and Met Opera productions.

RHINEBECK CRAFTS FESTIVAL

Shop from more than 200 artists and makers at this popular annual craft festival held on the Dutchess County Fairgrounds. Vendors sell everything from jewelry, apparel, and ceramics to gourmet snacks, wine, and spirits, which means there are tons of cool collectibles to tote home.

HUDSON VALLEY CIDER WEEK

ciderweekhv.com

Fall foliage is such a big deal in Hudson Valley that locals have to wait until June to celebrate their apples in peace. Frankly, it's worth it, considering the countless number of cider makers that have popped up in the past few years. Unlike most festivals that take place over a weekend on the fairgrounds, this is more of a destination-based weeklong festival where you can sample excellent local ciders at bars, restaurants, markets, orchards, and cider house tasting rooms.

WESTCHESTER WINE AND FOOD FESTIVAL

winefood.westchestermagazine.com

For the food obsessed, listen up: this is your festival. The weeklong festival consists of seven curated events, such as Italian wine tasting, a burger and beer blast, a food truck festival, and special winemaker dinners. Of course, no food festival is complete without a Grand Tasting event, where you can try it all under one roof.

TASTE OF COUNTRY MUSIC FESTIVAL

tasteofcountryfestival.com

When you're already escaping urban blight with a rural weekend getaway, why not go full country? This massive annual festival taps all the top country talent, like Rascal Flatts, Keith Urban, Little Big Town, Brooks & Dunn, and emerging artists you should know. It takes place at Hunter Mountain, and you can even make a full weekend of it by camping out on the grounds.

MOUNTAIN JAM

mountainjam.com

Going 15 years strong, this annual four-day music festival doesn't get as much national acclaim as Bonnaroo or Coachella, but the roster of headliners is certainly head-turning. Think: Willie Nelson, The Avett Brothers, Father John Misty, Kurt Vile, Peter Frampton, and Gary Clark, Jr.—you know, a little country, a little rock 'n' roll.

CLEARWATER MUSIC FESTIVAL

clearwaterfestival.org

An eclectic mix of music, storytelling, education, and food, this longtime festival, going for more than 40 years, uses art as a medium to promote sustainability efforts and support Hudson River Sloop Clearwater, Inc., an environmental nonprofit organization that helps keep the Hudson River clean. Not only is it a good cause, but it draws acts like Mavis Staples, Ani DiFranco, and Jeff Tweedy.

AMERICAN ROOTS FESTIVAL

caramoor.org/music/american-roots

What is "American music"? Some say folk, blues, and jazz; others say country and bluegrass. But really, all of these genres contributed to the roots of American music, which is why they're all represented at this diverse music festival. Hosted at Caramoor Center for Music and the Arts, the festival's past headliners have included Aimee Mann, Rhiannon Giddens, Roseanne Cash, and The Milk Carton Kids.

DUSKLIT INTERACTIVE ART FESTIVAL

dusklit.com

When you think of a sensory deprivation chamber, it's not usually followed by a dance party or engaging with a kinetic sculpture. But at this annual interactive art festival, those three things

// The great outdoors are just a train ride away

have all coexisted in the same space. Challenging performing artists of all walks of life (poetry, dance, sculpture, etc.) to create immersive installations that play off the changing light of the setting sun, this is among The Seligmann Center's coolest events, where anything can happen.

JULY

WEEKEND OF CHAMBER MUSIC

wcmconcerts.org

This ongoing weekend series brings incredible live chamber music performances to unusual spaces throughout the Catskills, like a barn, a craft distillery, a farmers' market, and other places. Musicians ranging from cellists and violinists to clarinet and guitar players all travel in from around the world for this unique annual concert series.

HUDSON VALLEY HOT-AIR BALLOON FESTIVAL

Whether you've been toying with the idea of taking a ride or just want to see the sky littered with countless giant, glowing, colorful hot-air balloons, you can do both at this popular annual festival held at the Dutchess County Fairgrounds. While you can book both a full hot-air balloon ride and a helicopter ride, the festival also offers a rare opportunity to try a less pricey tethered ride for only $20. Beyond balloons, the festival also features live music, food and craft vendors, and carnival games.

AUGUST

HUICHICA FESTIVAL

huichica.com

An offshoot of festivals in Sonoma, California, and Walla Walla, Washington, this curated wine and music festival is so new, it's still under the radar. But it's bound to start getting noticed with indie headliners like Roky Erickson and The Mammals, plus a lineup of choice artisans, winemakers, and other local tastemakers.

SUMMER HOOT

hoot.love

Twice per year, The Ashokan Center in the Catskills plays host to a three-day folk roots music festival: Summer Hoot and Winter Hoot. While the Winter Hoot is all about hibernation, the Summer Hoot lives it up outdoors with an impressive lineup of artists like Tracy Bonham, Loudon Wainwright, and Natalie Merchant.

SEPTEMBER

HUDSON VALLEY GARLIC FESTIVAL

hvgf.org

BYO mouthwash and give up any romantic inclinations, because nothing is coming between you and the garlic at this festival. A Hudson Valley tradition for nearly 20 years, this festival brings together farmers, artisanal makers, and food vendors showing off the many varietals and iterations of this amazing allium.

HUDSON VALLEY WINE & FOOD FEST

hudsonvalleywinefest.com

Honestly, if Hudson Valley didn't have its own wine and food festival, it would be insulting to everyone. It's the epicenter of contemporary farm-to-table agriculture on the eastern seaboard and one of the most exciting wine regions having its moment. What's not to celebrate? If there's anything this book proves, it's that there's no shortage of delicious food options in Hudson Valley. If anything, there are too many to tackle, and that's what makes this festival so great: the ability to try it all in one convenient space.

BASILICA SOUNDSCAPE

basilicahudson.org

Internationally renowned and creeping up on its 10th anniversary, Basilica Hudson is more than a music festival. This genre-bending immersive art experience combines prolific experimental bands, incredible writers and literary readings, visual artists' installations, ritualistic performance art, a record show, food vendors, pop-up flea markets, and panel discussions. It's somewhat like a smaller-scale, less corporate version of SXSW meets Pitchfork Music Festival, but held in Hudson. Past headliners have included: Angel Olsen, Eileen Myles, John Maus, Amber Tamblyn, White Lung, and Swans.

☰ *Autumn*

OCTOBER

WOODSTOCK FILM FESTIVAL

woodstockfilmfestival.org

Considering the tiny size of Woodstock, it's kind of amazing that this independent film festival is not only approaching its 20th anniversary but manages to bring out a star-studded attendee list each year that has included A-list actors like Daniel Day-Lewis, Steve Buscemi, Edie Falco, Natalie Portman, and more. With independent films, panels, and special events throughout the towns of Woodstock, Rhinebeck, Kingston, Rosendale, and Saugerties, this is where you can get a first look at subversive flicks with commentary straight from the directors and actors who made them. Individual tickets are cheap ($10), but they sell out quickly, so stock up in advance.

AHIMSA YOGA AND MUSIC FESTIVAL

ahimsayogafestival.com

If you've ever visited Hunter Mountain during peak season, it's hard to image the bustling year-round resort being the same place that hosts a yoga and meditation festival. Then again, low season in early November, when all the crowds roll out, is probably the perfect time to chase your bliss. Perhaps that's why this incredibly popular festival brings in so many practitioners of all levels for a weekend of spiritual tranquility, meditation, and yoga. Workshops range from kundalini pranayama breathwork and Ayurvedic medicine to sound healing, music meditation hikes, acroyoga, and Thai massage.

CATSKILLS WINE AND FOOD FESTIVAL

catskillsfestival.com

Why choose between food and music festivals when you can have both in the same place? That's the idea behind this festival newcomer, which brings New York City celebrity chefs like Josh Capon, Alex Guarnaschelli, Michael Chernow, and Daniel Holzman to cook and demo alongside a lineup of performances from indie bands like The Revivalists, Moon Taxi, and Lord Huron.

Ghostly Getaways: Haunted Attractions
Cemetery Tours
SLEEPY HOLLOW CEMETERY

540 North Broadway, Sleepy Hollow • sleepyhollowcemetery.org

I just checked and it turns out that nighttime cemetery tours are still totally creepy. No better time to take one than during Halloween, when you can visit the gravesites of famous residents like Andrew Carnegie, Washington Irving, Elizabeth Arden, Brooke Astor, and William Rockefeller, plus hear cautionary tales about the victims of "the Mad Murderer of Sleepy Hollow" and other ghost stories.

SLEEPY HOLLOW HORSEMAN'S HOLLOW

Philipsburg Manor, 381 North Broadway, Sleepy Hollow

When it comes to Halloween, the lower Hudson Valley does not mess around. Taking a cue from local literary legend Washington Irving's famous villain, the Headless Horseman, in his iconic tale, "The Legend of Sleepy Hollow," Philipsburg Manor transforms into a historic haunted trail that will entertain you at best and terrify you at worst.

GREAT JACK O'LANTERN BLAZE

Van Cortlandt Manor, 525 South Riverside Avenue, Croton-on-Hudson

Forget your pumpkin spice latte; this incredible Halloween festival puts all other seasonal festivities to shame. More than 7,000 hand-carved pumpkins light up for 46 evenings between late September and mid-November, illuminating everything from Van Cortlandt Manor's 18th-century landscape and the thematic "Pumpkin Zee Bridge" to a 20-foot Pumpkin Carousel, a pumpkin-stacked Statue of Liberty, and a Pumpkin Planetarium.

JAY GHOUL'S HOUSE OF CURIOSITIES

lyndhurst.org

If you want to go to this annual event at Lyndhurst Mansion, act fast—it sells out quickly every year for good reason. Each year, the mansion is transformed into a Halloween wonderland, hosting a 40-minute immersive theater production where guests are invited to solve a case based on classic mystery novels. Along with getting to live out your dreams of being a detective in an Agatha Christie novel, the event provides a rare opportunity to explore the first floor and basement of the iconic mansion at nighttime.

SPOOKY LODGINGS

GHOST HUNTING WEEKENDS AT SHANLEY HOTEL • 56 Main Street,
Napanoch • 845-217-3112 • thehauntedshanleyhotel.com

Ever dream of becoming a ghost hunter? Then book a night at this haunted hotel that has been featured on *Ghost Lab* and *Ghost Hunters* for its paranormal activity. Not to be confused with the haunted Stanley Hotel in Colorado, famously featured in the movie *The Shining*, The Shanley has its own spooky history dating back to 1845, and supposedly it has frequent cameos from its permanent ghostly residents. You can book a night and a paranormal investigation tour any time, but Halloween provides the extra incentive to dress up in costume while doing it.

BURN BRAE MANSION • 73 High Road, Glen Spey • 845-856-3335 •
burnbraemansion.com

This turn-of-the-century mansion originally belonged to former Singer Sewing Machine company president George Ross Mackenzie and is notoriously haunted (at least according to *Ghost Hunters*, actress Linda Blair of *The Exorcist,* and nearly every person that has ever slept there. But who's counting?). This means that if you want to go all out for an appropriately terrifying Halloween group weekend, this is the place to do it. Round up your friends and book an overnight paranormal expedition, or try to score tickets for a murder mystery dinner (act quickly, these sell out fast). Can't swing either? Burn Brae hosts an epic haunted forest every October, right behind the mansion. And even if you're too chicken to hit the trail, you can wait for your friends at the end of the path, where there's local beer and cider, live music, and craft vendors.

MOHONK MOUNTAIN HOUSE • 1000 Mountain Rest Road, New Paltz •
845-765-3286 • mohonk.com

In a positive light, this 150-year-old Victorian lakeside resort could be a ringer for the one in Wes Anderson's film *The Grand Budapest Hotel.* On the other hand, it was also the rumored (and hotly contested) inspiration for Stephen King's Overlook Hotel in *The Shining*, so it's a pretty creepy spot to visit in the fall for Halloween. It doesn't rank anywhere among the most haunted places in America, but it's pretty old, so it's fair to assume it's probably haunted. Either way, Mohonk is downright stunning during fall foliage season, with 1,200 acres of natural beauty courtesy of the Shawangunk Ridge. Unsurprisingly, that makes this one of the pricier destinations, but it is incredibly scenic, with a certain historic charm unmatched by modern properties.

continued

// Burn Brae Mansion is among the top destinations for Halloween thrills in the Catskills

THE BEEKMAN ARMS · 6387 Mill Street, Rhinebeck · 845-876-7077 ·
beekmandelamaterinn.com

Dating back to 1766, The Beekman Arms lays claim to being the oldest inn in America.
So it shouldn't come as much of a shocker that they allegedly have some haunted guests
overstaying their welcome in the basement. Find out for yourself by taking one of their
weekly haunted tours that includes ghost stories and other tales of guests who have stayed
there during its 250-year tenure. If you make a weekend of it, the property may be old,
but the accommodations have fortunately received a modern upgrade, with plush bedding
and air conditioning. Bonus: as a nice gesture, the property stocks each room with a
complimentary decanter of sherry.

HAUNTED MILL AND MONSTER'S BALL AT THE WASSAIC PROJECT

wassaicproject.org

Part creepy haunted house, part eccentric art installation, Maxon Mills turns into a seven-story hall of creepy curiosities the last Saturday before Halloween. During the day, the haunted mill tones things down with kid-friendly activities before transforming into an adults-only costume party at night backed by DJs and fueled by (alcoholic) spirits.

The Right Way to Fall Foliage

Fall foliage in the Hudson Valley and Catskills is such a big deal that there are daily trackers alerting leaf peepers of what stage the trees are in. If you're going to travel out of your way to go gawk at nature, make sure you do it correctly by factoring in the best places to get photos, engaging with nature, and cramming as many apple cider doughnuts in your mouth as possible.

Best Outlooks to Instagram

UPPER DELAWARE SCENIC BYWAY

upperdelawarescenicbyway.org

Dubbed "The Most Scenic Highway in the East," this 50-mile two-lane stretch reminiscent of Big Sur in California winds along the Delaware River on the New York-Pennsylvania state border. Its stunning panoramic views of the river and mountains are good any time of year, but they are in rare form during fall foliage season. Pull off at Hawk's Nest or one of the other roadside stops to get your snaps.

SHAWANGUNK MOUNTAINS

mtnscenicbyway.org

This scenic byway is actually a looped connection of four routes, roughly a 20-minute drive each, passing through landmarks like Mohonk Preserve, Minnewaska State Park Preserve, Rondout Creek, and Wallkill River. So when the mountainous landscape shows off its brilliant technicolor coat, the winding route offers countless photo ops for an idyllic autumn.

BEAR MOUNTAIN STATE PARK

Whether you hike the Bear Mountain trail loop to the Perkins Memorial Tower lookout or take the scenic drive, the unobstructed panoramic views stretching to the Manhattan skyline and the Catskills are ranked among the area's best.

BASH BISH FALLS STATE PARK

Situated on the western edge of Massachusetts, just past New York's Taconic State Park, this is one of the few spots you'll have to cross the state border to get to. But it's only a 40-minute drive from Hudson, which isn't too crazy to get to a jaw-dropping 80-foot waterfall (the highest in Massachusetts). The loop is an easy 1.5-mile hike, and the falls makes for an incredible photo against the fall foliage.

>> **For More Information:** Get the lay of the land on the Hudson Valley's best scenic outlooks on page 152.

Hot-Air Balloons

Sailing in a hot-air balloon is not a budget-friendly activity by any means, but there's a reason why it's on so many bucket lists: it's downright breathtaking. Whether it's a romantic weekend or you want to see fall foliage from 3,000 feet in the air, these three balloon operators can take you there.

ABOVE THE CLOUDS

Randall Airport, 100 Airport Road, Middletown • 845-360-5594 • abovethecloudsinc.com

FANTASY BALLOON FLIGHTS

Randall Airport, 100 Airport Road, Middletown • 845-856-7103 • fantasyfliers.com

BALLOON NY

Columbia County Airport, 1142 Route 9H, Ghent • 607-435-9839 • balloonny.com

Ziplining

NEW YORK ZIPLINE CANOPY TOURS AT HUNTER MOUNTAIN

7740 Main Street, Hunter • 518-263-4388 • ziplinenewyork.com

Flying through fall foliage sounds so much cooler than taking a few snapshots from the ground, doesn't it? This zipline company operates three courses at Hunter Mountain, including an adventure tower, a mid-mountain canopy tour, and the SkyRider: the longest, fastest, and highest zipline in North America.

// Weekenders love to hit the slopes at mountains throughout Hudson Valley and the Catskills

CATAMOUNT SKI/AERIAL ADVENTURE PARK

17 Nicholson Road, South Egremont, MA • 413-528-1262 • catamounttrees.com

Just barely crossing the Massachusetts line into the Berkshires, this is an easy tack-on activity for a fall foliage weekend in Hudson or nearby Taconic State Park in Copake Falls. Boasting more adventure courses and a larger park than Hunter, this zipline operator lets you soar through the foliage with sky-high views of the Valley and Berkshires.

KITTATINNY CANOES AND CAMPGROUNDS

3846 Route 97, Barryville • 800-356-2852 • kittatinny.com

Kittatinny doesn't have as many adventure courses or ziplines as other operators, but you'll be hard-pressed to find more outdoor activities in one place. In addition to being the only zipline on the Delaware River (a great place to hit up during peak fall foliage season), it's also home to activities like canoeing, kayaking, rafting, tubing, paintball, and camping. Kittatinny's ziplines operate on a classic dual racing drop line (no adventure course), sailing down a half mile to drops of 3,000 feet and speeds up to 60 miles per hour.

Where to Get Cider Doughnuts

VERA'S MARKETPLACE

3091 US 9 #102, Cold Spring • 845-265-2151 • verasmarketplaceandgardencenter.com

What makes for a perfect cider doughnut? That's for you to decide. But Hudson Valley locals think this place serves some of the best and are willing to wait in snaking lines for it.

TANTILLO'S FARM

730 Route 208, Gardiner • 845-256-9109 • tantillosfarm.com

Pick your own apples at this fourth-generation family orchard, along with a pack of cider doughnuts top-ranked by *Hudson Valley Magazine*.

SOONS ORCHARDS

23 Soons Circle, New Hampton • 845-374-5471 • soonsorchards.com

Cider doughnuts are great, but cider doughnuts with a hard cider tasting is next-level. You can have both at this family-owned orchard that also produces its own line of artisanal hard cider and pommeau, served in its on-site tasting room.

PENNING'S FARM CIDERY

4 Warwick Turnpike, Warwick • 845-987-9922 • penningscidery.com

You might have to face a line filled with screaming children in strollers to get the cider doughnuts at this popular orchard, but afterward, you can enjoy them in a kid-free environment at their hard cider tasting room.

THOMPSON'S CIDER MILL

335 Blinn Road, Croton-On-Hudson • 914-271-2254 • thompsonscidermill.com

Among the prettiest cider mills in Hudson Valley, you can get more than your fill of the harvest here, with cider doughnuts, sweet cider, and their small-batch hard cider, all inside a scenic Victorian-style red barn.

 # *Winter*

DECEMBER

SINTERKLAAS FESTIVAL

Rhinebeck/Kingston • sinterklaashudsonvalley.com

Every December, Rhinebeck lights up with a mass of glowing stars to mark the final send-off for its month-long Sinterklaas Festival. A tradition dating back to the original Dutch settlers, this folkloric festival is somewhat like the nondenominational precursor to the story of Santa Claus. What it entails is a daylong block party featuring music, theater, dance, and a Children's Starlight Parade, complete with two-story-tall puppets and hundreds of star-toting people.

HOLIDAY MANSION TOUR AT LYNDHURST

lyndhurst.org

Lyndhurst Mansion is a looker any time of the year, but it's particularly dazzling toward the end of the year when it gets dolled up for the holidays. Dozens of Christmas trees are scattered throughout the mansion (hey, they're not short on space) along with authentic holiday period furnishings dusted off from the Gilded Age that belonged to its former tenants, the prosperous Gould family. Tickets for this event (as well as Halloween) tend to sell out quickly, so make sure to buy well in advance.

JANUARY

TROUT TOWN WINTERFEST

Roscoe

After holiday festivities die down, everyone goes into hibernation mode. But if you happen to be in Roscoe in January, you'll be thankful that the good folks at Roscoe Beer Company had the sense to put together a winter festival. Also, it puts a positive spin on an otherwise bleak winter with fun activities like live music, horse-drawn sleigh rides, ice-carving demos, snowman contests, a giant bonfire, and most importantly: specialty beers.

// Trout isn't the only attraction in Roscoe—don't miss the craft beers at Roscoe Brewery

FEBRUARY

WINTER HOOT

The Ashokan Center, 477 Beaverkill Road, Olivebridge • hoot.love

Stuck in snowy New York instead of being a snowbird on the beach this winter? This lesser-known folk music festival in the Catskills gives you a good reason to ditch the city. Chiller than its summer counterpart, the biannual three-day festival is a celebration of art, music, film, food, and nature with headliners like Natalie Merchant, Tracy Bonham, and Loudon Wainwright.

Itineraries

1. No Reservations in Peekskill

Procrastinators unite! Only an hour's train ride from Manhattan, Peekskill is among the easiest destinations to pull off as a last-minute day trip when you can't be bothered to plan anything.

Getting There

1 hour to Peekskill Train Station via Metro-North from Grand Central ($12–24 each way).

Getting Around

Most Peekskill attractions are within walking distance, but both Lyft and Uber have decent local service, should you need it.

☰ *Morning*

Hop on an early Saturday or Sunday morning Metro-North train at Grand Central, which drops off directly in front of Riverfront Green Park. It's a short walk to Main Street to hit up area shops like Bruised Apple Books or Marketplace at The Flatz.

☰ *Afternoon*

If you've been itching to get outdoors but don't want to make a gear commitment, rent a bike from Pedal Peekskill (pedalpeekskill.com) and take a ride through the Blue Mountain Reservation. Or you can walk the riverfront to Peekskill Brewery, where you can taste incredible beers in their taproom before grabbing fresh ice cream at The Hudson Creamery.

☰ *Evening*

Grab a meal at Birdsall House (which has a decent happy hour) or Taco Dive Bar, or see what's playing at Riverfront Green Park, across from the Metro-North station, before you head back to the city (not a bad place to get stuck, in the event you miss a train).

Peekskill Highlights

BIRDSALL HOUSE · 970 Main Street, Peekskill · 914-930-1880 · birdsallhouse.net

Craft beers and gastropub favorites make this a popular spot among locals and travelers. Hit the beer garden during summer happy hour for cheap brews and discount appetizers.

BLUE MOUNTAIN RESERVATION · 435 Welcher Avenue, Peekskill

For a seasoned New Yorker who regularly pounds the pavement, it's a manageable mile-long walk from the Peekskill Metro-North train station to reach this 1,500-acre park within the 12-mile Briarcliff-Peekskill Trailway. Roughly 20 hiking and biking trails of all levels are here (the Dickey Brook Trail and Boundary Trail are easier; climbing to the summits of more challenging peaks like Mount Spitzenberg or Blue Mountain will earn you excellent views).

PEEKSKILL BREWERY · 47 South Water Street, Peekskill · 914-734-2337 · peekskillbrewery.com

Yep, it's that same label you've probably seen on tap at your local bar or in the case at the bodega. Their Peekskill taproom and restaurant is where you can try the flagship brews plus limited-edition styles with elevated bar bites. During the summer, they open a pop-up outdoor beer garden with live music.

2. The Best of Beacon

So, you think you know Beacon? Renowned contemporary art museum Dia:Beacon and massive outdoor sculpture park Storm King are probably both on your radar (you'll want to commit a whole day to each of those alone), but if you want to soak up a whole weekend of art, food, culture, and a touch of nature, there's tons to explore here.

Getting There

1 hour 30 minutes via Metro-North to Beacon or Cold Spring from Grand Central ($14–34 each way).

Getting Around

Once you get off the train, it's a short walk to the attractions along Main Street or to Dia:Beacon. Lyft and Uber both operate here, though service is spottier than what you'd find around New York City. Local taxi services usually have cars by the train station, so bring cash in the event you need to pick up a ride.

☰ Friday

AFTERNOON: Friday rush hour is a quick and easy trip via Metro-North, which runs on peak schedule out of Grand Central Terminal.

EVENING: Inventive farm-to-table restaurant Kitchen Sink Food & Drink is located at the beginning of Main Street, close to the train station, making it easy to slide in for a leisurely dinner before the 10 p.m. cutoff.

☰ Saturday

MORNING: Start with a cup of coffee from Trax Espresso, then pick up fresh baked goods from Ella's Bellas before hitting Main Street to visit the independent galleries, boutiques, eateries, and shops like Hudson Beach Glass, Zakka Joy, KAIGHT, and Hudson Valley Vinyl.

AFTERNOON: Book an afternoon boat trip and hiking tour to learn about the fascinating ruins of Bannerman Castle or take a challenging hike to the top of Mount Beacon Park to see excellent views of the Valley.

EVENING: After a long day outdoors, keep it casual with a burger and craft beer at Meyer's Olde Dutch. Cap off the evening with a visit to Hudson Valley Brewery, which serves its small-batch beers until 10 p.m. on weekends.

Sunday

MORNING: Fill up with a scratch-made brunch at Beacon Bread Company, which pulls in farm-fresh ingredients from around the Valley.

AFTERNOON: Weekends are perpetually busy at Dia:Beacon, but since you're staying in town, you'll have a leg up on getting there before the masses. Been there, done that? Take a cab to nearby Cold Spring to swing by the Cold Spring General Store before visiting lesser-known spots like Magazzino and Manitoga.

EVENING: If you're still in Beacon, grab one last beer on the patio at 2 Way Brewing, which is only a few minutes' walk from the train station, before heading back to the city. You can also pick up the Metro-North one stop away in Cold Spring.

Beacon Highlights

BANNERMAN CASTLE · bannermancastle.org

Explore the ruins of Bannerman Island, an abandoned armory located on Pollepel Island, just off the banks of nearby Breakneck Ridge. Take a guided hiking or kayak tour departing by boat from Beacon. Check ahead for specialty evening events like live theater performances, concerts, and movie screenings throughout the summer.

COLD SPRING GENERAL STORE · 66 Main Street, Cold Spring · 845-809-5522 · coldspringgeneralstore.com

It's a short 13-minute Lyft ride south to get to the nearby town of Cold Spring, where this general store curates handmade artisan products like kitchenware, snacks, cookbooks, and knickknacks, all sourced within New York State.

DIA:BEACON · 3 Beekman Street, Beacon · 845-440-0100 · diaart.org

Think of it as the MoMA for Beacon. Explore immersive experimental and conceptual works from groundbreaking artists like Louise Bourgeois, Richard Serra, Bruce Nauman, and Walter De Maria.

HUDSON BEACH GLASS · 162 Main Street, Beacon · 845-440-0068 · hudsonbeachglass.com

Watch live glassblowing at this working artist studio and shop, featuring functional and sculptural hand-cast pieces by local artisans.

MAGAZZINO ITALIAN ART · 2700 Route 9, Cold Spring · 845-666-7202 · magazzino.art

This space boasts a massive collection of Postwar and Contemporary Italian art. With contents handpicked from the Olnick Spanu Collection, this free 20,000-square-foot museum is a unique opportunity to see formal, conceptual, and immersive pieces from solely Italian contemporary artists outside of Italy.

MANITOGA · 584 Route 9D, Garrison · 845-424-3812 · visitmanitoga.org

Take a tour of the studio and home of modernist industrial designer Russel Wright, a stunning, experimental, glass-walled estate dubbed "Dragon Rock," built into the site of an abandoned quarry overlooking a 30-foot waterfall, pool, and 75 acres of natural woodland landscape.

MOUNT BEACON PARK · 788 Wolcott Avenue, Beacon

No car needed for this challenging hike that picks up about 2 miles east of the Metro-North Beacon train station (cut the walk to the trail by taking a cab) and scales 2,000 feet in elevation. The payoff is worth the trek—the incredible views stretch across the valley.

Where to Eat and Drink

Find the majority of Beacon's best dining along Main Street, a short 8-minute walk from the Metro-North train station.

2 WAY BREWING · 18 West Main Street, Beacon · 845-202-7334 · 2waybrewingcompany.com

Only a block away from the Beacon train station, this microbrewery is ideal for a quick drink on the way in or out of town. If the weather's nice, grab a seat on the outdoor patio.

DENNING'S POINT DISTILLERY · 10 North Chestnut Street, Beacon · 845-476-8413 · denningspointdistillery.com

Pick your poison—bourbon, gin, brandy, or vodka—this distillery does it all. Swing by on a Friday or Sunday for a tasting or snag a tasting/tour combo on Saturdays for $5. Not the type to drink neat? No sweat, have them whip up one of their seasonal cocktails.

ELLA'S BELLAS · 418 Main Street, Beacon · 845-765-8502 · ellasbellasbeacon.com

Vegans and the gluten-free crowd are safe at this adorable bakery and café, but those without dietary restrictions will find the quality stands up impressively against any other baked good.

HUDSON VALLEY BREWERY · 7 Main Street, Beacon · 845-218-9156 ·
hudsonvalleybrewery.com

Try some of Hudson Valley's most insane experimental brews, like apple cider doughnut sour IPA, farmhouse ales fermented with sourdough yeast and aged in oak, and a sour black double IPA. Pair with food from local pop-ups like Allan's Falafel, Momo Valley, and Samosa Shack.

KITCHEN SINK FOOD & DRINK · 157 Main Street, Beacon · 845-765-0240 ·
kitchensinkny.com

You never know what will end up on this restaurant's weekly changing menu, but you can trust it will be fresh and farm-y. That's because the majority of ingredients come direct from Chef Brian Arnoff's family farm, Truckload Farm and Orchard. He puts them to good use in feel-good comfort dishes accented by a few white tablecloth tricks, paired with a beverage list highlighting predominantly local craft brews, ciders, and wines.

MEYER'S OLDE DUTCH · 184 Main Street, Beacon · 845-440-6900 ·
meyersoldedutch.com

Whether you're getting the *New York Times*-approved double-patty burger and crispy chicken sandwiches or their daily specials like General Tso's crispy tofu sandwich or falafel with harissa carrot slaw, you'll be happy to know that you can make only good choices at this popular casual spot.

Where to Stay
For Summer Camp Vibes
MALOUF'S MOUNTAIN CAMPGROUND · Beacon · 845-831-6767 ·
maloufsmountain.com

If you want to camp and get a little hiking in, Malouf's Mountain Campground has a shuttle that picks up direct from the Beacon train station with tents, firewood, and meals available for an impromptu campout on the cheap ($70–90).

For Something Fancier
INN AND SPA AT BEACON · 151 Main Street, Beacon · 845-205-2900 ·
innspabeacon.com

Situated conveniently on Beacon's main strip, just a short walk from the Metro-North train station, this boutique inn and hydrotherapy spa has all the deluxe services for an easy day trip or a cozy weekend.

// Take your brunch riverside: Roundhouse is conveniently located next to Beacon Falls

ROUNDHOUSE BEACON · 2 East Main Street, Beacon · 845-765-8369 · roundhousebeacon.com

Housed in a former textile manufacturing warehouse, this design-centric property doesn't have the kind of frills worthy of a staycation. But it's modern, elegant, and the complimentary buffet breakfast is exceptionally good.

3. Wining and Dining in New Paltz

Despite its small footprint, New Paltz has a surprising number of great restaurants, bars, and cute shops sprinkled throughout the town. For those traveling without a car, it's conveniently walkable, with restaurants tucked away throughout winding alcoves for a quick food-focused weekender off the beaten path.

Getting There

BY BUS | 1 hour 48 minutes from Port Authority. Bus is the shortest and easiest route besides driving, with regular service running between Port Authority and SUNY New Paltz via Trailways NY ($19-65). The luxury charter shuttle Line offers drop-off service between the New Paltz Park and Ride and Manhattan Thursday through Monday ($39 each way).

BY CAR | 1 hour 28 minutes from Manhattan. Driving isn't a necessity for getting to/around New Paltz, but it does offer more flexibility for off-site excursions in the nearby Shawangunk Region and Wallkill Valley.

Getting Around

If you're taking the bus, it drops off conveniently in downtown New Paltz within walking distance of major restaurants. To get to nearby destinations, ride-hailing services like Uber and Lyft are both accessible. But if you plan to head out into the country, it's best to just rent a car.

☰ Friday

AFTERNOON: Whether you drive or take the bus, you'll get there about the same time, which is roughly around dinner.

EVENING: Dig into Hudson Valley gastropub goodness at Garvan's. Unwind at Jar'd Wine Pub, a cavernous little spot that often has DJ dance parties on the patio.

☰ Saturday

MORNING: Make your first stop Main Street Bistro, where you can find solid breakfast staples done right, such as poached eggs with sundried tomatoes, pesto, Asiago, and hollandaise, or buttermilk pancakes with cranberries, almonds, powdered sugar, and maple syrup. Down to double up on breakfast? Sift through local artisanal cheeses at The Cheese Plate before taking a stroll around town to walk it off.

AFTERNOON: Take a quick 3-mile rural detour to nearby Twin Star Orchards, home of Brooklyn Cider House, where you can do an afternoon's hard cider tasting, chow down on wood-fired pizzas, and pick apples when they're in season.

EVENING: Stop for happy hour beers at Arrowood Outpost, the New Paltz tasting room of this farm brewery in nearby Accord. Get a reservation at A Tavola Trattoria, a fine Italian restaurant with a Hudson Valley slant. Spend the rest of the evening hitting up local craft breweries Bacchus and Clemson Brothers Brewing.

☰ Sunday

MORNING: Sleep off that hangover, then stumble into brunch at farm-to-table spot Huckleberry (which has an excellent outdoor patio) or New Orleans–inspired joint The Parish (also has an excellent outdoor patio).

AFTERNOON: Spend the afternoon strolling along Main Street, record shopping at Rhino Records, Jack's Rhythms, or indie label Team Love, picking up quirky gifts at lifestyle shop Cocoon, browsing books at Inquiring Minds, and heading down to the Wallkill River along Huguenot Street. Hit the road and head back to New York City rested, well-fed, and ready to tackle the week.

New Paltz Foodie Highlights

ARROWOOD OUTPOST · 3B Church Street, New Paltz · arrowoodfarms.com

Everything that goes into this farm brewery's beers is local, from the water sourced from the limestone caves in Rosendale to the hops, yeast, herbs, fruit, and vegetables grown right on the farm. Arrowood even has its own apiary that produces honey for their honey porter. If you're without wheels to get to this farm brewery's main facility in Accord or just want to double up on your beers, its New Paltz outpost has a tasting room conveniently in the center of town where you can taste them all.

CLEMSON BROTHERS BREWERY · The Gilded Otter, 3 Main Street, New Paltz · 845-256-1700 · gildedotter.com

Get a taste of popular Middletown brewery, Clemson Brothers, at this outpost brewpub featuring their changing lineup of craft beers.

GARVAN'S · 215 Huguenot Street, New Paltz · 845-255-7888 · garvans.com

Approachable New American dishes with a Hudson Valley angle, featuring seasonally driven ingredients with inventive spins.

HUCKLEBERRY · 21 Church Street, New Paltz · 845-633-8443 · huckleberrynewpaltz.com

This cozy little restaurant and cocktail bar tucked down a shady side street features approachable favorites with Hudson Valley ingredients, best taken on its private outdoor patio.

TWIN STAR ORCHARDS · 155 North Ohioville Road, New Paltz · 845-633-8657 · twinstarorchards.com

Backdropped by a stunning view of the rolling tree-filled landscape and a serene pond, this producer is best known for the heirloom and rare apple varietals used to make its award-winning dry, sour, funky, and raw-fermented hard ciders. On weekends, the cider house serves wood-fired artisanal pizzas. During fall harvest, the orchard opens up as a U-Pick, so you can stock up on apples during peak foliage season.

Where to Stay

Within New Paltz, you won't find as many cutesy bed-and-breakfasts as in other Hudson Valley towns, but here are a few choice picks:

For That Hudson Valley Farm Life

AUDREY'S FARMHOUSE · 2188 Bruynswick Road, Wallkill · 845-895-3440 · audreysfarmhouse.com

Stay in a renovated 18th-century Dutch farmhouse and cottage furnished with a blend of photo-friendly antique and contemporary interiors. Enjoy the on-site farm-to-table spot The Greenhouses Restaurant.

For a Home Away from Home

MOONDANCE RIDGE BED & BREAKFAST · 55 Shivertown Road, New Paltz · 845-255-4161 · moondanceridge.com

This cozy bed-and-breakfast ranks among the top local picks, each room outfitted with a private whirlpool bath and electric fireplace.

For the Crunchy-Healthy Getaway

HUNGRY GHOST GUEST HOUSE · 35 Cragswood Road, New Paltz · 508-579-1600 · hungryghostguesthouse.com

Relax and recharge at this retreat featuring comfy accommodations; a custom menu of organic, vegan, and gluten-free dishes; and a beautiful forested backdrop within reach of major New Paltz attractions.

4. Bikes and Booze in the Black Dirt Region

The 5,500-acre pocket of Western Hudson Valley known as the Black Dirt Region is named after its distinctive nutrient-rich soil, the remnants of a 12,000-year-old shallow lake formed during a glacial period that grows some of the region's most incredible produce. Soak up the bucolic landscape, plus its boozy bounty of farm breweries, cideries, vineyards, and spirits makers, with a leisurely bike ride through the Heritage Trail that cuts through the terrain. Along the way, make time to swing through the nearby villages of Goshen, Warwick, and New Hampton for great eats and a drive-in movie.

Getting There

BY CAR | 1 hour to Warwick or Goshen from Manhattan.

Getting Around

A car is really your best bet if you want to explore the Black Dirt Region; Lyft/Uber tends to get spotty out here for bouncing between farmland destinations. But if you plan to just do the Heritage Trail in Goshen, you can easily make it a car-free weekend (1 hour 30 minutes to Goshen via Coach USA Shortline bus for $18–60).

Friday

AFTERNOON/EVENING: Rent a car and head to the Iron Forge Inn in Warwick, a historic farmhouse with an upscale farm-to-table restaurant. Get a nightcap in Goshen at the local gastropub, Craft 47, then hit the hay.

Saturday

MORNING: Fill up with a quick breakfast at Noble Coffee Roasters. Pick up a bike at Joe Fix Its and hit the Heritage Trail.

AFTERNOON: Bike to Rushing Duck Brewing (6 miles, about 30 minutes), where you can order a flight of cool craft beers. Grab lunch at Allan's Falafel (0.7 miles, 5 minutes) or continue to Long Lot Farm Brewery (2.3 miles, 15 minutes), a microbrewery serving better-than-average beers.

Prefer cider or spirits instead of beer? Take the trail to Orchard Hill Cider Mill in New Hampton (4.9 miles, 30 minutes), a functioning apple orchard with a country market, sea-

// Orchard Hill's farm-style ciders have developed a cult following at bars around NYC

sonal U-Pick, and tasting room where you can try their line of heritage hard ciders, pommeau, and cocktails. Or head to Orange County Distillery at Brown Barn Farms (5.1 miles, 29 minutes) to try their line of a dozen spirits that includes everything from standards to experimental barrel-aged gin, unoaked rye, and maple-flavored whiskey, served neat or in a craft cocktail.

Pick your path, then head back to Goshen, swinging by Trailside Treats to cool off with a refreshing ice cream.

EVENING: Shower and unwind, then drive to Pennings Farm Cidery in Warwick (25 minutes) to try seasonal ciders in a kid-free zone and pick up a growler to go. It's a 3-minute drive to the farm-to-table spot The Grange for an intimate dinner before hitting the Warwick Drive-In Theater (across the street from Pennings) for a double feature under the stars.

Sunday

MORNING: Enjoy a leisurely brunch at the Stagecoach Inn in the solarium, offering sunny views of their private back garden (don't miss the baked French toast—it's unreal).

AFTERNOON: Continue your Black Dirt tour de booze by traveling through the rolling farmland to Glenmere Brewing in Florida, checking out local spirits at Black Dirt Distillery in Warwick, or trying ciders and wines at Applewood Winery in Warwick before heading back to the city.

Black Dirt Region Highlights

ALLAN'S FALAFEL · 115 Main Street, Chester · 845-469-1714 · allansfalafel.net

Israeli food in rural New York? Yep, and it's even better than some of the stuff you'll find in Manhattan (not to mention way more affordable). Everything is made fresh from scratch in-house, with spices and oils shipped in directly from the homeland. Think: super-creamy hummus, farm-fresh tabbouleh, and slow-roasted kebabs with extremely generous portions.

APPLEWOOD WINERY ·

82 Four Corners Road, Warwick · 845-988-9292 · applewoodwinery.com

Even if you haven't heard of this Hudson Valley winery, chances are you might know its sister cider brand, Naked Flock Hard Cider, which makes frequent cameos in the New York City bodega beer coolers. And even if you

// Allan's Falafel serves authentic Israeli mezze better than most NYC joints

have, no better time than the present to give them both a try at its Warwick tasting room.

BLACK DIRT DISTILLERY · 114 Little York Road, Warwick · 845-258-6020 · blackdirtdistillery.com

This 4,000-square-foot farm distillery churns out incredible bourbon, applejack, and rye, using locally grown corn and aged in American barrels. Try them all at their tasting room inside Warwick Valley Winery and Distillery, where you can sample all of it, plus local ciders and wines, under the same roof.

THE GRANGE · 1 Ryerson Road, Warwick · 845-986-1170 · thegrangewarwick.com

With only 19 seats and usually one cook working in the back, this intimate farm-to-table restaurant has a homey, open-kitchen vibe. Most of the ingredients on its seasonally changing menu are locally sourced, with plenty of those same vegetables and artisanal products sold within the restaurant's market store.

HERITAGE TRAIL

This forest-lined 14-mile trail is a mostly flat, easy bike ride that stretches across Orange County from Goshen to Harriman. The road is well-paved with asphalt, making it a popular trail for bikers and pedestrians. Pick up the trailhead in Goshen just outside Trailside Treats Creamery.

IRON FORGE INN · 38 Iron Forge Road, Warwick · 845-986-3411 · ironforgeinn.com

Don't miss this elegant farmhouse restaurant and taproom housed within a historic Colonial-era inn. Its surroundings might be old (dating back to 1760), but the menu couldn't be fresher, thanks to local ingredients and modern techniques.

JOE FIX ITS · 20 Main Street, Goshen ·845-294-7242 · joefixits.com

Conveniently two blocks away from the Goshen trailhead, this bike shop has about 30 rentals for all levels to hit the Heritage Trail.

GLENMERE BREWING · 55 Maple Avenue, Florida · 845-651-1939 · glenmerebrewingco.com

Tucked away in the back of an industrial corridor of the tiny village of Florida is this micro-brewery that's small in size but big on flavor. Serving only eight drafts within a tasting room the size of most New Yorkers' bedrooms, what Glenmere lacks in square footage they make up for with award-winning brews (two of which snagged gold medals in the 2018 New York State Craft Beer Competition). What differentiates this brewery from the rest is its commitment to buying local ingredients for its beers from farmers in the nearby Black Dirt Region for super-fresh pours that pack a punch.

LONG LOT FARM BREWERY · 153 Johnson Road, Chester · 845-214-7033 · longlotfarmbrewery.com

There are so many craft breweries in New York State that you might even bypass one without knowing. That's how this nanobrewery often gets overlooked. Housed within a fifth-generation farm, this lesser-known gem has an impressive selection of six taps featuring beers made on-site with local ingredients straight from the farm and its neighbors around the nearby Black Dirt Region. Plus, there's the bonus of being able to brag to all your friends about the cool farm brewery you found that no one else knows about.

ORANGE COUNTY DISTILLERY AT BROWN BARN FARMS

· 286 Maple Avenue, New Hampton · 845-374-2011 · orangecountydistillery.com/brownbarnfarms

Something of an oasis within Orange County's iconic Black Dirt Region, this distillery's tasting room is literally in the middle of nowhere inside a converted barn on a farm, surrounded by acres upon acres of rolling greenery. It feels like a well-kept secret. Tapping only local ingredients for its dozen varieties of whiskies, gins, vodkas, and cocktail garnishes, this is a great place to kick back until the evening, when the distillery hosts live music, comedy, their on-site food truck, and the occasional bonfire.

ORCHARD HILL CIDER MILL • 29 Soons Circle, New Hampton • 845-374-2468 • orchardhillnyc.com

Situated within the Soons Orchards U-Pick farm, Orchard Hill has picked up a solid reputation among cider connoisseurs for its heritage hard ciders and New York-style pommeau, a riff on the classic Normandy blend of apple juice and brandy, aged in French oak barrels. Try them in the tasting room, then hit up the farm store for fresh fruit, vegetables, and tasty housemade snacks for the ride home.

PENNINGS FARM CIDERY

• 4 Warwick Turnpike, Warwick • 845-987-9922 • penningscidery.com

Along with being Hudson Valley's go-to for U-Pick apples and seasonal cider doughnuts, Penning's has become a hot spot for super-fresh heritage ciders with modern, experimental flavors like wild-fermented, honey-hopped, or infused with fresh ginger-beet and maple-vanilla. Another unexpected bonus: the cider house is totally kid-free. This means you can feel free to kick back with some hard ciders, wood-fired pizza, and a beautiful backdrop of

// Try innovative, farm-fresh cider flavors like ginger-beet, honey-hopped, and maple-vanilla at Pennings Farm Cidery

rolling orchards and carelessly drop a bunch of f-bombs without offending the sensibilities of young families.

RUSHING DUCK BREWERY • 1 Battiato Lane, Chester • 845-610-5440 • rushingduck.com

Rushing Duck becomes quite the scene on weekends when beer geeks pile in from around the Tri-State Area to load up on cans and growlers at this coveted brewery. Even if you're not a collector, there's certainly plenty to try among its 21 taps, from big IPAs and robust porters to experimental sours, barley wine, and nitro stouts. Order a pint from the bar and a plate from Bistro on the Go, a food truck parked outside that's run by local restaurant Christopher's Bistro.

TRAILSIDE TREATS CREAMERY · 28 St. James Place, Goshen

Trailside Treats isn't the kind of artisanal ice cream shop worth traveling out of the way for, but it's the beloved seasonal stop-off that locals and travelers alike can both look forward to each summer. It's also a convenient marker for picking up Heritage Trail, so it's a win-win to swing by after a long and sweaty bike ride.

Where to Stay
For an Elegant Overnighter

STAGECOACH INN · 268 Main Street, Goshen · 845-294-5526 · stagecoachny.com

Originally built as a farm home in 1747, this historic inn features bespoke, Pottery Barn chic interiors with luxe touches like an in-room fireplace, Molton Brown soaps, and down alternative bedding.

For a Homey Bed-and-Breakfast

WARWICK VALLEY B&B · 24 Maple Avenue, Warwick · 845-987-7255 · wvbedandbreakfast.com

Nestled within walking distance of historic Warwick, this seven-room Colonial Revivalist bed-and-breakfast has a comfy-cozy, home-away-from-home vibe. Unlike your own home, however, this one has a delightful innkeeper who serves a farm-fresh full breakfast in the morning before you go on your way.

5. The Best of Hudson

You'll want to devote a full weekend to Hudson, and even then, it will still feel too short. There's a reason this place is on the tip of everyone's tongues: it's the best of all worlds. Aside from being among the easiest car-free destinations, Hudson is blessed with Brooklyn-approved artsy enclaves, upscale boutiques, incredible restaurants, and close proximity to the river and mountains.

Among the most pedestrian-friendly upstate destinations, Amtrak drops off directly in front of Henry Hudson Riverfront Park (a great place to watch the sunset), steps away from major local attractions like experimental performing arts venue Basilica Hudson and coveted craft brewery Hudson Brewing Company. Its main strip, Warren Street, is where you can eat, drink, and make impulsive purchases of fancy apothecary goods, fashion, and curated interiors. Nightlife tends to go on a bit later here than in other Hudson Valley towns, with notable acts at Helsinki Hudson and lots of bar-hopping you won't find in other Hudson Valley enclaves.

Getting There

2 hours 26 minutes. Amtrak offers direct daily service to Hudson from Penn Station ($29–45 each way).

Getting Around

Once you get off the train, almost everything is in walking distance (around a mile). Lyft/Uber service is better than most Hudson Valley towns, should you need it. If you want to check out the town of Athens across the river, Hudson River Cruises (hudsoncruises.com) operates

// Stroll by restaurants, shops, and studios lining Hudson's 1-mile Columbia Street strip

round-trip ferry service from Hudson on Friday and Saturday evenings seasonally, Memorial Day through Labor Day ($15 round-trip, cash only).

Friday

AFTERNOON/EVENING: Hop on Amtrak at New York's Penn Station. Depending on how you time it, you'll make it in time for dinner or a nightcap at Wm. Farmer and Sons or Lil' Deb's Oasis.

Saturday

MORNING: Walk down Warren Street to motorcycle-themed coffee shop MOTO Coffee/Machine, then pick up artisanal snacks at Olde Hudson Market and Café.

AFTERNOON: Take a detour to the Olana State Historic Site, one of Hudson Valley's most fascinating estate tours. Then check out the seemingly endless sprawl of lifestyle, designer, and vintage boutiques; interior design studios; apothecaries; galleries; and eateries of Hudson's Warren Strip, like Flowerkraut, Valley Variety, 2 Note Hudson, Kasuri, and more.

EVENING: Hit Hudson's riverfront just before sunset to catch incredible views along the water. Secure a reservation in advance at Aeble or Fish & Game (both are notoriously popular), followed by a show at Helsinki Hudson. Finish with drinks at BackBar, or if you want to make friends with the locals, head to beloved dive bar, The Half Moon.

Sunday

MORNING: Bounce around Warren Street one last time, making a final pit stop for brunch at Grazin' Diner or Le Gamin Country.

AFTERNOON: Wait, it's time to go already? Chances are you didn't conquer everything this trip, but that's just another reason to come back. If you have enough time, stop by Hudson Brewing Company for a quick drink before hitting the train, conveniently located across the street.

Hudson Highlights

2 NOTE HUDSON • 255 Warren Street, Hudson • 518-828-0915 • 2notehudson.com
Browse handmade natural, organic bath and body products developed by two musicians who blend unique fragrances inspired by compositions like lavender, black pepper, and sandalwood or vetiver, patchouli, and vanilla.

FLOWERKRAUT · 722 Warren Street, Hudson · 518-821-6176 · flowerkrauthudson.com

Find thoughtfully curated ceramics, apothecary goods, flowers, and probiotics (yep, you read correctly) at this artsy flower shop-boutique concept shop.

HELSINKI HUDSON · 405 Columbia Street, Hudson · 518-828-4800 · helsinkihudson.com

Half music club, half restaurant, you really net a two-for-one on an evening out at this popular Hudson spot. Heavy with Southern influence, the menu sweeps from the Low Country to Texas, which is convenient when you want shrimp and grits, fried chicken, and barbecue under the same roof. Afterward, make your way into the theater to catch a live show that might be anything from blues and jazz or a drag queen performing cabaret.

OLANA STATE HISTORIC SITE · 5720 Route 9G, Hudson · 518-828-1872 · olana.org

Not to overshadow all the other historic estate tours, but Olana is arguably one of the coolest. An architectural anomaly, the Middle East–inspired Victorian mansion filled with antiquities was originally owned and concepted by Frederic Edwin Church, an American landscape painter and pivotal figure within the Hudson River School known for his romantic representa-

// Designed and decorated from his travels abroad, Frederic Edwin Church's iconic estate, Olana, is considered ahead of its time

tions of the Hudson Valley and the Catskills. Given his affinity for landscapes, it should come as no surprise that the views here are even more incredible than the estate.

OLDE HUDSON MARKET AND CAFÉ . 449 Warren Street, Hudson • 581-828-6923 • oldehudson.com

Would you really expect anything less than awesome for a Hudson market? I didn't think so. If it's a high-quality, gourmet pantry item, chances are this place has it for stocking up on snacks, gifts, and ingredients to tote home.

Where to Eat and Drink

You could make an entire weekend just eating your way around Hudson.

AEBLE . 449 Warren Street, Hudson • 518-697-7987 • aebleny.com

After training at top kitchens throughout San Francisco and New York, Culinary Institute grad Charles Brassard returned to the Valley to join Hudson's growing restaurant scene. Modern, cheffed-up dishes dominate the curated menu, putting local ingredients at the forefront (as if there's any other way). Think: grilled pork chops with roasted corn succotash, red collard greens, and chorizo vinaigrette; heirloom tomato salad with grilled nectarines, miso aioli, shaved red onion, basil, and manchego cheese.

FISH & GAME . 13 South 3rd Street, Hudson • 518-822-1500 • fishandgamehudson.com

Acclaimed New York City restaurateur Zak Pelaccio was on top of the Hudson trend years before it was cool, opening this James Beard Award–winning farm-to-table spot in 2013 on the heels of his two wildly successful concepts Fatty Crab and Fatty 'Cue. Leaving the city life behind, Fish & Game is thriving, gaining national recognition and putting Hudson squarely on the map. Menus change frequently to stay afloat with the local harvest, presented with rustic Italian touches like grilled Wild Hive polenta with garlic butter, snails, and black truffle; housemade linguini with crab, basil, and salted chili; and chestnut panna cotta.

GRAZIN' DINER . 717 Warren Street, Hudson • 518-822-9323 • grazinburger.com

Nestled along the far end of Hudson's Warren Street strip is a nondescript throwback diner that looks like a scene ripped from a movie. It's the home of Grazin', a restaurant offshoot of grass-fed Black Angus farm Grazin' Angus Acres in nearby Ghent. Naturally, burgers are the star of the menu, loaded with farm-fresh ingredients and served with hand-cut French fries. If the prices raise an eyebrow, don't balk; each burger is made with sustainable beef that's Animal Welfare Approved, making it an ethical (and delicious) choice worth the extra dough.

// Many of Hudson Brewing Company's beers can only be found on-site at its bar in Hudson

HUDSON BREWING COMPANY · 99 South 3rd Street, Hudson · 518-697-5400 · hudsonbrew.com

Directly across from the Hudson Amtrak station, this small farm brewery is an easy walk-in and within stumbling distance of most attractions. Located in a revitalized warehouse, the tasting room has 11 brews on tap plus a pineapple cider, all inspired by Hudson's rough, storied past as a shipping city.

LIL' DEB'S OASIS · 747 Columbia Street, Hudson · 518-828-4307 · lildebsoasis.com

The summertime cookout vibes never end at this colorful James Beard Award–nominated bar and restaurant situated just at the tail end of Hudson's main strip—even in the dead of winter. Tapping into the flavors of Latin America, southeast Asia, and, occasionally, Alabama (just go with it), the eclectic menu doesn't stray too far from its artsy and tropical backdrop. It's worth swinging by, even for a drink, particularly for its impressive wine list peppered with some fun and funky varietals that wine geeks will appreciate. Just make sure you watch your tab or stop by an ATM on the way in; this place is cash only.

MOTO COFFEE/MACHINE · 357 Warren Street, Hudson · 518-822-8232

Part coffee shop, part motorcycle showroom, this hybrid concept is best known for its ridiculously good espresso and made-to-order breakfast sandwiches and waffles.

>> **Know Before You Go:** Many restaurants keep limited or seasonal hours, often closing Monday through Wednesday or adding more time slots in summer. If you're planning a food-centric weekend, check for the most up-to-date information and try to reserve whenever possible.

Where to Stay

Blame all the vacationing celebrities, but unfortunately Hudson definitely isn't the most budget-friendly place to visit (particularly during peak season, when it sells out frequently). But if you can swing a few extra bucks or want to have a memorable stay, do it up at these spots.

For Something That Looks Damn Fine for Its Age

TIGER HOUSE · 317 Allen Street, Hudson · 518-828-1321 · tigerhousehudson.com

A former hunting lodge dating to 1901, this unique Dutch Jacobian-style property is now a haven for stylish New York City weekenders escaping to Hudson. *Ornate* is an understatement—common areas are brimming with stunning original woodwork and authentic fixtures that give this a timeless elegance many places can only try to replicate (the plant-filled solarium is a great place to take your morning coffee or read a book). Each of the five spacious rooms is furnished with individual personality to include fine details like antique four-poster beds, gas fireplaces, large soaking tubs, and private terraces.

For Something That Will Make Your Cool Friends Jealous

RIVERTOWN LODGE · 731 Warren Street, Hudson · 518-512-0954 · rivertownlodge.com

Is it a movie theater or a motel? Well, in a former life, this renovated property has been both. Tucked away at the end of the Warren Street strip, the Rivertown Lodge is the latest iteration of a historic building that spent its first 30 years as a cinema (hence the Deco-style marquee), followed by another 40 years as the Warren Inn Motel (conveniently remodeled into 27 catwalk-style rooms). Nodding to its colorful past, the hotel is outfitted to have a clean, minimalist, mid-century vibe with curated touches that your designer friends will love.

>> **Know Before You Go:** Despite all the expensive private galleries, hip dining, and cool cocktail bars along the main strip, if you walk two blocks over, it gets immediately desolate and rough. Stick to well-lit and populated areas, and don't be shy about calling a cab if anything feels questionable.

6. Summer in Trout Town, USA

Given that the tiny town of Roscoe greets you with a giant sign declaring itself Trout Town, USA, it's pretty clear that this is a town that loves its fly-fishing, and so do the majority of its visitors. Centered within the Catskill State Park adjacent to the Beaverkill River, Roscoe is a convenient place to commune with nature for a weekend. If you're not a seasoned fisherman and not interested in picking up a lesson (there are plenty of outfitters to choose from), don't fret. Hiking, biking, kayaking, foraging, and other outdoor activities are all within reach.

While you're in town, take advantage of the local agriculture along with that coveted trout at quality farm-to-table restaurants popping up between Roscoe and nearby towns like Livingston Manor.

Getting There

2 hours by car via Route 17. Like most Western Catskills destinations, you'll need wheels to get there and properly explore the area.

Getting Around

The main strips of these Catskills towns are only a couple blocks long, so plan for a lot of driving between destinations. Keep in mind that reception in the Catskills gets very, very spotty, so take advantage of Wi-Fi where you can find it to have GPS directions nailed down.

Friday

AFTERNOON: Hit the road from Manhattan toward Livingston Manor, which will take about 2 hours via Route 17. Depending on traffic, you should arrive around dinner or in time for a nightcap. Keep in mind that the latest things are open is 10:30 to 11 p.m. and plan accordingly. If you want to do classic tent camping in the woods, you'll want to leave earlier in the day to ensure there's enough light to set up.

EVENING: Refuel on the twinkling backyard patio with artisanal wood-fired pizzas at The Kaatskeller, a casual spot you won't need to dress up for, followed by drinks in the rustic tavern at local hot spot, The Arnold House.

Saturday

MORNING: Grab coffee and freshly baked German-style pastries at Brandenburg Bakery. If you want to hike in the afternoon, swing by Morgan Outdoors for the latest trail conditions and to grab any equipment you might have forgotten. Then stock up on sandwiches and snacks for your afternoon outdoors at Main Street Farm.

AFTERNOON: Hit the trails suggested by Morgan Outdoors if you planned last-minute. Or book ahead to take advantage of nature walks with The Outside Institute or trying your hand at fly-fishing with a half-day lesson with Catskill Flies in Roscoe. Before dinner, swing by Prohibition Distillery to stock up on craft vodka, gin, and whiskey (they close at 7 p.m. and you'll want to keep that booze handy for later).

// Shop for local condiments, snacks, and other artisan goods at Main Street Farm

EVENING: Clean yourself up and get decently presentable for dinner at Northern Farmhouse Pasta, which serves fresh, house-made noodles made with local, seasonal ingredients.

Sunday

MORNING: Head to The DeBruce for an elegant Catskills brunch, featuring panoramic views of the mountains and picture-perfect dishes made using locally foraged ingredients.

AFTERNOON: Stop by Catskill Brewery for an afternoon beer tasting, picking up any growlers or bottles to take home, then take your time heading back to the city to leave enough time to unwind before the Monday grind.

Roscoe and Livingston Manor Highlights

CATSKILL FLIES · 6 Stewart Avenue, Roscoe · 607-498-6146 · catskillflies.com

Upper Beaverkill Valley is the Catskills fly-fishing country, and within the heart of it is the town of Roscoe. So if a day of hanging out in waist-high waders on the river trying to catch trout sounds up your alley, reserve a day learning how to cast, how to tie knots, and other basics of fly-fishing with a private instructor. Fly-fishing, in general, tends to run on the pricier side, but Catskill Flies is on the cheaper end of the spectrum (rates run about $120 for a half day; $200 for a full day, which includes the instructor, equipment, and lunch).

MORGAN OUTDOORS · 46 Main Street, Livingston Manor · 845-439-5507 · morgan-outdoors.com

Before you hit the trails, swing by this outdoor store to pick up equipment rentals and get insider tips on the best spots to hike and updated trail condition information.

THE OUTSIDE INSTITUTE · theoutsideinstitute.org

From plant walks and foraging to beekeeping and botany, Catskills outdoor expert Laura Silverman offers frequent group events and curated private tours across the board.

Where to Eat and Drink

THE ARNOLD HOUSE · 839 Shandelee Road, Livingston Manor · 845-439-5070 · thearnoldhouse.com

Channeling the heyday of the Catskills' 1950s and 1960s resort era, this 13-room vintage revival boutique hotel meshes mid-century modern chic with rustic cabin coziness. For vin-

// Many properties have their own woodland trails, like this pastoral walkway at The DeBruce

tage design and antique geeks, this stylish property will give you all the feels. Not much has changed over the past 50 years in its basement tavern, except the menu that now features cool craft cocktails, local brews, and a Catskills-inspired assortment of elevated bar bites.

BRANDENBURG BAKERY · 66 Main Street, Livingston Manor · 845-439-0200 · brandenburgbakery.com

Considering how tiny Livingston Manor is, it's truly shocking how there can be so many delicious food options in one village. Don't ask questions, just go with it. After building up a cult following among local farmers' markets, this German-style bakery is among the latest newcomers adding to the local food scene (by the way, the pastries are out of this world).

CATSKILL BREWERY · 672 Old Route 17, Livingston Manor · 845-439-1232 · catskillbrewery.com

Catskill Brewery will soon become such a familiar sight on beer menus around the Catskills that when you start to notice it at Brooklyn bars, you'll wonder how you overlooked it in the first place. Don't miss the barrel-aged Flemish-style red ale that has a sour complexity worthy of pairing with an elegant dinner.

THE DeBRUCE · 982 Debruce Road, Livingston Manor · 845-439-3900 · thedebruce.com

Disconnect at The DeBruce, a luxe bed-and-breakfast thoughtfully curated with crisp linens and fluffy comforters, design-centric furnishings, and priceless natural views of the Catskills. Dining here is a little unusual—the kind of fine dining you'd find in the city or at another upscale destination: an intimate 28-seat dining room and nine-course tasting menu for dinner and à la carte breakfast menu that's on the pricey side for outsiders but a relative steal as an inclusive amenity for overnight guests.

THE KAATSKELLER · 39 Main Street, Livingston Manor · 845-439-4339 · thekaatskeller.com

Scratch-made, wood-fired pizzas topped with super-fresh ingredients from local artisanal makers like farm butter, raw Catskill honey, and smoked Beaverkill trout, plus inventive cocktails and craft cider and beer. Is it any shocker this place situated in the middle of the rural Catskills brings out locals and tourists from all over the area?

NORTHERN FARMHOUSE PASTA · 65 Rockland Road, Roscoe · 607-290-4064 · northernfarmhousepasta.com

The formerly sleepy town of Roscoe is on the up-and-up thanks to a slew of breweries, distilleries, and inns starting to open, including this artisanal pasta shop that sells seasonally driven noodles packed with ingredients like wild ramps, zucchini blossoms, and roasted summer corn.

MAIN STREET FARM · 36 Main Street, Livingston Manor · 845-439-4309 · mainstreetfarm.com

This cutesy market café and pantry serves a solid menu of made-to-order sandwiches, gourmet goodies from local makers, and other food-centric souvenirs worth toting home. Don't miss the trout sandwich, with fish straight from nearby Beaverkill Creek.

PROHIBITION DISTILLERY · 10 Union Street, Roscoe · 607-498-4511 · prohibitiondistillery.com

Roscoe is a hamlet best known for its fly-fishing, but over the past few years it has generated another reputation for its growing food and beverage scene, thanks to pioneers like this distillery that opened in 2013. As suggested, the distillery pays homage to New York's history during the Prohibition Era, crafting award-winning artisanal vodka, gin, and bourbon under the label "Bootlegger"—they go down smooth as silk. Their tasting room features tours of the microdistillery on-site, open year-round. During the summer, the back alley transforms into an outdoor bar for seasonal cocktails and local bites.

Where to Stay
For a Weekend in the Woods

ROSCOE CAMPSITES · 2179 Old Route 17, Roscoe · 607-498-5264 · roscoecampsite.com

Whether you want to pop your own tent or nestle into a woodland cabin along the Beaverkill, this campsite makes it easy to do it all. Plus, if you want to tack on outdoor activities like biking, hiking, or water sports, the campsite has plenty of rentals available so you can make the most of your weekend in the woods.

For Something Kinda Weird

WILLOWEMOC WILD FOREST YURT · 60 Browns Road, Livingston Manor · 845-439-4367 · willowemocwildforestyurt.com

Not as rustic as a standard tent, yet not as polished as a luxury retreat, this shabby chic yurt and safari tent nestled within the Catskill Forest Preserve offers a unique and peaceful getaway for communing with nature. Unlike other campground resorts, the property is a mom-and-pop spot with limited lodging that makes it feel truly disconnected from the regular world. Accommodations are cushier than your average sleeping bag and mat experience, but if you're looking for glamping luxury, this is definitely on the crunchier side (eco-friendly lights are solar-powered and there are no electric outlets or heating options like more modern, upscale yurts and safari tents).

For Something Stylish

THE RED ROSE MOTEL + TAVERN · 21677 Old Route 17, Roscoe · 607-290-4333 · theredrosemotel.com

Built in 1938, this storied motel and tavern has seen many transformations throughout the years. Its most recent iteration: a stunning renovation that channels the timeless rustic aesthetic of the Catskills and vintage Americana. The establishment finally reopened its doors in 2018. Think: wood-paneled walls, sportsman motifs, cozy wool blankets, antiques peppered throughout, and endless views of the great outdoors. Downstairs in the tavern, you'll find a full selection of local wines, beers, spirits, and tasty bar bites made with farm-fresh ingredients.

7. Hipster Weekend in Kingston

Just across the river from the upscale Rhinebeck is its scrappier sibling city, Kingston, which is quickly growing a reputation for attracting artsy weirdos with its laid-back, DIY vibe. In the historic uptown Stockade District, beautiful graffiti murals are peppered throughout the aging industrial buildings. This is where you'll find indie rock music venue BSP Kingston, the local LGBTQ community center, and a stream of new boutiques, bars, cafés, and art supply stores congregated in the main square. On the other side of town, in the downtown Rondout neighborhood, pop into quirky galleries, shop for antiques, stroll along the waterfront, and grab a glass of wine. Here's how to fit it all into one weekend.

Getting There

BY CAR | 2 hours. Car is really the best option, particularly if you want to explore any outside attractions.

BY BUS | 3 hours via Trailways NY. Renting a car will be your best bet for exploring the area, but Trailways NY offers direct service between the Port Authority Bus Terminal and Kingston, leaving roughly every 30 minutes ($54.50 round-trip).

BY TRAIN | 2 hours via Amtrak to Rhinecliff ($27–40), followed by a 20-minute taxi ride across the bridge. Though temptingly shorter than the bus, taking the train will knock you with pricey taxi fares crossing the river to Kingston.

Getting Around

Lyft and Uber both operate here, though service is still much spottier than what you'd find around New York City.

 Friday

AFTERNOON/EVENING: Depending on which transit you take, you'll end up in Kingston around dinnertime or nightcap hour. Swing by Kingston Wine Co. to pick up a special bottle for later (remember: shops close early), then head to Brunette, Lis, or öl Beer and Bites for dinner, followed by a stroll along the waterfront of the Rondout Creek.

 Saturday

MORNING: Head to Kingston's historic Stockade District for coffee and freshly baked pastries at Outdated Café, then kick around the neighborhood's array of indie boutiques, galleries, restaurants, and original Huguenot settlement.

AFTERNOON: If you want to stay in town, swing by any of the boutiques, wine shops, galleries, or antique shops in the Rondout neighborhood, like Clove & Creek, Hops Petunia, or Jay Teske Leather Co. But for a quick detour, check out nearby Saugerties, where you can explore the downtown shops, snap a photo of the Hudson River from the Saugerties Lighthouse, or explore Opus 40, a permanent art installation nestled in a former private quarry.

EVENING: Make your way to the Stockade District in Kingston, where you can browse books over a happy hour beer at Rough Draft Bar & Books before dinner at inventive farm-to-table spot Wilde Beest or the more casual gastropub Boiston's. After, check out the bill at BSP Kingston, UPAC, or Tubby's Kingston to see which shows are on.

☰ Sunday

MORNING: Grab a leisurely brunch at Duo Bistro and hit up their market, Duo Pantry, next door to stock up on artisanal cheeses, freshly baked pastries, and other curated local goods. If you're into street art, take a stroll around the neighborhood to find all sorts of cool murals lining the buildings and alleyways of Kingston.

AFTERNOON: On the way out of town, swing by any of the boutiques, wine shops, galleries, or antique shops you might have missed, like Lovefield Vintage, Bop to Tottom, Oak 42, or Ester Wine and Spirits.

Kingston's Hip Highlights

BSP KINGSTON • 323 Wall Street, Kingston • 845-481-5158 • bspkingston.com

Indie bands like The Black Lips and Thurston Moore routinely grace this rock club, along with events like zodiac-themed dance parties, live band karaoke, and screenings of cult classics like *The Dark Crystal.*

KINGSTON WINE CO. • 65 Broadway, Kingston • 845-340-9463 • kingstonwine.com

Even by snobby Brooklyn standards, this is an incredible wine shop. Along with coveted locally made artisanal wines and ciders, Kingston Wine Co. has an impressive selection of curated wines, ciders, and sakes from around the world, including lesser-known regions like Czechia, Georgia, and Greece, plus trendy pét-nat, fortified, and heritage styles.

TUBBY'S KINGSTON • 586 Broadway, Kingston • tubbyskingston.com

More interested in seeing a scrappy garage rock or psych band than a major headliner? This is your joint. Along with its regular lineup of shows, this dive venue often hosts weekly events like karaoke and collage nights.

ULSTER PERFORMING ARTS CENTER · 601 Broadway, Kingston · 845-339-6088 · bardavon.org

If you're the type of person who frequently donates to NPR, you'll most likely enjoy the lineup of acts at this premier performing arts theater that has featured everyone from David Byrne and John Malkovich to the Mystical Arts of Tibet. Dating back to 1927, this 1,510-seat former movie palace and vaudeville house was turned into its current iteration as a performing arts theater in 1979 and has become a major stop for touring concerts, plays, dance performances, and other stage acts.

Where to Eat and Drink
For Coffee and Fresh Pastries

DUO BISTRO · 299 Wall Street, Kingston · 845-383-1198 · duobistro.com

Centrally located along the main strip in Kingston's trendy Stockade District is a sunny bistro staple worth putting on your weekend bucket list. Approachable and seasonally driven New American dishes are gently studded with inventive touches like tempura fried squash with berbere spice and mushroom risotto with roasted seitan. Don't have time for a full sit-down dinner? Pop into Duo Pantry, the sister grocer concept set up conveniently next door, which offers fresh pastries, bread, and curated items from across the Hudson Valley and Catskills.

OUTDATED CAFÉ · 314 Wall Street, Kingston · 845-331-0030 · outdatedcafe.com

Don't be surprised if you walk in with the intention of only buying a cup of coffee and walk out with a handful of antiques. It's the blessing and the curse of a curated café and antique shop, where everything is beautiful and most of it is for sale. Spare some time to dine in, so you can try creative sweet and savory vegetarian breakfast items like polenta with eggs or tofu, heirloom tomatoes, greens, and tomato jam, or grab-and-go their rotating selection of baked goodies like peach lemon doughnuts or matcha cupcakes with orange buttercream. While you wait, rifle through the antiques decorating the café, which include things like vintage art supplies, signs and trinkets, and other curios.

For an Afternoon Drink While Browsing for Books

ROUGH DRAFT BAR & BOOKS · 82 John Street, Kingston · 845-802-0027 · roughdraftny.com

Hanging out in a bookstore would be so much better if you could cozy up with a beer or glass of wine—which is why this place was invented. Thumb through the latest curated titles while unwinding with a little booze at this bookstore in Kingston's historic Stockade District.

For Hipster-Approved Booze

BRUNETTE · 33 Broadway, Kingston · 845-802-0837 · brunettewinebar.com

It's all natural at this cutesy Parisian-style wine bar in the Rondout neighborhood of Kingston, which is basically a modern dog whistle for hipster wine geeks. To some, that might sound pretentious. But to most Brooklynites, it sounds like a lovely Friday night. Keep an eye out for cool collaboration events like pop-up shops, soul nights, and oyster parties.

LIS BAR · 240 Foxhall Avenue, Kingston · 845-514-2350 · lisbar.com

Situated in Kingston's up-and-coming Midtown District, this cool craft cocktail bar is unique in that it has a definitively Polish approach to its farm-to-table menu. Think: chilled beet soup with dill, elevated pierogies, and kishka-style hot dogs, along with a Polish-inspired Negroni using Bison Grass vodka.

ÖL BEER AND BITES · 85 Broadway, Kingston · 845-514-2527 · hettaglogg.com

Traditional Nordic mulled wine lovingly handcrafted in Kingston under the label HETTA. Give it a try, along with local craft beers, at their bar öl Beer and Bites.

For Food Fancy Enough To Be Considered Art

WILDE BEEST · 310 Wall Street, Kingston · 845-481-4181 · wilde-beest.com

A newcomer to the Kingston dining scene, Wilde Beest is among the latest hot spots driving farm-to-table into the next generation. Think: inventive combinations brimming with unique ingredients like smoked trout with goat cheese mousse and fresno piri piri; black bass with cucumber-dill syrup, sour cream, and lemon skordalia; and cardamom panna cotta with spiced beer cake and apple pudding. The dishes might be preciously plated à la fine dining, but the atmosphere has a breathable Brooklyn vibe, typically backed by a rotating soundtrack of hand-picked records ranging from David Bowie to Erykah Badu.

Where to Stay

You'll score a deal in Kingston by booking at a chain hotel or Airbnb, but for something a little more personal (albeit pricier) check out these art-centric properties near Kingston.

THE GALLERY INN · 93 Broadway, Kingston · 845-514-3998 · thegalleryinnkingstonny.com

For an artsy stay, you can't get much closer than an inn located within a converted gallery space. Steps away from the Rondout neighborhood waterfront, this cozy, apartment-style suite has a home-away-from-home vibe with the bonus of proximity to Kingston's vibrant art scene.

THE FORSYTH B&B · 85 Abeel Street, Kingston · 845-481-9148 · theforsythkingston.com

This *Vogue*-approved property combines the comfort of a historic home with style and modernity worth humblebragging about on Instagram. Luxe touches like a California king bed, deep soaking tub, and fresh-made breakfast from a trained chef make it so comfortable that if you end up staying in all weekend, you won't even be mad about it.

BOHEMIAN INN · 44 Partition Street, Saugerties · 917-538-9572 · bohemianinn.com

Is there anything more fitting for a hipster weekend than staying in a place called the Bohemian Inn? Each room at this adorable Victorian bed-and-breakfast nestled 20 minutes outside of Kingston in the up-and-coming town of Saugerties has a bespoke vibe inspired by the owner's favorite travel destinations, from Jaipur and Havana to Saint-Tropez and Athens.

8. Hop Through History in Hyde Park

Among the countless Gilded Age estates lining the Hudson River, the Valley has a number of homes that once belonged to presidents, first ladies, and influential dignitaries. Now immortalized as National Historic Sites, you can brush up on American history by taking a tour of the lifestyles of the rich and presidential. Hyde Park has become essentially a National Historic Site trail, with the trifecta of the Franklin D. Roosevelt Home and Presidential Library, the Eleanor Roosevelt Center at Val-Kill, and the Vanderbilt Mansion National Historic Site all within reach of one another.

Getting There

1 hour 40 minutes by car. If you're only doing estates, the National Park Service has a free shuttle that operates seasonally May through October, picking up at the Poughkeepsie Metro-North train station and dropping off at stops along both Roosevelt and Vanderbilt sites. Check the nps.gov website for the most current schedule.

Getting Around

Rent a car. Aside from the NPS museum shuttle, getting around Hyde Park without a car is a challenge. Buses exist, but they run very infrequently, and Lyft/Uber aren't very robust. If you have a Zipcar membership, you can reserve a car at the Poughkeepsie train station, or reserve with a commercial car rental service for pick-up upon arriving at the station.

≡ Friday

AFTERNOON/EVENING: Decide where you're staying as your base ahead of time (it won't be in Hyde Park—there's not much there worth sticking around for, beyond the historic sites). New Paltz, Rhinebeck, and Kingston are all less than 30 minutes driving time to Hyde Park. If you're a serious history geek, Rhinebeck has a number of historical restaurants and inns dating back to the Colonial era. But the crowd tends to be older and more posh, so keep that in mind if you want to enjoy any nightlife.

≡ *Saturday*

MORNING/AFTERNOON: Touring the campus of the Franklin D. Roosevelt Home, Presidential Library, and Museum will take up the whole day. Make sure to book tickets in advance and fill up with a solid breakfast or grab lunch, because the café menu is not really worth mentioning. If you need a break for lunch, Hyde Park Brewing and Eveready Diner are both decent options within 10 minutes' drive of the museum campus.

EVENING: Check out the restaurants inside the Culinary Institute of America for an early dinner. This is where some of the world's best chefs get their start, and these restaurants are where they earn their chops (the prix-fixe menu is reasonable, too). Afterward, go roller-skating at Roller Magic or catch a feature at the Hyde Park drive-in (you can't remember the last time you've done either?).

≡ *Sunday*

MORNING: Make sure to grab breakfast before you head to the Vanderbilt Mansion National Historic Site; you should get tour tickets in advance during peak season. Afterward, take a walk around the grounds. It's adjacent to the Hudson River, offering great views for a quick snapshot.

AFTERNOON: Head to Eleanor Roosevelt National Historic Site, which is on the southeast side of Hyde Park on the way out of town. If you have time, try to swing by Plan Bee Farm Brewery or Mill House Brewing Company in Poughkeepsie on the way back to the city for a taste of local goodness.

Hyde Park Highlights

ELEANOR ROOSEVELT NATIONAL HISTORIC SITE • 54 Valkill
Park Road, Hyde Park • 845-229-9422 • nps.gov/elro • grounds are open daily from sunrise to sunset; the visitor center is open 9 a.m.–5 p.m. daily May through October; closed Tuesday and Wednesday November–April • free

Eleanor Roosevelt is one of the few first ladies whose legacy transcends her husband's presidential tenure. A committed humanitarian and activist, her work carried on long after her husband left office and even after he passed away. Though she had spent many years by his side at his estate on Albany Post Road, Eleanor had her own property down the way at Val-Kill. Learn more about her world through a fascinating guided tour, and then find out how her efforts continue today at the Eleanor Roosevelt Center.

// Explore the home of former President Franklin Delano Roosevelt in Hyde Park

FRANKLIN D. ROOSEVELT HOME, PRESIDENTIAL LIBRARY, AND MUSEUM · 4079 Albany Post Road, Hyde Park · 800-337-8474 · fdrlibrary.org · hours change seasonally; check website for more information · $20

Now celebrating its 75th year, this historic attraction is unique in that you get three major stops in one place: the home of former president Franklin D. Roosevelt and his wife, Eleanor Roosevelt; a museum dedicated to their lives and political tenure; and one of 14 presidential libraries in the United States that serve to maintain nonpartisan national archives of American history.

VANDERBILT MANSION NATIONAL HISTORIC SITE · 119 Vanderbilt Park Road, Hyde Park · nps.gov/vama · hours and tour schedules change seasonally; check the NPS website for the most up-to-date information · $10

It was a great time to be a Vanderbilt during the Gilded Age. At least that's the takeaway as you stroll through the gorgeous fineries of aristocratic life as a millionaire in late 19th-century America. As one of the region's oldest Hudson River estates, Vanderbilt is blessed with not only a beautiful mansion (there's certainly nothing shabby here when it comes to American Beaux Arts design), but also a picturesque riverside location and an incredible manicured landscape filled with formal gardens.

>> **Know Before You Go:** The mansion is only accessible by guided tour. During peak season, these tours are quite popular on weekends and holidays and sell out quickly.

Where to Eat and Drink

Dining isn't super-robust around here (and the options at the on-site cafés at the historic sites aren't great), so if you're doing the historic trail, pack a lunch. If you've got wheels, check out:

For a Decent Burger and Brew

HYDE PARK BREWING COMPANY · 4076 Albany Post Road, Hyde Park · 845-229-8277 · hydeparkbrewing.com

Hyde Park Brewing doesn't have destination-worthy brews, but you'll be grateful for their better-than-your-average craft beer and burgers, located conveniently across the street from the FDR Library.

For an Authentic Diner Experience

EVEREADY DINER · 4184 Albany Post Road, Hyde Park · 845-229-8100 · theeverydiner.com

Load up on generously sized, classic American dishes at this throwback chrome diner situated about 5 minutes north of the Hyde Park museum strip.

For the Unexpected Foodie Experience

CULINARY INSTITUTE OF AMERICA · 1946 Campus Drive, Hyde Park · 845-452-9600 · ciafoodies.com

Brush up your knife skills by taking an immersive weekend or weeklong boot camp at one of the best culinary schools in the world. Courses range from seafood and grilling to skills development and working with the specialized flavors of the Hudson Valley. If you only have time to pop in, the school has five restaurants open to the public and an excellent gift shop for finding cool kitchenware.

Where to Stay

THE BEEKMAN ARMS · 6387 Mill Street, Rhinebeck · 845-876-7077 · beekmandelamaterinn.com

Proudly claiming to be the oldest inn in America, The Beekman Arms certainly has receipts to back it up. Dating to 1766, the inn and tavern has actual documentation of its check-in records from the American Revolution. Given its lengthy tenure and reputation, The Beekman Arms has hosted countless famous guests, including former presidents George Washington, Franklin D. Roosevelt, and Bill Clinton. The property may be old, but the accommodations have fortunately received a modern upgrade, with plush bedding and air conditioning. Bonus: as a nice gesture, the property stocks each room with a complimentary decanter of sherry.

Acknowledgments

This book wouldn't have been possible without the help of the following people, who deserve perpetual praise and only the best things in life.

First of all, I'd like to thank myself. This was a behemoth of a project and I threw everything into it. I hope you like it as much as I do. If not, I have your money already, so tough luck!

To my mom, Pam, and grandma, Celia-Ann: Thank you for always believing in me and encouraging me to write.

To Erin Hartz: Thank you for being my sister, my lifeline, and my best friend, while rooting for me to reach the finish line. I'm so glad that you were able to be part of the journey while I painstakingly researched, wrote, and finalized this book.

To Blair Hopkins: Thank you for being my photographer, adventure co-pilot, and emotional guru. Traveling wouldn't have been the same without you, and I'm proud to immortalize your work and our memories in this book.

Huge thanks to my patron saints: Josh and Kayla Cagan, Laura Yee, Michael Zumbrun, Jeffrey Ward, Katie Bezrouch, Adina Hilton, Laura Collins, Nicole Dudka, Kate Bernot, Elena Kherson, Diana Murphy, Michelle Mermelstein, Caitlin Bergo, Kali Jacobs, Kyle Gorman, Hilary Pritchard, Shannon Heidkamp, Kelli Korducki, Jaydee Decker, Carol Flatto, Aliah Greene, Danielle Kalamaras, Shannon Bandur, Royal Lichter, and Mike Fenn.

Gigantic thank-you to the tourism boards of Dutchess County, Orange County, Sullivan County, Columbia County, and Ulster County; ILoveNY; and Finn Partners. This book would not be possible without your tremendous support and efforts to connect me with the best of New York State.

Most importantly, thank you to the Hudson Valley and Catskills, for there would be no book at all without these two amazing regions. I'm excited to share all the independent business owners, farmers, artists, and makers that contribute to such a wonderful place.

Index

* Illustrations are in *italics*.